THE GREAT
MEDITERRANEAN
COMFORT FOOD
TOUR

5 MONTHS TRAVELING

10 COUNTRIES TO DISCOVER EUROPE'S

MOST MOUTHWATERING

CULINARY INDULGENCES:

A MEMOIR

Karen McCann

CAFÉ
SOCIETY
PRESS

For more information:

enjoylivingabroad@gmail.com

ISBN: 9798364750280

For all the generous, warmhearted cooks
who invited me into their kitchens
and nourished my sprit with comfort food.

Praise for
The Great Mediterranean Comfort Food Tour

"Karen McCann's book is the perfect homage to two of the greatest things in life – food and travel."
George Mahood, author of *Free Country*

"A rollicking culinary adventure seasoned with a dash of history, a sprinkling of heart-warming characters, and a liberal shot of humor."
Jackie Smith, author of *TravelnWrite*

"A lighthearted food tour around the Mediterranean … a delight to read, amusing, witty, and informative."
Joan Fallon, author of *Daughters of Spain*

"A culinary exploration of each area's unique contribution … served up with a dash of wit that made me laugh even as I took notes about what dish to try next." Dru Pearson, author of *Europe on a Dime*

"Entertaining stories with wit and wisdom. Her stories always leave me feeling lighter, happier, and more relaxed. Oh! And there's food!"
Nancy Solak, www.areluctanttraveler.net

"We've been traveling the world full-time for over nine years, and Karen's books have played a big part in our trip planning. This new book lays out the perfect itinerary for eating your way along the sun-kissed Mediterranean!"
Debbie and Michael Campbell, The Senior Nomads, authors of *Your Keys, Our Home*

CONTENTS

THE ROUTE

"Is there anything, apart from a really good chocolate cream pie and receiving a large unexpected cheque in the post, to beat finding yourself at large in a foreign city on a fair spring evening, loafing along unfamiliar streets in the long shadows of a lazy sunset, pausing to gaze in shop windows or at some church or lovely square or tranquil stretch of quayside, hesitating at street corners to decide whether that cheerful and homey restaurant you will remember fondly for years is likely to lie down this street or that one? I just love it. I could spend my life arriving each evening in a new city."

– Bill Bryson

INTRODUCTION

When all the stars align to make a long trip practical, I clear my calendar, walk to the train station, and head off into the unknown, bringing with me nothing but one small suitcase and my husband.

I call it research for my work as a travel writer. That's the truth. But not the whole truth.

Sure, I'll chronicle the fun stuff in articles, blog posts, and books, describing quirky settings, oddball characters, and road food that proves particularly transcendent, ghastly, or weird. (Yes, Portuguese pig's ears, I'm thinking of you in the latter categories.) But my real reason for hitting the road is to have the kinds of adventures I dreamed about when I was a kid.

The journey I want to tell you about began — as so many of mine have — in a Spanish café. I've lived in Seville for the better part of two decades; among its other delights, this ancient city provides a great jumping off place for train travel around Europe. My husband, Rich, is never happier than when he's working out the logistics of complicated overland routes requiring multiple forms of public transportation, preferably through regions signposted in alphabets neither of us knows. On the morning in question, we were sitting at a small, marble-topped table, sipping espresso, toying with ideas for the next big railway summer.

The ideas were getting more and more outlandish, and for us, that's a fairly high bar. We'd hiked the Himalayas, swum in the waters of the Amazon (the river, not the online retailer), done volunteer work in Africa, slept (or tried to) in haunted hotels, and interviewed a man who saw Bigfoot. So far, the only given about the next big trip was that it would last for months and involve a railway journey through obscure parts of Europe. Obviously we'd have to narrow it down a bit. But how?

And then Rich had his brainstorm.

"Have you noticed," he said, setting down his cup and leaning forward, "that every time you write about food, your readers love it? What if we made that the theme of the trip? Everybody likes Mediterranean food, right?"

Instantly the journey took shape in my mind. "We'll call it the Mediterranean Comfort Food Tour," I said. "Travel by train and ferry around the Mediterranean rim, sampling some of the world's best cooking in its native habitat."

"I'm in!"

"We'll explore local culture through the cuisine," I went on, growing ever more enthusiastic. "Food always has an interesting backstory, one that tells you a lot about the people who eat it. Wines, too!"

"You had me at comfort food," he said.

The idea seemed perfectly sound to me but aroused a surprising amount of consternation among my more sensible friends. Of course, over the years they'd often watched in horror as I set off for remote places with dubious infrastructure, even more dubious medical systems, and cuisine rumored to be as indigestible as it was unpronounceable. Perhaps their skepticism was understandable.

"So you'll be eating your way around the Mediterranean rim," one commented. "I assume all the clothes you're packing will have elastic waistbands?"

"I expect to double my body weight," I said cheerfully. "And I'll be so contented I won't care."

But to be honest, I didn't really expect to gain much weight. I always walk a great deal, and that goes double on long journeys. And being a light eater by nature, I doubted the trip would turn into an orgy of overconsumption. But my friends were far from convinced.

"Is this going to be like that guy in Supersize Me?" somebody asked. "You'll have to stop halfway through because the diet is so unhealthy?"

"Hey, this is Mediterranean comfort food," I replied. "I'll probably come back with cholesterol so low my doctors will force me to eat more cheeseburgers."

"OK, I have to ask," said another. "What exactly do you mean by 'comfort food.'"

I explained that to me — and, coincidentally enough, to the authors of the Merriam-Webster Dictionary — it's "food prepared in a traditional style having a usually nostalgic or sentimental appeal."

You've probably got a list of your own special favorites: grandma's chicken soup, homemade chocolate chip cookies fresh from the oven, that spaghetti your roommate used to cook up on Friday nights. Whatever they are, some foods are special to you; thinking about them makes your mouth water and wraps a soft cocoon of contentment around your heart, if only for a moment.

Those feel-good sensations are hardwired in all of us, but the foods that prompt them run an amazingly broad gamut. Take Marmite, for instance. To me, it's like slathering your toast with over-salted tar, but millions of people in the UK, Australia, and New Zealand swear by this yeast-extract paste; I've known expats to spend a fortune special-ordering the stuff. Equally baffling to me is the Mississippi Delta craze for

Koolickles, pickles brined in various fruit flavors of Kool-Aid. Then there's France's beloved andouillette sausage, which Rich ordered once in all innocence, discovering to his horror that it was stuffed with pig tripe and strings of intestines that writhed out onto his plate like living worms. Different strokes!

Of course, I realize for some, the words "comfort food" conjure up a darker meaning. For them it's not about pleasure but a desperate attempt to offset pain by binging on unhealthy substances during life's bleakest moments. As one Huffington Post article put it, in what I consider the most revolting metaphor of the decade, "it's a dietary bandage we've all used." Yuck, no!

The author added, "In the U.S. we understand that when someone is stuffing their face with French fries and doughnuts it's a signifier for, 'I'm overwhelmed, please avoid eye contact.'" To me, frequent indulgence in that kind of frantic gluttony is a worrying form of self-harm. And no, that's not even remotely what my journey was about.

"I'm not talking about comfort food as pathological escapism," I assured my friends. "If I wanted to binge like that I'd be planning the All-American Fast Food Tour. To me, the Mediterranean diet is one of those rare instances when we humans got it right. We created great food that's actually good for you. Every meal is satisfying, yet leaves you already happily anticipating the next."

"So you're going to travel around eating and writing about it?"

"More or less." Admittedly, this part of the plan was a bit hazy.

What I really wanted to do was go into kitchens, interview chefs, get their recipes, and record the entire process with photos and videos. But why would any sane cook allow a stranger to bumble about underfoot, getting in the way of the fast-paced, complicated task of prepping, cooking, and serving? And weren't chefs famously reluctant to share their secret recipes with the world?

The more I thought about it, the less optimistic I felt about my chances. Yes, I was sure I'd eat well. And I could always write "here-I-am-trying-the-freshly-caught-octopus" articles, linking to recipes on other people's cooking blogs and YouTube channels. I could have some fun with that.

But could I do better?

As it turned out, I could. To my astonishment, cooks everywhere welcomed me into their kitchens. They shared their time, their techniques, and their recipes, often introducing me to their families and talking about what inspired them in their work.

You can find all the recipes, photos, and videos on my website, and I hope as you read this book, or when you've finished it, you'll go take a look. It's fun to see the cafés, farms, restaurants, homes, gardens, and urban rooftops where memorable meals were created. You'll meet the cooks and listen to their advice about making moussaka, risotto, wild goat, bourbouristi (snails), dragon pie, and other unforgettable fare. And you'll have all the recipes so you can try making everything yourself. Each recipe is shown using both metric and US measurements.

I'd originally planned to include the recipes in this book, but then I realized the print edition would become enormously long and ridiculously expensive to produce. And I don't know about you, but I've never figured out how to download or print a recipe from my Kindle. So it occurred to me that it would be more practical to collect everything online — recipes, videos, photos, my blog posts, links, notes — and let you freely access everything in one place: EnjoyLivingAbroad.com. There you'll find the entire online cookbook under Mediterranean Recipes.

So to recap, this is not a recipe book. Nor is it a traditional guide to restaurants in cities you're likely to visit. While I identify many delightful eateries by name, often I was in obscure villages, remote farmhouses, private homes (you'll learn how I arranged that later), and tiny mom-and-pop cafés. Trying to visit such lesser-known locales isn't easy in the best of times, and I fear some of my favorites may have closed forever during the pandemic. Many aren't on social media so I can't check on them from afar, and I don't want to send you on a wild goose chase.

But this book isn't about following in my footsteps, it's about exploring on your own. It's full of simple, tried-and-true ways you can discover great food wherever you may roam. You'll obviously find this easier in Mediterranean countries with a hundred generations of great cooking under their belts, but the principles apply everywhere in the world. Yes, even suburban America.

Here's one tip that will come as no surprise: it's hard to go wrong with Mediterranea

n food. Back when the Mediterranean Sea was the center of Western civilization, the seafaring city-states on its shores were constantly trading, raiding, and invading each other. In their spare time, they ate each other's food and swapped recipes, bringing home newfangled ideas like olive oil, wine, cheese, and pasta, enriching their communities with new culinary pleasures.

Like so many Americans, I didn't grow up with the idea that cooking and eating were pleasurable activities. The twentieth century brought a lot of serious (if sometimes misguided) science into the kitchen. My harried mother devoted endless hours to calculating protein, carbohydrates, and vitamins to make sure she'd provided her husband and six kids with sufficient fuel — ideally without triggering a run to the hospital (we had diabetes and allergies in the family), running afoul of the Catholic Church's fasting requirements, or causing an outright revolt among the populace. Eating was a lot more about "should" than "good."

This attitude is common in the USA, where our view of food gets all tangled up with anxiety and moral judgement. I blame our Puritan heritage. In word association games, if you say "chocolate cake," the most common response among Americans is "guilt." Not so the Europeans. The French say "celebration." And in Spain, when chocolate cake arrives on the table, everyone exclaims, "*Que rico!*" (How rich!). I've never heard a Spaniard say, "*No, realmente no debería*" (No, I really shouldn't).

In Mediterranean Europe, food isn't automatically treated as an enemy. Au contraire, food is welcomed as a friend. People with long histories have long memories, and you never forget times of scarcity. In Seville, for instance, the twentieth century saw some very dark days known as the Hunger, desperate years following the Spanish Civil War, when nobody had enough to eat.

"When I was a kid," a Sevillano friend in his sixties told me, "we always kissed the bread before we ate it." Remembering lean times means treating food with respect and affection, even when it's no longer scarce.

Many of the foods we consider Mediterranean classics were born out of such shortages, created by poor families in every country and era as parents struggled to feed their kids in a region with sandy soil, searing summer heat, and frequent wars. People ate what they could raise, make, or catch: olives for oil, seeds, beans, cereals, fruits, vegetables, occasionally fish, some cheese and yogurt, and once in a great while, a little meat. In the mid-twentieth century, the rest of the world discovered what Mediterranean families had known for centuries: this diet helps people to live longer, healthier, happier lives.

This book is a celebration of Mediterranean comfort food and the cooks who have passed down their recipes for generations. It's not just about ingredients and techniques; it's about approaching every meal with gusto. For me, it all comes down to this simple truth: Mediterranean food reminds us it's fun to be alive. When I'm fortunate enough to be sharing it with congenial companions, especially on the road, I find myself flooded with gratitude and joy.

From the moment this trip was first discussed, I was eager to learn more about Mediterranean cooking and share my discoveries with my readers. I knew that throughout the journey I'd report some of the highlights on my blog, but there would be far more oddball adventures, amazing recipes, and quirky backstories than I could possibly squeeze into my short weekly posts. From the beginning, I looked forward to the day I could sit down and start writing this book, so I could fill you in properly on all the good stuff.

But before any of that could happen, I had to pick a direction, figure out what to pack, and hit the road.

SPAIN

1. Getting Ready / *Planning and Packing*

They say preparation is everything, but when it comes to long journeys, my best advice is simple: don't overdo it. Filling your head with a million details means you'll soon be drowning in a sea of data, losing track of vital notes when you need them, and running the risk of having your head explode before you set foot outside the door.

On the other hand, the world is a very large place and you have to start somewhere. Over the years I've found it works best if I sketch out a rough route and then secure lodgings for the first few nights. After that initial Airbnb, overnight ferry, sleeper train, or hotel, it's the open road. Or railway lines. Or waves. You get the idea. From then on I wing it, reserving accommodations just a night or two in advance, keeping life as flexible as possible.

This is one of the many things that convinces my more sensible friends that I am seriously bonkers.

"I don't know how you two travel the way you do," a Californian friend told me. "If I didn't know where I was going to stay for the evening?" He shuddered. "I couldn't deal with that. If things don't go exactly as planned, I have a meltdown."

He had just returned from Morocco and was soon telling me about the night he got spooked while wandering around an old marketplace there. His wife and their two travel companions weren't ready to leave, so my friend headed back to the hotel alone in the dark. Needless to say, he became hopelessly lost. Eventually, in desperation, he stopped the most respectable-looking person on the street and asked for directions.

"You will get lost again. Ask one of these fellows—" the man gestured toward some nearby male prostitutes "— to guide you, and pay him a little for his trouble."

My friend was aghast, possibly worrying he was expected to sleep with one of these men just to have help finding his way back to the hotel. Seeing his distress, the Moroccan added kindly, "They're just looking for some money. It will be fine."

And it was. The youth politely escorted my friend to the hotel and went away happily pocketing a modest tip. The question of exchanging sexual favors never came up.

In travel as in everyday life, it's pretty clear that we're all operating under Murphy's infamous law: whatever can go wrong will go wrong, and at the worst possible moment. Of course my friend got lost on the way back to his Moroccan hotel; did anyone not see that coming? Our best laid plans are always being thrown out the window by the capricious workings of fate. The only part we have any control over is how we deal with it. Or as author Ally Condie put it, "In the end you can't always choose what to keep. You can only choose how you let it go."

One of my favorite examples of this occurred many years ago when Rich and I were running late for a connecting flight in Paris and arrived just as the plane's doors were closing. My demands to reopen them fell on deaf ears. I may have expressed my sentiments with unbecoming force. Someone fetched the manager.

After listening to me rant a while, he said firmly, "Madam, we will put you on tomorrow night's flight. But for now, you have no alternative but to spend the next twenty-four hours in Paris."

I was drawing breath for a quelling retort when his words sank in. Twenty-four hours in Paris? Why, yes, I could live with that. Fifteen minutes later I had a reservation at my favorite hotel and within the hour I was happily sipping vin in a sidewalk café.

So my point — you knew I'd get around to one eventually — is that for me staying flexible is the best way to navigate an unpredictable world.

But still, some decisions do have to be made before setting out on any long journey. It didn't take long to realize that covering the entire Mediterranean rim was impractical; that would require at least a year, and I was hoping to leave in April and return to Seville somewhere around the end of summer. Rich and I agreed we'd focus on the European portion of the Mediterranean, and the route began to take shape.

From Seville we'd head north through Spain, traverse southern France and northern Italy, then meander down the east coast of the Adriatic Sea through Slovenia, Croatia, Bosnia and Herzegovina, Montenegro, and Albania before turning inland to North Macedonia and mainland Greece. From Athens it would be easy to catch ferries out to some of the Greek islands, eventually flying home from Crete. This meant traveling from countries I knew to the wilder reaches of Europe, from the familiar paella and pasta fazool to mysterious dishes with names like burek, mlinci, and σαλιγκάρια.

I spent hours studying the map taped to the wall above my kitchen table. What regions, I wondered, had cuisine that would make my taste buds jump up and dance with joy? Time to do some research.

Tracking down Seville's best cuisine, and the stories behind it, had taken me years of patient research in the city's 3000 tapas bars. (I know, tough work, but somebody's got to do it.) Now God in Her wisdom and mercy had given us Google, but I still believed the best place to start was asking my friends for information and advice.

"You'll be going to Istria, of course," said one.

"Where?"

She eyed me pityingly. "Northern Croatia's truffle country."

What? They have truffles in Croatia? Who knew?

"There's a little restaurant," she went on. "It's not easy to get to, but the food …." She trailed off, rolling her eyes heavenward in blissful memory.

"Make a note of that one," Rich said.

Finding delectable comfort food in Mediterranean countries wasn't going to be a problem; the very names on the map were making my mouth water. I could hardly wait to sample parmesan cheese in Parma, Bolognese sauce in Bologna, Kalamata's black olives, and the mustard of Dijon. The difficulty lay in whittling down the list of foods and destinations I was quickly amassing. For help with this, the first resource I always turn to — and here I'm giving away a closely held professional writers' secret — is Wikipedia

One morning, for instance, I kicked back with a large mug of coffee and Wikipedia's Albanian cuisine page. It explained earnestly that the food in the north of Albania is "rural, coastal, and mountainous," while their southern neighbors prefer fare that is "rural, mountainous, and coastal." Possibly this distinction had lost something in translation. I was fascinated to discover Albania had just surpassed Spain to become the country with the highest number of coffee houses per capita in the world. Way to go Albania! I took a big swig from my mug and soldiered on.

Eventually the article began describing actual dishes, starting with desserts. I was beginning to admire their priorities. It turned out Albanians still enjoy the first known dessert in the world — a mix of grains, fruits, and nuts called Noah's Pudding because it commemorates the Ark's return to land. Now that's a dish with a long backstory.

As the list of countries grew clearer in my mind, I began checking out specific regions and towns. Over the years I'd found myself gravitating toward mid-sized cities, with populations around 200,000 (give or take 100,000). I like the fact they're small enough to navigate on foot; unfamiliar public transit systems have a tendency to reduce me to a state of bumfuzzlement (a lovely word meaning confusion and perplexity). Best of all, most midsized cities have enough quirky cafés, interesting shops, funky buildings, loony street art, and random characters to keep me entertained as I stroll along.

When considering any city, I looked up their cooking classes, food tours, and/or private dining experiences such as EatWith — which is a sort of culinary version of Airbnb where you go to a chef's home for a private dinner party. The EatWith website lets you see photos of the food and setting, bios of the hosts, menus, and plenty of other details to give you a sense of what's on offer; it can be exclusive for you and your friends, but if not, you can see who else will be coming. You pay ahead of time by credit card, so there's no awkward fumbling for tips in a strange currency. The whole evening feels like a normal dinner in someone's home that just happens to be in Zagreb or Barcelona.

When I first heard about EatWith, I could hardly wait to try it, but my more levelheaded friends were less than enthusiastic about the idea.

"Why would you want to go to a stranger's home and eat with people you don't know?" one asked incredulously.

"The hosts aren't picked at random off the street," I protested. "They're professional chefs and fabulous cooks who open their homes to small groups for private dining. It's like a pop-up restaurant or a small supper club."

"Yes, but you all sit together. There's no telling who would be next to you."

"That's the fun part!"

My friend just rolled her eyes. I eventually persuaded her to join me, and to her surprise we had a grand time. She's now a huge fan and seeks out EatWith dinners wherever she travels. As do I. There are similar groups out there, most notably the Traveling Spoon, as well as smaller, regional companies. You can Google "private social dining experiences" to explore your options.

A few years ago I met with some of the leaders of EatWith in their San Francisco headquarters and learned how carefully they vet the cooks.

"Everyone has to submit a video of themselves preparing a meal and serving it to a group," the quality control manager explained to me. "I can tell just by the angle of their knife whether they really know what they're doing." That's when I realized I would never qualify as an EatWith host. I'm from the slap-dash, make-it-up-as-you-go tradition of culinary arts. I had no idea how I was supposed to be holding my knife.

For me, the best part of EatWith is that your hosts join you at the table, so you have hours to sit together over a bottle of wine and talk about their cuisine and culture. These evenings have ranged from pleasant to uproariously convivial; some led to lasting friendships and a few required a quiet recovery day afterwards. EatWith cooks tend to be extroverts who like nothing better than showing off their culinary skills. How hard could it be to talk my way into their kitchens on this trip?

One thing I'd discovered in my travels was that comfort food — in fact, all food — is best enjoyed at a leisurely pace. Traveling slowly in easy stages via public transportation would make it easier to appreciate gradual shifts in the cultural and culinary landscape. And it would let me linger in convivial towns, depart promptly from those that were less sympatico, and allow time to detour at whim to investigate culinary oddities in their native habitat. Absolutely nothing was set in stone — except for one destination.

Four years earlier, my husband — and I say this lovingly — had become obsessed with a rural Albanian restaurant called Ali Kali. "The owner brings in your food riding on the back of a horse," he told me excitedly. "Ali Kali means Ali's Horse. It's fantastic. We've got to go."

He showed me YouTube videos of a wiry man in Bermuda shorts riding bareback into the center of an outdoor restaurant brandishing skewers of meat hot off the grill. When the horse dropped to its knees, Ali leapt down and strode among the tables, serving sizzling chunks of lamb to grinning Albanian families. Everyone was clearly getting a tremendous kick out of the whole performance.

I'd mentioned Ali Kali to many friends, and not all of them shared Rich's enthusiasm. Some considered horseback food delivery to be dubious on many levels, starting with taste, hygiene, and the morality of training animals to perform tricks. But I had learned to trust Rich's instincts for finding remarkable food experiences. However wildly we might divert from the original rough itinerary, I knew from the start that Ali Kali was a fixed star on the horizon.

By now the departure date seemed to be zooming toward me at warp speed. I began working feverishly to create some order out of the piles of Post-it notes and scribbled-on cocktail napkins littering my desk. I ruthlessly deleted whole countries I'd visited before — sorry, Slovenia and Montenegro — and organized my thoughts into a few, densely packed pages headed "Tentative Itinerary." Under the name of each country I listed the most interesting cities, culinary specialties, EatWith hosts, food tours, and random oddities too intriguing to pass up.

Meanwhile, I was doing the same kind of fierce final editing with my wardrobe. As a semi-minimalist, I travel with just one roll-aboard suitcase and a roomy purse I can sling on bandolero-style. I pack the same amount for a weekend or many months on the road, bringing sturdy, fast-drying, no-iron garments that can stand up to frequent use and the eccentricities of Airbnb washing machines. Comfort is my first priority, although I also strive for a reasonable degree of stylishness — by which I mean not looking as if I were on my way to a safari, the gym, or bed.

Having narrowed down my clothing choices, I began laying everything out on the guest room bed. A few garments fell short of roadworthy cleanliness and were tossed into the washing machine. Forty-five minutes later I was staring at the remains of my new grey cardigan exclaiming in horror, "What happened here?"

Recently purchased and lightly worn, the go-with-everything cardigan had not survived its very first washing. Yes, before you ask, I'd scrupulously followed the cold-water-only instructions on the label. Yet what was once a long and supple garment was now short and boxy, with arms that would be snug on a ten-year-old. As directed, I attempted to "reshape and dry flat," but no matter how vigorously I tugged, the cardigan simply sprang back into its preferred child size. I could almost hear it snickering at my futile efforts.

When you're living out of a single small suitcase for months at a time, every garment has to pull its weight, fitting over and under various other layers. Tight clothes are always impractical, and doubly so on this trip, when some serious eating would be taking place. While I was hoping my weight wouldn't balloon out of control, I doubted my arms were going to shrink back to the size they were in fourth grade.

With the untimely demise of the gray cardigan, my packing list now included a light jacket, a pullover sweater, my seventeen-pocket travel vest, three pairs of trousers, three shirts, two long-sleeved t-shirts, two tank tops, loose yoga pants for workouts and sleeping, a scarf, sneakers, walking shoes, slippers, undergarments, and socks. Personal essentials were tucked into my toiletry kit, and I'd stockpiled five months' supply of prescription medications. My electronic devices included my iPhone, a Kindle, and the laptop I'd need for blogging along the way.

My readers often write to point out how difficult it is to whittle down your wardrobe when you don't know precisely what lies ahead. Yes, it is tough. But it becomes a lot easier when you give up trying to cover every possible contingency. The trick is to take basic, versatile clothes, dress in layers, and assume if you suddenly decide you need something — a warmer sweater, say, or a sun hat — you can pick it up along the way. On long trips, I always make a few wardrobe adjustments.

"My biggest problem," one reader wrote, "is packing all the medications I want on hand just in case something flares up."

The secret is to take minimal amounts — the tail end of a tube of ointment, enough pills for five days —rather than toting full containers of every contingency medication. If the problem persists, or should something new crop up, Europe has excellent pharmacists who are able to dispense many medications that in the US would require a doctor's prescription. Obviously if you might suddenly need something critical and difficult to get, like a specific heart medication, you'll want to carry plenty with you. But otherwise, reducing the volume of just-in-case meds can save valuable weight and space.

You're likely to find plenty of pharmacies and other useful shops all along your route. This makes it practical to pack small, travel-size toiletries that you can replace when they're used up. You can't always count on finding your favorite brands, but hey, trying new stuff is all part of the adventure, right?

Ten days before our April departure date, with the packing and rough itinerary more or less under control, Rich and I went to lunch with our friend Haris. He'd grown up in Crete's capital, Heraklion, which I'd earmarked as the end point of the trip, and I wanted his take on the island's culinary traditions. As he spread a map of Crete on the table, I asked, "What's the most popular comfort food?"

"*Hohli bourbouristi.*"

"And that would be…?"

"Snails cooked in rosemary. Look, there is a recipe on the back of the map." He flipped it over to show a photo of glistening snails, three recipes, and several paragraphs of general culinary advice for visitors.

"Great map!" I exclaimed. "Where did you get it?"

Haris grinned and tapped the logo in the map's corner. "McDonald's."

He asked about the route, and I explained to him the plan called for catching the new high-speed train to Valencia, heading north to Barcelona and on to southern France, and then continuing around the Mediterranean rim, ultimately arriving in Crete.

Haris began to look worried. "But that means you'll get to Crete when — in August? You really don't want to do that." He shuddered. "The heat. The crowds. It will be terrible."

Rich and I looked at each other, then back at Haris. "Should we reverse the entire journey?" I asked. "Go to Crete first?"

Haris's face lit up. April, it seemed, was a heavenly time on the island. Mild temperatures, few tourists, everything in bloom. It didn't take long for him to convince us of the wisdom of making his home town the starting point.

As soon as lunch was over, Rich and I rushed back to the apartment. While he booked airline tickets to Heraklion, I got to work reversing our tentative itinerary. Instead of moving from the familiar to the exotic, I'd be plunging right into the unknown. OK, sure, why not?

I reminded myself that every trip worth taking involves uncertainty, surprises, and the peculiar challenges author Kurt Vonnegut called "dancing lessons from God." It's this very sense of mystery and suspense that keeps us turning the pages of our own travel journals, eager to see what's going to unfold in the next chapter.

2. Seville / *Ham of God*

During the run-up to departure, I spent as much time as possible with friends in Seville, soaking up warm feelings of companionship to sustain me on the road. Sooner or later, someone would always ask, "How can you stand to be away for months at a time? Don't you long for your own bed?"

Of course I do, especially when I find myself in some funky hostel with pillows harder than my suitcase and blankets so heavy I can barely roll over or so skimpy I have to sleep in all my clothes. But having traveled to more than sixty countries and lived in several, I'd grown comfortable with the idea that, as the seventeenth-century poet Matsuo Basho wrote in his travel diary, "Every day is a journey, and the journey itself is home."

Whenever people asked if I was going to miss my own bed, I suspected what they really wanted to know was whether I'd miss them — along with all the other friends and family who make up the fabric of my life. Of course I would, I'd miss them terribly, and I made sure to let them know it. But being an expat means partings and reunions are woven into the fabric of my life. And I would hardly, as many seemed to think, be existing in an emotional vacuum. Not only would I have Rich's congenial companionship, but I'd be meeting countless others along the way. These social connections might last minutes, an evening, or a lifetime, but I'd learned even the shortest could boost my spirits and nourish my soul.

My Spanish friends are dumbfounded by this attitude. In Seville's traditional culture, nearly everyone's closest bonds are with family and friends they've known since baptism. Those relationships are the bedrock on which they build their lives. Rather being relegated to the outer margins of their spare time — after work, shopping, and the gym — their personal life comes first. (What a concept!)

Having the family home as the center point of life means there's generally a matriarch running things. Where some cultures (say, America, to pick one at random) are obsessed with young women, in the Mediterranean region middle aged and older females wield the real power in the extended family. These matriarchs hold society together and command respect at an age when, in other communities, they'd be isolated and ignored.

You can see why I love living in Seville.

Of course, not everyone in Spain — let alone the rest of the world — exists in the cozy embrace of that kind of close circle. Most of us can scarcely imagine what it's like to live out our lives surrounded by people who love us and want to see us every day and twice on Sunday. The sad fact is the world was in the grip of a loneliness epidemic long before anyone went into lockdown because of Covid-19.

In 2018, for instance, the Japanese government began trying to figure out why half a million of their nation's young people, known as *hikikomori,* were living in acute social withdrawal. At an age when most of us were learning to make our way in the world, these youngsters are hunkering down at home, in their room, refusing to go outside or have any human contact for six months or more at a stretch. For some, it's become a way of life extending into middle age. The impulse is understandable; we've all had days when we were tempted to stay home and pull the covers over our head. Apparently the *hikikomori* feel like that every day.

And they're not alone. Well, yes, technically they are alone, but metaphorically speaking they have plenty of company. Similar worrying statistics have been reported in Great Britain, Denmark, New Zealand,

Australia, and elsewhere. In the US, more than half of all adults, and nearly eighty percent of young adults, are classified as lonely. Feelings of isolation are on the rise in all age groups across the globe — yes, sadly, even in Spain and other Mediterranean countries. I wondered if I would see evidence of it during my travels.

Lack of human companionship certainly wasn't an issue for me in Seville, a city famous for its vibrant social life. As usual before leaving town, I enjoyed a round of long, wine-soaked farewell lunches and dinners with expat and Sevillano friends. Everyone wanted to share some final snippet of advice about places to go and things to eat, and these discussions were usually accompanied by a bottle of wine and a plate of Spain's most beloved comfort food, jamón (ham).

When I first arrived in Seville I was a vegetarian and could not understand why everyone was rhapsodizing about the dark red ham sliced from the massive hind legs of pigs that hung like clusters of bats from the ceiling of every tapas bar in town. Like most Americans, I'd grown up thinking of ham as the fleshy pink stuff in deli sandwiches. Spanish jamón could not be more different if it came from another animal altogether, possibly one from a parallel universe.

Jamón is a robust red cured meat marbled with white fat and "cut thin as cigarette paper," as the 1903 Gourmet's Guide to Europe put it. Bite-sized slivers are carefully arranged on a plate and carried to your table with the reverence of an acolyte delivering the Holy Grail. It has a robust yet elegant scent, rich flavor, and a texture that manages to be both toothy and tender. In Seville, it's consumed on morning toast, with beer at lunch, as a prelude to dinner in the evening, and as a late-night snack on the way home from a congenial gathering. The blissful expression on my friends' faces as they conveyed morsels of jamón to their mouths was one of the reasons I eventually abandoned my vegetarian diet.

I wasn't the first to forswear my principles and start eating jamón. In fact, during the Spanish Inquisition, thousands did just that in an often-futile attempt to save themselves from the flames of the *auto-da-fé*.

It all started in the fifteenth century when young Queen Isabella of Castille secretly married her second cousin, King Ferdinand of Aragon. There was a pesky little technicality in Church law prohibiting marriage between second cousins, and to get around it she produced a document allegedly conveying a special dispensation from Pope Pius II — which would have been somewhat more convincing if the Pope hadn't died five years before it was written. However, everybody decided to pretend it was all on the up and up, and the young couple got married and began to unify (or take over, depending on your point of view) the city-states that would eventually form the nation of Spain.

The Church, having turned a blind eye to the dubious status of the royal marriage, naturally expected the Queen's loyalty in return. High-ranking clergy began to whisper in her ear that unification would never work properly while diverse faiths were tolerated, as they had been in the region for centuries. For the good of the kingdom — and everybody's soul — why not make Catholicism mandatory for all her subjects? And while she was at it, how about authorizing a special team of Church officials to root out heretics, pagans, witches, sexual deviants, and other undesirables?

And so it came to pass. Thousands sensibly packed up and relocated to other countries. But thousands more elected to stay and become second-class Catholics known as *conversos* (if they were Jewish) or *moriscos* (if Muslim). They figured it would be easier to pretend to be Catholic than to uproot their families and businesses and start over somewhere else.

They were so wrong.

Neighbors, church officials, and government inspectors kept a constant, suspicious eye on the new converts, just waiting for them to slip up. Along with all their other religious beliefs, the converts had to disavow the ancient pork taboos of both the Jewish and Muslim faiths. As camouflage, savvy converts kept a ham leg hanging by the kitchen window, let their neighbors see them buying pork shoulders from the butcher, and waxed enthusiastic about the superiority of *manteca* (pork lard) over olive oil. Sometimes a mere whiff of olive oil in the kitchen, reported by a grouchy neighbor, could bring a *converso* or *morisco* up on charges before the Inquisitors.

Enforcement waxed and waned over the centuries, but the Inquisition remained in effect until 1834. It was not Spain's finest 356 years.

But we can't blame ham for its unwitting role in the sordid events of that era. Spanish *jamón* pre-dates the Inquisition by centuries, possibly millennia, and remains the nation's favorite food. It's the culinary mainstay of nearly every social gathering, and (according to my Sevillano friends) essential to maintaining a healthy physique. And before you start snickering about that, scientific evidence (from a Spanish study, of course) provides some support for the claim.

High-quality Spanish ham contains considerable amounts of oleic acid, which promotes the production of HDL, the "good cholesterol" that offsets the bad. Some years ago, when my cholesterol crept above 200, my Spanish doctor never mentioned statins or Omega 3 fatty acids, he simply told me to up my intake of red wine, dark chocolate, and good *jamón*. And while I suspect the oatmeal and fish oil capsules I added to my diet played a role, I can't ignore the possibility that *jamón* did some of the heavy lifting in getting those numbers back into the healthy column.

The greatest health benefits are attributed to top-notch *jamón iberico de bellota*, ham from free-range pigs with *patas negras* (black hooves) raised on a diet of acorns in southern Spain's oak forests. But even lesser versions are pretty good. *Jamón* has become one of my favorite comfort foods, and I ate a lot of it in the run-up to departure that spring.

My farewell lunches also included heaping portions of another

Spanish classic, *paella*. This started out as a cheap and easy way to feed field hands in rice-growing Valencia. As lunchtime approached the workers would capture whatever form of protein was wandering around — generally rabbits, chickens, and snails — and cook it up with rice and a few threads of saffron to give the dish a lively yellow color.

In modern times, *paella* is still customarily made by men, although the ingredients are usually purchased in markets, and it's no longer a worker's weekday meal but the centerpiece of a leisurely Sunday lunch. While the guys are all bustling around the kitchen or outdoor grilling ring, the female members of the party are expected to lounge about in the garden or living room sipping wine, topping up each other's glasses, and murmuring, "I could get used to this!"

Rich's first foray into *paella*-making occurred at a Spanish friend's home, but his efforts to come to grips with the process were frustrated by Javier's casual insistence that you just put in "as much as is needed" of each ingredient. The pan itself (the *paella* or PAELLERA, for which the dish is named) serves as a measuring tool. Preparations begin with the cook pouring a river of dry rice down the middle of the pan. "The width of the rice is the same as the distance between the rivets on the handles," Javier explained to Rich. "And the depth should match the height of the rivets." Next came chicken broth, and when Rich asked how to add, Javier's answer was, of course, "as much as is needed."

Since then Rich has taken *paella* classes with Victor Silvestre, a young chef with a cooking school at Seville's Triana Market. According to Victor, the only true *paella* is *Paella Valenciana*, which is made with rabbit, chicken, and snails; all other versions are merely rice dishes. Not all Spaniards are such die-hard purists. In fact, snails and rabbits have largely been abandoned in favor of more popular ingredients such as shellfish and artichoke hearts.

But flexibility only goes so far. There is one ingredient capable of rousing the wrath of the populace, as British celebrity chef Jamie Oliver learned a few years ago.

Oliver kicked off the uproar known as "Paellagate" by tweeting, "Good Spanish food doesn't get much better than paella. My version combines chicken thighs & chorizo."

The outrage was so intense, you'd have thought Oliver's recipe called for cyanide and radioactive waste. I knew traditionalists considered chorizo taboo in *paella* because its strong taste overwhelms the rest of the flavors, but I had no idea what a cultural hot button it was. One tweet ranted, "Hello @jamieoliver this is not paella, this is terrorism, you'd be better off making nuggets out of your fingers." Another showed a plate with fried eggs, sausages, and rice covered with ketchup, with the snarky caption, "Great work @jamieoliver. I also cooked paella. Hope you like my version." Fighting words!

"They went medieval on me man. It was serious," said the chef. "It trended *for weeks*. And I had death threats and all sorts because of a bit of sausage." He added unrepentantly, "By the way, just FYI, it tastes better with chorizo." At the risk of inviting death threats from my Spanish readers, I'll confess right now that I agree. I love chorizo in my *paella*. There I've said it and I stand by it. Don't hate me.

There is, however, one genuine abomination that moves even me to wrath, and that's frozen *paella*. The secret to this dish is making it fresh and serving it immediately, before the short, round-grain rice (usually *bomba*, which is similar to *arborio*) turns starchy. If a restaurant displays a poster out front offering six kinds of *paella*, you can be sure they're pulling it out of the freezer, and you're not getting the real deal. The Spanish consider *paella* too heavy to eat for dinner but perfect for Sunday lunch, because afterwards everybody can retire for a nice, long siesta until the afternoon's heat begins to subside.

Andalucía's hot climate has deeply affected all aspects of life, including its cuisine, so you won't be surprised to learn *gazpacho* was invented here, along with two lesser known but equally delicious cold soups, *salmorejo* and *ajo blanco*. Refreshingly cool on parched throats during a sizzling day, they also provide a practical way for thrifty cooks to use up leftovers.

If you haven't had the good fortune to encounter *gazpacho* in its native Seville, you may be used to the international version: coarsely chopped vegetables in a watery tomato base. Here on its home ground, *gazpacho* is pureed in a blender (in the old days, of course, it was mashed by hand) until it becomes smooth enough to drink from a glass. Recipes generally involve ripe tomatoes, green peppers, cucumber, garlic, extra virgin olive oil, vinegar, and salt. *Salmorejo* is somewhat similar, composed of tomatoes, garlic, olive oil, vinegar, and salt plus some stale bread, which gives it a thicker, creamier texture. Often *salmorejo* is topped with scraps of *jamón ,* chopped hard-boiled egg, and a drizzle of olive oil.

Chef Victor told me that two thousand years ago, these soups started out as field rations for Roman soldiers. They mashed together olive oil, a little onion, salt, and vinegar, creating a thick liquid providing rehydration and electrolytes as the men marched through the sweltering countryside in heavy armor. After Columbus returned from the New World, tomatoes were added for nutrition and a pop of flavor. In the twentieth century, refrigeration allowed these soups to be served chilled. Today, *salmorejo* is my go-to meal on days when it's too hot to eat much.

The soup that's most fun to surprise my visitors with is *ajo blanco*, invented in the nearby city of Málaga. While Spanish speakers easily translate the name as "white garlic," nobody ever guesses the ingredients. Spoiler alert: it's made of ground almonds, garlic, stale bread, extra virgin olive oil, vinegar, and salt. It passes through the blender in stages, resulting in a smooth yet slight grainy texture. This one's served in a bowl with a few green grapes hidden in the bottom, providing a wow finish.

Seville's scorching summer weather is one of the many reasons people like tapas, small portions that are just right when you want a little something but can't face up to a big meal. And although in recent years the city has enjoyed a foodie revolution that has fancy eateries springing up everywhere, there are still plenty of modest café-bars offering classic fare at affordable prices. Often prepared by someone's *abuela* (grandmother) using her *abuela's* recipes, the city's favorite tapas include *solomillo al whiskey* (pork loin in whiskey sauce), *colo de toro* (stewed bull's tail), *carrilladas* (pig cheeks), and *tortilla de españa* (a dense omelet with potatoes).

I was chowing down on plenty of these traditional dishes during my farewell meals with friends. Everyone kept asking if I was packed yet, and I kept explaining that I had everything laid out on the guest bed next to my suitcase, and I would do my actual packing the day before departure. Yes, I was pretty sure everything would fit in my bag.

Thinking about my travel wardrobe, I tried not to be bitter about the loss of my grey cardigan and my inability, in the short time available, to find a suitable replacement. I reminded myself that every trip has a few bumps and bounces in the run-up to departure. If losing the cardigan and reversing the order of our route were the only potholes in the road, I could hardly complain.

And then, three days before our departure date, Rich mentioned that he needed to go over to the clinic to have something checked out.

These are not words anyone wants to hear. Ever. And that goes double when you're about to leave for months on the road. We hotfooted it over to the clinic, and soon a doctor was bending over Rich, making the traditional "Hmmmm" sounds that indicate deep thought, although possibly about nothing more significant than where he was going to go for lunch that day.

Don't worry, I'm not working my way up to some blood-curdling medical horror story. The problem turned out to be a minor, benign skin issue on Rich's back requiring a small surgical procedure. When it was over, I asked the doctor about follow-up care, figuring he'd hand me a tube of antibiotic ointment and a fistful of Band-Aids and we'd be on our way.

"It will need to be cleaned every day."

"OK, show me how to do that."

He looked at me as if I'd offered to pitch in and perform open-heart surgery. "No. Impossible. It must be done by a medical professional."

"How often?

"Every day."

Every day? Was he kidding? How were we supposed to manage that on the road?

"For how long?" I asked.

"Not long. Two weeks, maybe three."

Three weeks? "Should we delay our trip?" I'd already filled him in a little on our plans.

He considered briefly then shook his head. "You say you are going to Crete? You can find a clinic there." Yes, that didn't sound daunting at all. Eventually, and very grudgingly, he agreed every other day might be sufficient.

Rich and I spent the long walk back to our apartment discussing whether we should postpone our departure, but he was determined not to let such a minor medical issue derail our plans.

After all, we'd dealt with illness and injury on the road before. There was the time I broke my finger in the Peruvian jungle, when the nearest medical clinic was days away by boat. All it needed was a splint, so Rich made me one. Problem solved. Another time Rich ate bad shrimp in Mexico and was ill for days, living on Coca-Cola and crackers. Finally

I said, "I've got the name of a local doctor..." At the prospect of receiving medical care in a tiny town in rural Mexico, Rich sat bolt upright in bed, exclaiming, "No! I'm feeling a LOT better." In minutes he was dressed, within hours he was walking around, and the next day we resumed our journey.

One of the comforting things about traveling in Europe was knowing how easy it is to access good medical attention. Healthcare in most European countries consistently ranks higher than that of the US (which is currently number thirty on the list). I usually start at the nearest pharmacy; they're legally qualified to dispense a broad range of advice and medications. In the unlikely event nobody at that pharmacy speaks English, I find one near the train station, where they're used to dealing with foreigners and tend to know multiple languages. If the issue is beyond them, pharmacists can often direct you to a physician, as can your hotel or the nearest embassy or consulate.

Getting good care in Crete was certainly possible; it was just a matter of figuring out exactly where to find it. The minute we got home, Rich grabbed his laptop and began researching private clinics in Heraklion and the next several cities under consideration.

"It will be fine," he muttered, eyes glued to the screen.

"Of course it will," I replied. I made a mental note to pack Band-Aids and look up the Greek word for antibiotic. (It's αντιβιοτικό, in case you're wondering.)

And then it was the eve of our departure. Rich and I dropped in at a favorite neighborhood tapas bar for some wine and a final plate of *jamón*. Then we walked back to the apartment and spent the rest of the evening tidying rooms, closing shutters, and reviewing the contents of our suitcases, reassuring ourselves once again that all was ready.

As I climbed into bed, I found myself wondering how this trip would change me. That I would return a slightly different person I had no doubt. The truth is, as I wrote in a post back in 2015, "When we set out in search of adventure what we really discover is ourselves. All journeys are inner journeys. The excitement of exploration lets us shed our ordinary preoccupations long enough to feel the rapture of being alive." Filled with anticipation bordering on rapture, I could scarcely sleep that night.

Rising before dawn, I pulled on the clothes I'd laid out in readiness, slung my purse over one shoulder, and grabbed the handle of my suitcase. After so many long months of preparation, it was time go.

Rich and I set out through the dark, chilly stillness to the railway station. The early train to Madrid would let us catch the afternoon flight to Crete; we'd be there by dinner time. Already I could feel my reality shifting. I did not lose one drop of the love I felt for my friends, my work, my apartment, or the ancient city I lived in, with its passion for *jamón* and family and fun. I didn't forget the deeply worrying state of the world or my obligation to do my small bit to help fix the mess. But with each step, I found myself falling into the sweet simplicity of a life in motion. As Jack Kerouac put it, "Nothing behind me, everything ahead of me, as is ever so on the road."

GREECE

3. Heraklion / *Gifts from the Wine-Dark Sea*

My first night in Crete started out well, but by the end of it, I was groaning and muttering to Rich, "I have learned my lesson. I am never, ever going to tell another person that I'm a travel writer on a food tour."

Our flight had arrived on the island at twilight, touching down gently at Heraklion's main airport, Nikos Kazantzakis International, named for the Crete-born author of *Zorba the Greek*. "The perfect traveler," wrote Kazantzakis, "always creates the country where he travels." I don't claim to be a perfect anything, but yes, I take full responsibility for creating what happened that first night in Heraklion.

The evening had turned dark and chilly by the time the taxi dropped us in front of our Airbnb apartment, where our engaging young host, Marina, and her boyfriend, Alex, were waiting to greet us. Their English was fluent and their welcome infused with *xenia*, the ardent hospitality for which the Greeks have been famous for thousands of years.

Xenia (literally guest-friendship) is serious business, requiring both host and guest to treat one another with courtesy and respect or risk the wrath of Zeus, avenger of wronged strangers. In modern times lapses in *xenia* rarely get punished with a lightning bolt or having your liver pecked out by eagles (and frankly, I can think of a few instances where I'd like to have seen this happen). But Greek hosts still go out of their way to be helpful. Everyone knows you really don't want to get on the wrong side of Zeus.

As Marina finished showing us around and handed over the keys, Rich asked, "Can you recommend somewhere we can go for dinner?"

"Yes, of course." She and Alex exchanged glances, then she added, "We are going out to eat now ourselves. Would you like to join us?"

Why not?

Twenty minutes later the four of us were ensconced at a table in a busy taverna near the waterfront, and Alex was offering to order for us all. He conducted a lively consultation with the waiter, who soon returned with a carafe of cold white wine and hot, crisp-fried zucchini. Next came a salad of cucumbers and tomatoes topped with thick wedges of feta cheese and large chunks of the barley rusks known locally as *dakos*, bread that was baked twice to make sure it was hard enough to chip a tooth (don't ask me why). A basket of softer bread appeared along with a dip that Alex and the menu both called mashed fava beans, but which inexplicably contained no fava beans whatsoever, being composed entirely of yellow split peas and a little seasoning. No matter, it was all great and I tucked in with pleasure.

Marina and Alex were soon in full possession of the facts about the Mediterranean Comfort Food Tour and offered various suggestions about places to go and foods to sample. Marina asked about my work as a writer and told me she was currently managing fifty Airbnb apartments. No wonder, I thought, that under her cheerfulness she looked exhausted.

Alex didn't appear to have a job at the moment, unless you counted ordering more food, which he continued to do with all the enthusiasm of one who is justly proud of his city's culinary delights, hopes to be immortalized in a book, and knows someone else is picking up the tab. Tiny, breaded sardines were followed by fried calamari and a whole, grilled *dorado* (golden sea bream), a fish so delectable the ancients associated it with Aphrodite, goddess of love. A second carafe of wine appeared as if by magic. I assured Alex with sincerity that everything was fabulous.

"In this country," Marina remarked to me in a casual undertone, "we keep bringing food until guests no longer continue to eat."

"Put down your fork," I whispered to Rich.

But even after Alex stopped ordering, there was more to come. It turned out that in Crete and much of southern Greece, restaurants had their own hospitality obligations, traditionally expressed by means of complimentary desserts and after-dinner drinks, usually small glasses of raki, the local brandy.

"I don't see how we can refuse," murmured Rich, manfully picking up his fork again to address the *ravani*, a sort of sponge cake made from semolina (coarsely ground durum wheat) that was blandly sweet and somehow both gummy and grainy at the same time.

Alex leaned forward and said, "But if you are writing about food you must try our lamb. I know a village…" He cast his eyes heavenward to express his appreciation for the extraordinary culinary blessings to be found in this humble hamlet. "We will all go tomorrow."

In a haze of wine-induced bonhomie, I accepted the invitation. But later, as we climbed heavily into bed, Rich said, "If we keep eating like this, I'm going to have a heart attack before we get to Athens."

"Don't be silly. Tomorrow won't be like this. We were eating low on the food chain tonight, mostly seafood. In the village, they will be serving lamb like there's no tomorrow. Because after that it's the last week of Lent, and nobody's getting any meat until Easter."

We'd arrived on a Saturday night, and the following Monday marked the start of Orthodox Holy Week, the run-up to Easter and the signal for the faithful to get serious about their Lenten fasting. Soon they'd be abstaining from olive oil, wine, and anything with red blood or a backbone. On the eve of such profound privation, no doubt the village chefs would go to extraordinary lengths to produce lamb dishes hearty enough to sustain everyone through an entire meatless week.

Rich groaned and got up to find the Pepto Bismol.

Luckily for our arteries, our livers, and our Pepto Bismol supply, the village lamb-eating expedition was scuttled by logistical complications. But I soon learned Alex was only the first of many who would go overboard in assisting me in my quest for comfort food.

Take for instance the staff of the private medical clinic we visited early Monday morning. Rich had spent days in close correspondence with them, and when he arrived that Monday, the staff greeted him with traditional Greek *xenia* and the fulsome enthusiasm of those welcoming a new customer who has expressed willingness to pay full price in cash.

In fact, Rich was treated like an old friend who also happened to be a member of the royal family and had just scored the winning goal in the final playoffs. The staff managed to refrain from picking him up and carrying him on their shoulders, but he was whisked past the reception line and taken directly upstairs to the office of Renia, head of the International Patient Department. Renia dropped everything to exchange handshakes, pleasantries, and initial paperwork with us, then went off to round up the doctor she'd earmarked for the job. He was a neurosurgeon, which seemed a trifle excessive for a simple dressing change, but at least I could be pretty sure he knew what he was doing.

Renia stayed with us every minute, supervising the procedure and chatting with me about what I hoped to see while in Crete. I got all the way to the cashier before I let it slip that we were on a Mediterranean Comfort Food Tour.

"But I know where you must go for the best fish in the city!" she exclaimed and ran upstairs to her office to fetch the restaurant's card, blithely ignoring the fact she was holding up the payment process not only for us, but for everyone behind us in line. Clearly she had a firm grasp of the virtue of *xenia* over mere business.

Renia and the neurosurgeon were extraordinarily kind and competent, but still, as we emerged from the clinic into the bright sunshine, Rich and I felt in need of a restorative second breakfast. I spotted an old-school coffee house with simple tables, no art on the walls, and a scattering of contented-looking guests. It was run by a blowsy woman with dyed blond hair and the kind of gravelly voice I always associate with Melina Mercouri, the *Never on Sunday* movie star who later became a member of parliament. The modest menu included a childhood favorite: grilled cheese sandwiches on white bread, served so hot the cheese was nearly liquified. Accompanied by gritty Greek coffee, it was just about perfect.

As I set down my cup, empty now of everything but the thick sediment in the bottom, I said to Rich, "But enough about you. Let's get serious about my hair." I'd had to cancel an appointment at my Seville salon to go to the clinic with Rich, and my look had crossed the line from casual to unkempt.

Finding a hairdresser in a strange foreign city is always challenging, and in Heraklion the search was further complicated by the need to decipher signs reading, "ινστιτούτο αισθητικής" and "αίθουσες ομορφιάς." I was doing my best to learn Greek characters, but I had to admit I often felt, as Nikos Kazantzakis put it, "May God forgive me, but the letters of the alphabet frighten me terribly. They are sly, shameless demons — and dangerous! You open the inkwell, release them; they run off — and how will you ever get control of them again!"

I decided to ignore the signs and peer through windows. Were there hairdressers at work? Did they look competent and not too relentlessly trendy? I didn't want to have to fend off suggestions that I get a tattoo, dye my hair blue, or shave the sides of my head to liven up my look. Eventually I found a small, family-owned salon, where I had the undivided attention of Nico and his two sons, both of whom, Zeus be praised, spoke English.

The younger son, Alex, handled the color; Vasili did the cut; both peppered me with questions about America and American movies. Alex was a big fan of horror films, and when I said nothing had ever scared me quite as much as *The Exorcist*, both young men eyed me blankly, but Nico (who spoke no English but had seen the film) jumped in. After I'd pantomimed Linda Blair's head spinning around, he enacted the floating-above-the-bed scene, provoking gales of laughter. The guys were great at their jobs and fun to be with, and we parted in a flurry of mutual good will.

By now it was lunchtime, and Rich and I headed to Mare, the fish restaurant Renia had recommended. This turned out to be a large, modern, upscale establishment on the waterfront, filled with extremely well-groomed Greeks and international visitors. The piped-in music was mostly instrumental interpretations of 1970s pop music; I have a vague recollection that "Don't Go Changin'" was playing as I walked in, but then again, it might have been "Feelings." Not exactly the kind of traditional place I normally seek out, but I was there, I was hungry, and I'd promised Renia to give it a try.

"Thank God I just had my hair done," I murmured to Rich as we sat down. My clothes were pretty basic, but I felt my coiffure could hold up its head anywhere. Craning my neck, I studied my reflection in the enormous, wrap-around windows, admiring the handiwork of Nico's boys.

Beyond the windows lay the Sea of Crete, the southernmost waters of the Aegean. Near the shore shone a brilliant, glittering turquoise. Further out, where the serious depths began, it turned the rich violet-purple of a glass of Shiraz, a living example of Homer's famous description of the "wine-dark sea." Scholars have argued for centuries over this phrase, objecting that seawater isn't dark red or purple but blue. They've advanced all sorts of convoluted explanations for Homer's repeated use of the phrase, including widespread colorblindness, the lack of the word "blue" in ancient Greek, an outbreak of red algae, or alkaline mineral deposits turning Greek wine dark blue. And in the end, all they actually needed to do was go look at the Aegean on a sunny day.

"I'm thinking the grilled octopus," Rich said, bringing me back to more immediate concerns. "It comes with caramelized onions and locust bean cream, whatever that is." (Looking it up later, I found that's a fancy name for carob seeds, which are primarily fed to animals; humans rarely eat them except when they're in the grip of famines, health food crazes, and haute cuisine one-upmanship.) I chose the shrimp and mussels in a light feta cheese and mustard sauce. Rich suggested a small carafe of house white to round out the meal.

What arrived was some of the most astonishingly delicious food I'd had in years. Everything was perfectly prepared; the octopus was succulent, the glistening shellfish fresh from the sea, the sauce of feta cheese and mustard delicate yet creamy. Thick-cut rustic bread was thoughtfully provided so we could sop up every last drop of feta, mustard, and locust bean.

As I leaned back, replete, thinking seriously about a siesta, two complementary desserts appeared on the table. Daringly, the chef had gone with the American classic red velvet cake and *sfakiani* pie, a sort of cross between flan and cheesecake that's a specialty of the Sfakia region along Crete's southern coast. Both were as fabulous as the main course. The waiter kindly provided a small carafe of *ouzo*, just to make absolutely sure we walked out in a blissful haze.

The Greeks have the perfect word for this state: *kefi*, which refers to the contentment and joy that arises when a moment is so overwhelmingly enjoyable you are completely transported by it. They say it most often happens when the company is good and the conversation engaging. I would add that superlative food (to say nothing of wine and ouzo) can also be a contributing factor in the confluence of pleasures creating this blissful sensation.

I decided we'd made a brilliant decision — thanks to Haris — about starting the trip in Crete. The weather was crisp and sunny, the people brimming with *xenia,* each day replete with *kefi.* And I was looking forward to an excursion that I hoped would be the highlight of our stay in Heraklion: a visit to Knossos, the 9000-year-old settlement known as "Europe's first city."

Knossos had its glory days around 1600 BC, when the population hit 100,000 and the legendary King Minos took the throne. To reassure supporters and intimidate his enemies, Minos asked the sea god Poseidon to send him a glorious bull, which he would then sacrifice in the god's honor. When a spectacular bull arrived, Minos couldn't bear to part with it, so he killed a lesser beast. Naturally this enraged Poseidon. In revenge, he made Minos' queen fall in love with the bull, mate with it, and give birth to the Minotaur, a creature with the body of a man, the tail of a bull, and an appetite for human flesh.

Note to self: Don't welch on the gods. It never ends well.

Minos imprisoned the Minotaur in an underground labyrinth. People reported hearing his bellows rumbling up from the depths, but he was never seen again.

Neither was the labyrinth. Some say it's still lying undiscovered beneath the vast palace complex. Many suggest the palace itself, with more than 1300 maze-like rooms, was the real labyrinth. Others insist there never was any labyrinth, and the Minotaur legend arose to explain the underground rumbling caused by earthquakes, which were particularly active in the years the story first appeared.

Clearly there was a lot to absorb about Knossos and its legends, and to learn a bit more before Monday's visit, Rich and I spent Sunday at the Heraklion Archeological Museum. Filled with some of the finest ancient artifacts on the planet, the museum's vast collection was so meticulously organized and beautifully presented that strolling from room to room gave me the heady sensation of walking through time itself.

I discovered that Knossos was first settled in the New Stone Age, when homes were made of sticks, mud, and dung, and the hot new trends were farming and domesticating animals. People were making a massive effort to figure out how to exert some control over the randomness of nature so they wouldn't be blindsided quite so often by it. When the Minoans came into power, they showed off their dominance over the natural world through the extreme sport of bull leaping. The museum had lively figurines showing young men and women engaging in this mad, dangerous game, but some questioned their realism.

"It's unclear," said one scholarly article, "whether the particular style (grabbing the bull by the horns, being lifted by the force of his head toss, and somersaulting onto the bull's back) seen in iconography is even possible."

Take it from me: yes, it is. Not that I've ever done it, of course, but I once saw bull leaping during the intermission of a bullfight in Mexico City. A troupe of intrepid little people performed a tumbling act with a young bull, grabbing his horns and somersaulting onto his back before sliding off over his tail and running around for another go. My point is: if those tumblers could do it, no doubt top Minoan athletes could, too.

One of my favorite figurines in the museum was the snake goddesses, whose proud face and bold stance showed she was a true bad ass. She bared her breasts, clutched a writhing serpent in each hand, and — in a surprise move — wore a cat perched on top of her head. Her identity remains in dispute; is she a domestic goddess, earth mother, or a snake-wrangling priestess? And what's with the cat?

By the time I finished touring the museum, I was itching to see the palace of Knossos itself. Sadly, this excursion turned out to be disappointing.

The palace of Knossos, which had been abandoned since Roman

times, had the misfortune of being excavated in the early twentieth century by Oxford's Sir Arthur Evans, whose enthusiasm for the site's picturesque potential far outstripped his attention to historical accuracy and archeological preservation standards. I found it hard to identify which parts were authentic, although I was pretty sure the reinforced concrete walkways and amateurishly reproduced wall paintings were not. Everywhere I looked there were signs admonishing me not to stop in the most interesting areas, for fear I might cause a bottleneck in the flow of tourists.

I tried to get caught up in the mystery, to envision what it must have been like when Europe's first city flowered, back in the days when bull leapers and snake goddesses were young. Instead, I spent most of the visit trying to guess which facts in the maddeningly scanty descriptions were trustworthy and which were flights of Sir Arthur's fantasy. My imagination had been so thoroughly captivated by the lively statues, murals, and figurines in the museum that I'd expected the palace of Knossos to have the same vigorous beauty and enduring charm. It didn't.

Still, it was a thrill just to stand on the site of Europe's oldest city, and to be fair, some sections were quite lovely. I wasn't sorry I went, but I was disinclined to linger. By mid-afternoon I was heading out of the palace ruins and back to the apartment to pack up in preparation for the next day's departure from Heraklion.

In the morning Rich and I rose early for our second and final visit to the clinic, where the staff again rolled out the red carpet, looking as if they were barely restraining themselves from showering Rich (and his wallet) with rose petals. I was going to miss their attitude when our standard of medical care settled back to normal. Doing my part in the *xenia* exchange, I thanked Renia profusely for telling me about the restaurant Mare, assuring her their fish was everything she'd said it was and more.

After that Rich and I collected our suitcases, locked the apartment, left the keys for Marina, and walked to the bus station. We'd decided to head west along the seacoast to Chania, Crete's second largest city, an ancient port surrounded by olive trees, citrus groves, vineyards, and dairy farms. As I stowed my suitcase under the bus and climbed aboard, I reflected, not for the first time, how delightfully simple life can become when you travel. My agenda for the day included nothing more demanding than arriving in Chania, having a bite of lunch, and letting the GPS on Rich's phone guide our steps to the next rental apartment.

As usual, Nikos Kazantzakis put it best. "I felt once more," he said, "how simple and frugal a thing is happiness: a glass of wine, a roast chestnut, a wretched little brazier, the sound of the sea. Nothing else."

4. Chania and Loutro / *Snails from the Crypt*

Before we go any further down the road in Crete, I think we need to stop for a moment to clear away some confusion about the cringeworthy word "cretin." This pejorative term, which implies in an offensive manner that someone is dumb as a rock, has nothing to do with the island of Crete or its inhabitants. *Crétin* is derived from the French word for Christian, which took on a nasty new meaning in the eighteenth century.

At the time, compassionate members of society were attempting to rein in bullies who were abusing those suffering from severe mental and physical impairments, particularly those caused by a common thyroid deficiency. The compassionate began referring to the bullies' victims as *chrétiennes* (Christians) to remind everybody that these unfortunate souls were baptized true believers like themselves and should be treated with common decency. (For now, I'm going to skip over the question of why non-Christians weren't entitled to equal measures of common decency; that's a topic for another day and another rant on my part.)

Proving once again that no good deed goes unpunished, the abusers quickly adopted the term *chrétienne* as an insult, and the shorthand version, *crétin,* took up permanent residence in the global vocabulary of slurs. As if that wasn't enough, healthcare workers began incorporating "cretinism" into medical literature as a synonym for congenital iodine deficiency. Health professionals are now discouraging the use of the word, but it's an uphill battle.

Knowing this, I think we can all agree it's high time to expunge the word "cretin" from our vocabulary, along with the term "cretinism" in reference to congenital iodine deficiency. The word "Cretan" (note the different spelling) refers to a person or thing from the island of Crete, and of course, implies absolutely no disparagement whatsoever. In fact, the people I met on the island were bright, competent, and engaging. Take for instance Yannis, the man who taught me how to cook snails.

Yannis ran a modest restaurant tucked into the back corner of a dusty parking lot in an unfashionable section of Chania, the city we visited after Heraklion. Quite literally if I'd blinked, I would have missed his place altogether. But as I strolled along the sidewalk, the corner of my eye caught a flash of yellow from a painted chair in dappled shade under some trees. Was this someone's private dining spot, I wondered idly. No; a second glace revealed more chairs and a scattering of tables. A restaurant, perhaps? The dogeared sign said helpfully, ΠΕΡΠΕΡΑΣ. Rich and I wandered over to take a closer look.

A tall, balding, affable man with a full beard and skinny pony tail greeted us warmly, and in less time than it takes to tell, we were ensconced at a table in the shade beneath the trees holding photocopied menus handwritten in English. I learned the name of the restaurant was Perperas and that it offered a surprisingly sophisticated array of dishes. Some specials had been meticulously lettered on a chalkboard in Greek and English but had subsequently been smeared into illegibility — presumably by someone's wayward child — and nobody had gotten around to repairing the damage, so I never discovered what they were.

A portly British retiree at the next table leaned over and advised me to order the grated zucchini patties sautéed in olive oil; I did, and he was right, they were excellent. We also had an oregano-dusted pie made of egg, cheese, and spinach, and *tzatziki*, thick Greek yogurt flavored with garlic and cucumber.

The food was beautifully prepared and absolutely delicious. I told

Yannis so, and he beamed with pride, lingering for a few minutes to chat about Cretan food customs. When he headed back to his kitchen, I gazed thoughtfully after him. He was affable, a great cook, and spoke excellent English. Would he let me invade his kitchen?

This wasn't the moment to ask. I'd learned from similar situations in Spain that it was always best to go back a second time and establish myself, however tenuously, as a repeat customer. And then ask. So Rich and I returned the next day, had another wonderful meal, and during a lull in the lunch rush, I sought out Yannis in his kitchen and popped the question. To my astonishment, he agreed.

"What dish would you like to see prepared?" he asked.

I didn't hesitate for a second. "Snails."

By now I'd learned the faithful could eat snails all through Lent because mollusks, lacking a backbone, weren't considered meat. However, making the island's most popular snail dish, *hohli bourbouristi*, required olive oil, which was strictly prohibited during this final week leading up to Easter Sunday. The one exemption was Holy Thursday, when those restrictions were temporarily lifted to celebrate the liturgical feast day commemorating the Last Supper. And as luck would have it, that was the very day I was talking with Yannis.

"Come back tonight," he said.

As you can imagine, I was tremendously excited and spent a good part of the afternoon brushing up on how snails are prepped and cooked. I learned a lot of grisly facts I'd have preferred not to know, and if you like eating snails, you may want to skip the next two paragraphs. The process is gruesome. More so for the snails, obviously, but humans of tender sensibilities will also find the subject distressing.

Still with me? Here goes. When the spring rains come, the snails' underground dens are flooded, forcing them to crawl out in search of drier ground. The unlucky ones are captured and imprisoned in mesh cages or a circle of salt, which they can't cross because salt is lethal to snails. Why? Snails that come into contact with salt rapidly absorb toxic amounts and begin secreting mucus like mad in an effort to wash it away. They become dehydrated and basically melt to death, ending their days as a puddle of slime.

The surviving captives spend about a week eating a bland diet of flour or dry pasta, which is said to make them excrete all their toxins. At this point, they're often thrown live into a pot of boiling water; the surface is soon covered with a white froth of snail saliva. Cookbooks advise keeping an eye out for the more enterprising or desperate members of the community, as they will try to climb out of the pot and must be rounded up and tossed back into the boiling water to perish along with their friends.

As you can imagine, the creepy backstory did nothing to enhance my appetite. "I'm calling this recipe 'Snails from the Crypt,'" I told Rich.

Not everyone takes my dim view of the process. In *The Happy Glutton*, French author Alin Laubreaux wrote, "Few rural delights can compete with that of running through the wet grass, after spring showers, or in the summer after a thunderstorm, in quest of the plump snails. They make their way through shivering grass-blades, or string out across the soft clay like fishing boats leaving port, followed by a silvery wake. In catching snails which one will cook oneself, one experiences the joy of the hunter who stalks his prey, anticipating stew, and that of the fisherman casting his line, with *matelote* [seafood stew] before his mind's eye."

Fortunately or unfortunately, I wasn't required to hunt down my own snails and neither was Yannis. He explained a family in a nearby village handled all that, delivering the snails to his kitchen clean, dead, ready to cook, and — unromantically — shrink-wrapped in plastic.

For one serving of *hohli bourbouristi*, Yannis took thirty large snails, gave them a final rinse in cool water, then dusted them with about a third of a cup of white flour. (He never counted or measured, so all quantities are my guesstimates jotted down at the time.) Then he poured a quarter of a cup of olive oil into a frying pan and set it on a gas burner. Pressing the fleshy foot of each snail into salt (even knowing they were already dead, this made me cringe a little on their behalf), he set each one carefully in the pan with its foot in the hot olive oil.

"They go in 'face down,' as we say," he told me. "The name *bourbouristi* comes from the Cretan *abouboura*, which means 'face down.'"

When the snails were sizzling nicely, he stripped the leaves off two springs of fresh rosemary and scattered them across the top, tossing a pinch of pepper in after them. Pouring half a cup of strong red wine vinegar over everything, he cooked the mixture for about three minutes until the liquid reduced to a thick sauce.

"Done!" said Yannis. He slid the snails into a shallow bowl, carried it outside, and set it down on the table in front of Rich with a flourish.

Rich eyed the bowl with the dubiousness of a man who wasn't that fond of snails and had spent all afternoon listening to the grim details of their journey from capture to cuisine. Gingerly, he picked up the nearest snail. Using the outermost tine of his fork, he delicately pried out the meat, popped it into his mouth, and swallowed. An expression of delighted surprise crossed his face. He nodded, kissed the shell in his fingers, and said, "These snails were not sacrificed in vain."

Sacrifice was the big theme in Greece during those final days of the run-up to Easter. As you may have heard — it's been talked about a lot over the years — Easter's backstory starts in the Garden of Eden when Adam and Eve ate the one fruit that was forbidden to them. In response, God kicked them out of their comfortable home and condemned them and all their descendants (that's the entire human race, folks) to live in a world filled with suffering, evil, and death. Like Zeus and Poseidon, the Christian God does not like to be crossed.

To secure God's forgiveness, Jesus made the ultimate sacrifice. But the effort, according to the nuns at my school, was ongoing; all the faithful, including us kids, were expected to pitch in and make sacrifices to keep on God's good side. And that went double during the run-up to Easter. Starting at the age of seven, I always gave up chocolate for Lent, and that was a pretty big sacrifice, let me tell you. But I figured hey, if that's what it took to defeat the forces of Satan, it was worth it.

And it was kind of thrilling to be part of something that important. Say what you will about old-fashioned Catholic schools — and I myself have said plenty; just ask any of my friends or bartenders — they did foster a sense of belonging. It was hard to feel isolated when you were answering the call to fight in Christ's army.

In Crete and many other parts of the world, they believe in taking that fight to the enemy. Fasting and personal sacrifice aren't considered enough to balance the cosmic scales; every year the faithful symbolically revenge themselves on the most hated figure in the New Testament: the apostle who betrayed Jesus to his Roman executioners. In a ritual that seems more pagan than Christian, an effigy of Judas Iscariot is strung up on Good Friday and put to the torch the following night.

"In recent years, crowds have used the effigies to represent politicians or businessmen who have wronged the people," reported an article in *Time*. "In Venezuela in 2008, a Judas dressed up as an Exxon representative ... was burned following the settlement of a legal fight between the nation and the oil giant. The tradition has also been a venue for misunderstanding, as a 2005 U.S. State Department report criticized Greece for its annual 'burning of the Jew.' Greece essentially responded by saying, 'you're idiots.'"

My blogger friend Jackie, an American living in Greece, had

recommend watching the burning ceremony in the small village of Loutro on the southern shore of Crete. The village, she explained, was quite isolated, clinging to the base of cliffs so steep that you can only get there by boat or, if you're incredibly hardy, by hiking over the mountains. That sounded intriguing, so on Holy Saturday, Rich and I hopped on a bus heading south to Sfakion where we could catch the boat to Loutro.

The first half of the bus ride was lovely, winding gently through towns, villages, and forests as the road skirted the foothills of Lefka Ori, the White Mountains. This impressive range, which occupies a large part of central Crete, earned its name by having snow-covered peaks in winter and showing bare, bleached limestone the rest of the year. As a landmark, it's impossible to miss. As a hiding place for Cretan rebels, it bamboozled the occupying armies of Venice, the Ottoman Empire, and Nazi Germany.

The second half of the journey took us past even more dramatic scenery, but I was unable to enjoy it properly due to the endless series of jolting, hairpin turns. My stomach tends to protest at being bounced around this kind of geography, and I normally placate it with small sips of Coca-Cola, but somehow I'd neglected to buy any for this road trip. I found it helped to keep my eyes shut as much as possible, although toward the end, my eyes kept flying open in alarm as the bus lurched down the final descent, an endless series of abrupt, looping zig-zags.

"Good Lord," I muttered to Rich through clenched teeth, "I haven't seen this many twists and turns since my last colonoscopy film."

It was a relief to stumble off the bus and stand on solid ground. The ferry soon arrived, and sunlight and sea spray restored my equilibrium. After twenty minutes the village of Loutro appeared, tucked into a broad, curved harbor. Fishing boats bobbed in the water, a walkway ran along the shore, and a series of whitewashed cafés, hotels, and shops sat wedged into the narrow strip of land at the base of the cliffs. As Rich and I stepped onto the pier, we were passed by workers hurrying ashore with carts piled high with deliveries. Following at a more leisurely pace, we soon came upon a pleasant little café, sat down, and ordered coffee.

Having a recombobulation coffee has become one of my most cherished travel rituals. Years ago Rich read a post in which perpetual traveler Wandering Earl mentioned that as soon as he arrived in any unknown place, he always stopped for a coffee to give himself a few moments to regroup. Once he'd caught his breath and figured out where he was headed and how to get there, he could move on with more confidence and ease. Rich and I saw the wisdom in that and immediately adopted the practice.

On the rare occasions we've neglected to stop for recombobulation, we've paid the price. For instance, there was the time we took a train across the border between Romania and Bulgaria, hopped into a taxi, and were halfway to our hotel before realizing we had no Bulgarian lev with which to pay the driver. The situation could have turned very awkward indeed; luckily the driver happened to be amused and understanding. Nowadays, we always stop to recombobulate, usually over coffee, before plunging into any unfamiliar town.

In Loutro, I was astonished to be served my καφέ in a French press, something I hadn't seen anywhere else on Crete. As I pushed down the plunger and breathed in the heady aroma, Rich pulled out his iPhone and learned our hotel was just a few minutes' easy stroll further along the walkway. Our room turned out to be at the top, requiring a very long hike up a steep set of stone stairs. I was very glad to be traveling with minimal luggage, as the lone staff member who checked us in down at the bottom didn't even make a pretense of offering to help us with our bags.

"I guess it's survival of the fittest around here," I muttered as I hauled my bag upwards.

Our modest room had a large balcony, and when I stepped out onto it, I immediately spotted the effigy of Judas Iscariot, just a short way further along the harbor, dangling from scaffold on a patch of white sand beach. Of course, nobody knows what this most hated of all Biblical villains actually looked like, but even so the portrayal seemed pretty wide of the mark. The head was a lumpy stuffed pillow case on which vaguely humanoid features— crossed eyes, goofy grin, curly mustache — were drawn with a felt-tip pen. The body was dressed in well-worn sweatpants, sneakers, and a t-shirt sporting a picture of a house cat and the words "Urban Tiger Radio, Where Sound Bites!" Clearly the villagers were having their fun with the effigy. Men and boys were busily stacking palm fronds and scraps of wood around the base for the evening's conflagration.

At dusk the traditional Orthodox liturgy was held in the village church just above the sandy beach with its scaffold. The church was so small people took turns going inside to pay their respects then gathered in the back courtyard, chatting quietly in small groups, trying to keep over-excited children from getting too rambunctious. Nearly everyone but us held unlit candles, and many of the kids carried fancy ones decorated with figures such as unicorns, Barbie, or Spiderman. Rich and I went inside to see the church, then stood at the back of the courtyard to await events.

Eventually the priest emerged and climbed up to stand on a bench beside the door. After saying a few words to the assembled faithful, he began to sing, reading the lyrics off a cell phone tucked into a hymnal, his voice amplified by a microphone held by an altar boy. When he stopped, men and boys took turns enthusiastically ringing the church bell.

Then came the ritual kiss of peace, and everyone lit their candles. The next thing I knew, the service was over and the congregation was hurrying out of the courtyard and down to the beach, where someone had already set the bonfire ablaze beneath the dangling feet of Judas Iscariot. The local boys, including those who had been piously assisting the priest just moments ago, dashed forward to fling fire crackers into the blaze, the small explosions making everyone jump and laugh. As flames consumed the effigy, fireworks burst overhead, lighting up the sky. Once again, evil had been vanquished.

The fire was a doozy, blazing long into the night and still smoldering at dawn when I rose and peered down from my balcony. Soon men from the village arrived to pour water on the embers, shovel the cold, sodden ashes into plastic bags, and carry them away. Someone came to smooth the white sand, making it ready for another day of sunbathing and swimming, all signs of sin and retribution tidied away for another year.

How many people, I wondered idly, actually lived here in Loutro? Opening my laptop, I Googled the village and read, "Population: 0." Wait, what? It turned out the town had no full-time residents anymore; during the spring and summer season, people came in from the nearby towns to service holiday makers, and in the fall, they pocketed their pay packets and went home.

This seemed a dismal fate for a village had been around for thousands of years. In ancient times, it had served as an important port for the Greeks and Romans, and later became a lair for Barbary pirates and Saracen slavers. In the thirteenth century the Venetians ran off these brigands and built a fort on the harbor, and it had been more or less respectable ever since. Today the village survives on the international tourist trade, with a bit of fishing on the side. Instead of the strong social bonds I'd assumed existed, this was a loose collection of locals from various villages who came together in Loutro solely to make a few euros during the high season. I felt rather deflated by this news.

Easter Sunday was a quiet affair. Orthodox families, released from fasting (or the pretense of fasting) gathered to feast on lamb, the traditional symbol of sacrifice and salvation. I'd reserved a table at a small, family-run restaurant on the hill above the church, and during the morning I dropped by to see the lamb turning slowly on the spit, looking uncomfortably like a human sacrifice.

I was reminded of old paintings of St. Lawrence, an early Christian martyr roasted to death over hot coals. He allegedly called out cheerfully, "I'm done on this side, turn me over!" Which earned him the title of patron saint to both cooks and comedians. The lamb on the spit had aluminum foil draped over its loins, just as old-school artists always placed white cloths discretely over St. Lawrence's nether regions.

"Boy, these guys really know how to work a theme," I said.

5. The Peloponnese / *Gourounopoula & Kalamata Olives*

Rich often says one of the curses of the modern era is that accurate data spoils so many great stories. "Just as I'm getting into my stride," he complains, "somebody pulls out a cell phone and points out some tiny exaggeration and then the whole conversation derails."

Claiming his gift of gab comes from having kissed the Blarney Stone twice, Rich follows the tradition of his ancestors as described by author Rashers Tierney: "The Irish way of telling a story is a complex and elaborate one, complete with wild exaggerations, a certain delight in improbable fantasy, and a heightened sense of drama." Rich feels stories should enrich our collective lives by conveying something wonderful and true, even if it's not strictly factual. One of the things he loved about Greece was how often we found ourselves in places where wild, impossible tales had (allegedly) taken place in ancient times.

A couple of days after Easter, Rich and I took a ferry north from Crete to the Peloponnese peninsula, landing in the quiet harbor of Gytheio, the setting for one of the steamiest love scenes in history. As soon as we'd checked into our waterfront hotel, I opened the window and pointed out the small, pine-covered island just offshore, now connected by a narrow causeway.

"There it is!" I said. "That's where Helen of Troy and Paris spent their first night together. You know, starting the Trojan war. The sex that launched a thousand ships."

"What, there in the woods?" said Rich. "Doesn't look like a very comfortable place for it."

"Well, of course, that's all fiction. Helen of Troy never actually existed. And there was no Trojan Horse, either. Homer made that stuff up for *The Odyssey,* based on old legends." He looked so disappointed that I hastened to add, "But Troy did exist, and there was a Trojan war. Actually there were seven different wars on the site over a period of several centuries..." I prattled on, but I could tell he wasn't listening. I'd lost him at "no Trojan Horse." He's right. Sometimes the facts really do get in the way of a good story.

Manfully setting aside his dismay at my tarnishing the legend of the Trojan Horse, Rich joined me on a walk through Gytheio, strolling past colorful houses, cheerful cafés, and compact, business-like fishing boats. Thousands of years ago it had served as the port of Sparta, which was twenty-five miles away, but that legendary city-state had long since fallen into decline and disappeared, taking much of Gytheio's strategic importance with it. Since then the port suffered the usual colorful catastrophes, and nowadays nobody quite remembers what led to its final demise — being sacked by Visigoths, pillaged by Slavs, or destroyed in the massive earthquake of 375 AD. After that It muddled along as a tiny fishing village until the nineteenth century, when the population swelled due to the arrival of refugees during the Greek War of Independence.

Now most of Gytheio's five thousand inhabitants made a modest living by fishing or serving as regional administrators, handling the affairs of the Mani Peninsula on which the town sits. The Mani is the second of three peninsulas jutting out of the southern shore of the Peloponnese; it's often referred to as the middle finger, and I probably don't need to tell you that people have had a lot of fun with that over the years.

Gytheio remained slightly and (to my eye, at least) pleasantly rough around the edges, with lovely but crumbling old buildings, rambling little back streets, and a working dock where it was still common to see the day's catch of octopi strung up to dry in the sun. There was a small public health clinic, where Rich had his bandage changed by a pleasant, highly professional medical staff.

I enjoyed the town but wasn't destined to linger. By noon the next day I had checked out of the hotel and was waiting on the curb to meet Jackie, an American expat who wrote about life on the Mani Peninsula in her lively blog TravelnWrite. She and I had been corresponding for years, and we were finally going to meet IRL (in real life).

Five years earlier Jackie and her husband, Joel, had acquired an old stone house with an olive grove in the hills near the seaside village of Agios Dimitrios. Their view of the sea included the very island where Helen of Troy was born — or would have been, had she actually existed. When she'd heard about the Mediterranean Comfort Food Tour, Jackie offered to come collect us in Gytheio and show us around. When they arrived, I soon discovered that Jackie was as energetic and effervescent as her online writing, and that Joel was a man of few words and endless patience. They showed us Greek-style *xenia*, introducing us to the Mani's best eateries, from old-school mountain cafés to smart new beachfront restaurants with long wine lists. Every fish we ate tasted as if it had leapt directly from the sea into the frying pan.

On our first morning in Agios Dimitrios, Rich and I left our rental cottage early to visit the town's clinic before meeting up with Jackie and Joel. By now we were old hands at navigating the Greek medical system and had long since given up the high-end private establishments to embrace the richer cultural experience — and free services — of the public medical sector. Everywhere we went, the facilities were clean, modern, and efficient; the wait time to see a doctor was never more than a few minutes, and the paperwork was so minimal they often didn't even ask Rich's name. Obviously I missed the fawning attention, the neurosurgeon, and the restaurant recommendations of the Heraklion clinic, but I was more than satisfied with the public health service's level of care.

So I was feeling quite optimistic as Rich and I set out on the forty-minute walk to the local clinic, enjoying the crisp morning air, the sparkling water of the sea, and the charming hodgepodge of houses that made up the village of Agios Dimitrios.

The clinic was surprisingly large and dimly lit. At the front desk, a tall, robust woman in medical whites and scuffed Crocs demanded to know, in gruff Greek then gruffer English, what we wanted. Rich explained what he needed. She gave him a long, hard look and gestured to some chairs in the gloomy corridor.

"You wait," she snapped.

She walked off and disappeared through a door. A moment later we heard someone cry out in pain.

"Oh, great," Rich said. "I got Nurse Ratched." He was referring, of course, to the heartless, tyrannical nurse who locked horns with Jack Nicholson's character in *One Flew Over the Cuckoo's Nest*. As you may recall, it didn't turn out too well for Jack.

Another howl of pain came from behind the closed door. There was a long silence (I tried not to think of it as ominous) and then the door opened. A very old man was pushed out in a wheelchair. His face ashen and slack. His left leg bristled with metal pins that stuck out in all directions, like Pinhead in the posters for the sci-fi horror series *Hellraiser*. It was excruciating just to look at that leg. And that face. The patient remained utterly motionless, as if drained of all life. A young man wheeled him away.

Nurse Ratched waved us in.

The treatment room was crowded with beds, desks, and equipment. At the back, a middle-aged man was sitting up on the edge of a bed, pressing an oxygen mask to his mouth, concentrating very fiercely on the task of moving air in and out of his lungs. The nurse looked at Rich and gestured to the bed closest to the door. As he started unbuttoning his shirt, she turned to me.

"Madam, you leave."

Right, like I was going to abandon Rich in this cuckoo's nest.

"No," I said firmly. "He needs me to look at his back and tell him what I see."

She set her jaw but evidently decided not to press it. A thin, silent, dark-haired woman — I assumed she was a doctor, but as no one introduced themselves or wore name tags, she might just as easily have been a member of the catering staff, a passing veterinarian, or a patient — came over and pulled off Rich's bandage. The two women exchanged a look.

"Where was this bandage changed?" asked Nurse Ratched.

"Gytheio," I said.

"Oh, Gytheio." She fairly spat out the word. Why? No idea. The Gytheio clinic had seemed highly competent to me — and considerably less terrifying than this facility. She flung the bandage into a medical waste bin emblazoned with a biohazard symbol. The dark-haired woman stuck a Band-Aid on Rich's back.

"Something wrong?" I asked.

"No. He's fine. Don't come back."

"You mean he doesn't have to have his bandages changed by doctors anymore?" The staff in Gytheio had advised us to keep it up for another week or so.

"No. Now go."

I didn't need to be told again. I had Rich out of there before he'd finished buttoning his shirt.

So that was our last official contact with the Greek medical system. Whew! Now we could return our full attention to exploring the Mani Peninsula.

The setting was breathtaking, rugged mountains rising up from a turquoise sea, wooded hills dotted with houses of rough grey stone, and thousand-year-old Byzantine churches with faded murals showing scenes of glory and salvation.

One night, Jackie asked us to be ready for dinner a bit earlier than usual, as she and Joel wanted to show us the sunset from the cliff above the coastal village of Trachila.

"There's a great little restaurant there, run by Petros," she explained. Joel put the car in gear and began threading his way through the mountains on a narrow road with dizzying drops to the sea and rocks below.

"We don't take everyone here," Jackie added. "Some people can't handle it. Last time we took guests here, Joel and one of our friends wandered over to the sea wall and noticed there was a fishing line dangling from the railing to the water. It's a common way of keeping the day's catch fresh. They asked Petros about it, and he pulled on it and brought up a live eel. The eel came flying onto the café floor, thrashing about. Petros ran back into the kitchen and came out with a huge carving knife and cut its head off."

"Was it on the menu as the evening special?" I asked Jackie with interest, trying to recall if I'd ever eaten eel.

"Fishing bait. Anyway, the smell of freshly slaughtered eel brought out every cat in the neighborhood, and the animals were running all over the restaurant. Petros's ninety-three-year-old mother, a very large woman who walks bent over — you'll see her tonight —she suddenly appeared with a huge spray bottle of water and ran around chasing away all the cats. Our guests thought it was a bit much."

"Sounds very entertaining," I said. "I can only hope we're that lucky."

Sadly, there were no dramatic incidents with flying eels, but we did meet the genial Petros and his mother. She looked like some powerful, crippled goddess, one of the Furies perhaps, dressed in black, stalking around in her slippers with a spray bottle, menacing any cats that even thought about straying into the café. The sunset provided a splendid backdrop to the meal of fresh fish, grilled sausage, a salad of cucumber, tomato, and feta cheese, and a small bowl of the deep purple-brown olives grown in nearby Kalamata.

On our last morning in Agios Dimitrios, I awakened to discover the village was in the grip of a sirocco and a power outage. In a sirocco, fierce sand-laden winds blow up from Africa's Sahara desert, turning the Mediterranean sky a gritty gray and (they say) driving people mad. During the Ottoman era, if you murdered someone during a sirocco, you got a lesser sentence due to extenuating circumstances. I somehow managed not to go berserk, even when I realized without electricity I couldn't brew my morning coffee.

Our landlord kindly provided a lift to the bus stop, conveniently located in front of a popular café run by an expat named Freda, who was widely known as the village's most resourceful resident. She didn't fail us now. Working by candlelight with a gas-powered burner, Freda produced French-press coffee, bread, and jam. Jackie and Joel, who had come to see us off on the bus, joined in this modest but very welcome meal.

"Does the sirocco always knock out the electricity?" I asked, reaching for the jam pot.

"Oh no, this is a planned outage," said Jackie. "Nothing to do with the sirocco. They must be fixing something. It may just be in this village."

It wasn't. As our bus trundled northward along the narrow coast road for thirty miles, the gritty gray sky persisted and every house in every village showed dark windows. I tried to ignore the gloominess of the sky and concentrate on the fact I was on my way to the city of Kalamata, which I'd earmarked from the start. I was looking forward to learning all about their famous olives. What was their origin? Were there legends about them? Ancient traditions? I could hardly wait to find out.

The visit to Kalamata did not start well. After the picturesque charms of Crete and the rugged magnificence of the Mani Peninsula, my first glimpse — and frankly, my second and third glimpses as well — suggested that Kalamata was a soulless wasteland of shabby, crumbling concrete buildings and vacant lots full of weeds, rubble, and litter. The sirocco and power outage did nothing to enhance the atmosphere. As the bus wheezed to a halt in the shadows under a stained metal portico, I began to have serious doubts about the town.

A fifteen-minute walk brought us to the rental apartment, where the hosts, Maria and George, opened the door and told us we couldn't come in. Explaining they needed more time to clean, George relieved us of our bags, and Maria said, "Go have coffee. Our favorite place, it is very close." She stepped out of the doorway and walked a few yards to the corner, pointing to a pair of enormous trees; in the dense shadows beneath the branches I could make out dark forms that just might be people and tables. "Come back at one-thirty."

Coffee sounded good, and come to think of it, I was pretty hungry. We headed over to the café Maria had pointed out. Rich, stepping smartly into the profound gloom beneath the trees, immediately walked into a low metal table, gashing his shin. He hobbled to a chair, sat down, and began sopping up the blood with his handkerchief.

I left him to it and went to the counter to discuss our order. That didn't take long; thanks to the power outage, they were serving nothing but coffee.

When ours arrived, Rich took one sip and nearly spit it out again.

"This isn't coffee." He glared into his cup. "It's gasoline."

"No, there's definitely some coffee in it because I have grounds stuck in my teeth." But I had to admit there was a strong aroma of gasoline along with the muddy taste of burnt grounds. It had no doubt been boiled on some leaky, gas-powered stove. I tried not to think about the health effects of drinking the stuff, or even breathing its fumes.

I set down my cup and looked around, trying to get a handle on the moment. A few silent, brooding men sat, each at his own table, hunched over a cup of ghastly coffee in the gloom beneath the trees. Beyond, I could see the gritty gray sky and a deserted street.

"Let's go," I said. "There has to be more to Kalamata than this."

At first, all I saw were streets lined with closed doors and lightless windows. Here and there, few brave restauranteurs were serving dubious coffee to silent customers at sidewalk tables. After twenty dispiriting minutes, Rich suddenly went on high alert.

"Do I smell food cooking?" he said.

He pushed through a door into the steamy warmth of a small restaurant, where the cook had, by some miracle, produced an array of hearty dishes. In a matter of moments Rich was smiling down at a plateful of moussaka, and I was breathing in the heady fragrance of chicken and green beans. I sighed with satisfaction and picked up my fork.

By the time I was chasing the last string bean around my plate, the electricity had come back on and the sun was breaking through the sandy clouds blanketing the sky. Emerging from the restaurant, I saw life had picked up again; people were stepping out of apartment buildings and bustling in and out of bright shops and inviting cafés. Rich grudgingly agreed the town might have some redeeming features.

Returning to the apartment, I discovered it was even nicer than it looked in the photos. (When does that ever happen?)

I was particularly delighted to see the bathroom held a relatively new front-loaded washing machine. Traveling with a minimal wardrobe, I always have laundry at the top of my to-do list. As soon as our hosts departed, I threw in a load that contained almost everything except what we stood up in.

Forty minutes later the controls said the cycle was over, and like a chump, I believed them. I opened the door and water came flooding out, leaving behind a sodden lump of soapy clothes. I eventually figured out how to run two cycles to get the clothes clean, but I often had to wring out the excess water by hand, and there were many more floods as the washer and I got to know each other better. I spent a lot of time mopping that floor.

Later, when I mentioned all this to George, he said this was perfectly normal. Really? In what universe? I will say this: the floor in that bathroom was spotlessly clean throughout our stay.

I'd booked a food tour for the following morning, and as instructed, Rich and I made our way to the downtown rendezvous point, the Church of Ypapantis (Jesus' Presentation at the Temple). This was the home of a miracle-working, seventh-century icon of the Virgin and Child that locals claim saved the city during the plague in 1841. So far I haven't been able to discover whether the icon was equally helpful during the Covid pandemic; let us pray it was. Among the many mysteries surrounding the painting is the origin of its name, "*kalá mátia*" meaning "good eyes." Naturally people think it's the source of the name bestowed upon the town and its famous olives, but rather disappointingly, reliable scholars insist Kalamata is a corruption of an older name, *Kalámai*, meaning "reeds." What fun is that?

Foreign visitors being relatively rare in Kalamata outside of the summer months, we were the only ones taking the tour, which was led by a cheerful young woman named Fotini. She took us around town, introducing us to cooks, bakers, and shopkeepers who treated us as a delightful novelty, dropping everything to settle in for a nice little chat.

Fotini, Rich, and I spent a delightful morning sampling cheese drizzled with honey, smoked meat, and fresh bread with fruit compote. At the herb market, she pointed out a basket filled with long, dry, lumpy, red-brown pods that looked like something you'd sweep off your back deck without a second thought.

"That's carob. During World War II, when we were occupied by the Germans, they didn't recognize carob or know what to do with it. So they failed to confiscate it along with everything else edible in the city. It was the mainstay of our diet during the occupation." She appeared to think this rather a good joke on the Germans. I tried to imagine subsisting for four years on a diet of carob, which I remembered from my college days as a disappointingly bland, low fat, caffeine-free alternative to chocolate. More recently I'd had it as locust bean cream at the fancy fish restaurant in Heraklion, but I suspected without the grilled octopus and caramelized onions it wouldn't be much of a treat.

An hour or so into the tour, I mentioned to Fotini that I hadn't yet had any coffee that morning and asked about stopping for a cup. She looked up and down the street as if searching for a spot. "How about right there?" I gestured toward an old-fashioned café just across the street.

Fotini hesitated. And this is where I got my first real introduction to Greek coffee etiquette. Like everything in Greece, this seemingly simple act had countless layers of meaning.

Most Greek coffee houses, known as *cafeneons*, are all-male preserves where guys gather to talk. In the days before TV and Google, they were the place to learn what was happening in the world. Today, men still meet there to discuss politics, business, sports, the in-laws, TV shows, their lumbago, and problems they're having with their teeth.

I felt I ought to object on principle to these masculine enclaves, but traveling through Greece I began to appreciate the practical benefit of giving men a place to hang out together. The worldwide epidemic of isolation has hit Greek men particularly hard; they're among the most socially isolated in Europe. That kind of severe loneliness is not just distressing, it's medically dangerous; studies show it cuts lifespans short as remorselessly as smoking, obesity, or alcoholism. For many the *cafeneon* was the only place to find social connection; it was quite literally a lifesaver.

In the old days women were expected to drink their coffee at home, and I'm sorry to say that in some rural areas this is still the norm. In more urban settings, most Greek women do go out, but they make a point of going to coffee houses they know are "open" or "mixed." I even saw one coffee house that was exclusively occupied by women. Could a woman go into one of the all-male *cafeneons* and get served? Yes, and I've done it accidentally; everyone was very polite. But gatecrashing the guys' clubhouse isn't nearly as amusing as it may sound.

Here's how Matt Barrett, an American travel writer, describes invading a *cafeneon* with his wife, who grew up on the Greek island of Lesbos.

"Andrea pulls me … into a *cafeneon* full of old men. Though she usually has no qualms about invading the sanctity of these men-only cafes, this time she hesitates at the door. "Is it open?" she asks me even though we can both see the place is full and loud male voices are echoing off the stone walls and high ceilings. I know what she means and I feel irritated that she would cross a boundary that no woman from the island would dare, and that I was her accomplice. I become self-conscious about my role in her incursion. I am a traitor to my race and my gender. My shirt is too orange, my shorts are too purple and holding my daughter I feel like a fool in the company of these old men who have fought for their beliefs and for their livelihoods in harder times. I notice on the wall two portraits of Aris Velouchiotis, the communist guerilla leader and hero who harassed the Germans and helped liberate the country after WWII, only to be hunted down and killed by the army of the right-wing government that the British and Americans decided should rule after the occupation...

"I am aware that I sit in a room full of old men who half a century ago wore their hair long, rode horses, wore cartridge belts and used vintage rifles against a powerful enemy with tanks and modern weapons and after attaining victory found themselves doing it all over again against their own country men, this time suffering defeat. It is unlikely that I will ever know the feeling of betrayal that these men have felt. One old man sits next to his cup of Turkish coffee, his mouth and the lines of his face point to the floor in a permanent frown. His eyes stare at a pop-art poster that looks completely out of place on the wall, though it is obvious to me that what he is seeing is the sadness of his own life. Lost loved ones, and broken dreams. I feel unworthy of the Turkish coffee I drink. To further drive in the point they have given it to me in a glass instead of the small white cups the old men drink from."

My point — and Matt's — is that in Greece, going out for coffee is about so much more than just a caffeine boost. Fotini's hesitation was understandable; I'd unwittingly trapped her between the conflicting demands of showing me *xenia* and respecting these men in their own *cafeneon*. She neatly solved the dilemma by installing us at an outside table and leaving us alone to drink our coffee. As ignorant foreigners, Rich and I could be excused for our transgression, while she, who knew the rules, could not. Well played, Fotini, well played.

For hours, Rich and I nibbled and sipped our way through the city, shaking hands, kissing cheeks, assuring each of the shop owners, cooks, and bakers that we would be happy to come back one day to see them again and sample more of their wares.

Fontini took us to a wall constructed of rough wooden planks that held a row of hooks surrounded by painted stick figures, hearts, balloons, and a rainbow. "This is the Happiness Wall," she explained, smiling. "People leave bags of food here for those who are too poor to buy their own. Those who need it can come and take the food without anyone knowing, so they don't have to feel ashamed in front of their neighbors." What a brilliant form of compassion, I thought. Why doesn't every town have one of these?

The tour's finale was lunch at a place known for its *souvlaki*, small chunks of grilled meat and vegetables, often described as Greece's answer to fast food. I ordered the roast chicken tucked into thick, hot pita bread and served with yogurt sauce. Delicious.

"This tour has been wonderful," I said to Fotini. "I was a little bit surprised, though, that we never talked about Kalamata olives. Somehow I assumed they'd be an important part of the tour."

She seemed startled by the question, then she shrugged. "When you've been eating something since ancient times, it is just a part of everyday life."

"OK," I said. I'd learned even Wikipedia didn't have much to say about Kalamata olives; apparently the trees have large leaves, are intolerant of cold, and are susceptible to Verticillium wilt but resistant to olive knot and the olive fruit fly. It's hard to parlay that into a fascinating backstory. Disappointed but soldiering on, I asked, "Are there any other local specialties you think I should try while I'm here?"

"Gourounopoula." Her face lit up at the very mention of it. "Roast pork with plenty of skin and fat." She leaned forward confidingly. "You know, back in the days of the Ottoman empire, we used it to plan a revolution. When we had feasts, we of course had to invite our Ottoman neighbors. But being Muslims, they didn't eat pork, so when we served *gourounopoula*, they stayed away. And we could plan our revolution, right under their noses."

Once again she seemed delighted at the way her city had snookered their enemies. Thanks to *gourounopoula* — and a few other factors, of course — the Greeks gained independence in 1829 after 400 years of Ottoman occupation.

"If you'd like to try it, I know the best place." Fotini led me to the corner and pointed. "There. The restaurant with the two giant trees." It was the place we'd drunk the gasoline-flavored coffee our first morning in town.

After she'd departed, Rich said firmly, "No way I'm going back there. I want a second opinion on this pork business." He consulted one of his apps. "There's a tourist information office not far from here. Let's ask them."

"Ah, *gourounopoula*." The woman at the tourist information office sighed ecstatically. "Yes, you must try it. The best is here." She pointed at the map. "At Barbayiannis."

The next day, we set out to find Barbayiannis. Map in hand, Rich led the way, walking briskly through the city, hampered only by the fact most streets weren't marked, and the few names that were posted didn't seem to match any of the street names on the map. He wasn't lost, of course; he just didn't know precisely where he was or how to get where he was going. Eventually I noticed a pig's severed head staring up at me from a large window. The rest of the body and a meat cleaver lay nearby. Could this be it? Rich bent down to peer at the pig, and I looked up and saw the sign: Μπαρμπαγιάννης Barbayiannis.

"We're here!" And then I did a doubletake. "Hey, this is the place we had lunch the first day, during the power outage!" What were the odds? Kalamata is a small city, just under 70,000, but still.

In we went and ordered *gourounopoula*. This was comfort food at its finest: a crispy outer layer of crackling surrounding meat so tender it fell apart under my fork. Even splitting a small portion we could barely finish it, and we utterly failed to do justice to the roast potatoes and Greek salad that accompanied it.

Barbayiannis means "Uncle John," and if the faded color photo on the wall was anything to go by, Uncle John was passionate about his pig meat. Judging by the clothes and cars, the picture had been shot decades ago, in the restaurant's parking lot. The foreground shows a grizzled man with bushy black eyebrows smiling happily as he prepares to swing a mighty meat cleaver down on the decimated remains of a roast pig laid out on a slab. Behind him stand two slender youths, possibly his nephews, who are half-turned away, clearly attempting to distance themselves from the scene. You can almost hear them thinking, "There goes goofy Uncle John again, hacking up another pig." Eyerolls. "So uncool, man. I hope nobody sees us out here."

In my view, the *gourounopoula* was totally cool, and every bit as wonderful as Fotini and the woman at the tourist office had suggested. For a while we ate in blissful silence. When I was sopping up the last bit of salty grease with a scrap of bread, I brought up the subject of where we should go when we left Kalamata.

"Are you still thinking about Sparta?" asked Rich.

I'd had Sparta on my short list from the start — actually, from the time I'd first read about it in fifth grade. Growing up in California during the make-love-not-war sixties, I found the fierce Spartan philosophy utterly alien and grimly fascinating. In that ancient military powerhouse, every male was raised as a warrior, and every woman sent her men off to battle with the admonition to return "with your shield or on it" — that is, victorious or carried home dead. No fear, no prisoners, no second chances.

Spartan training was brutal. Starting at age seven, boys were kept on such short rations they had to steal food to survive; if caught, they were punished harshly. Plutarch, a Greek historian during that era, wrote, "The boys make such a serious matter of their stealing that one of them, as the story goes, who was carrying concealed under his cloak a young fox which he had stolen, suffered the animal to tear out his bowels with its teeth and claws, and died rather than have his theft detected." Yes, the Spartans were the ultimate tough guys — or macho idiots, depending on your point of view. Personally, I lean toward the latter.

In 2006, Sparta became a hot tourist destination following the release of the popular film *300*, but everything I'd read suggested those visitors were doomed to disappointment. The original Sparta was long gone. After glorious victories in the Peloponnese war of 404 BC, the Spartans suffered equally spectacular defeats, and within a few hundred years the city-state was little more than a tourist destination, where vacationing Romans came to gawk at its quaint, old-fashioned ways. No doubt this was extremely galling for the Spartans of the day; their warrior ancestors must have been turning in their graves.

The final blow came in 396 AD when the Visigoths sacked the city and sold off all the survivors as slaves. The city was left in ruins, which apparently wasn't that much of a loss, as the Spartans were never ones to waste their time or resources on grand architecture.

They didn't leave much of a culinary legacy either. The only traditional dish I'd uncovered in my research was something called black broth, made with boiled pig legs, vinegar, and blood. You can see why the boys were out stealing foxes to upgrade their diet.

"I hate to say it, but I don't think it's worth visiting Sparta," I told Rich. "There's not much there *there*."

"Thank God," he said. "I was not looking forward to trying black broth."

He pulled up a map on his phone, and after considering various options, we decided not to linger on the Peloponnese but to make our way north to Piraeus, the port of Athens. From there we could catch a ferry to Lesbos Island, birthplace of the Greek poet Sappho, and then go on to Ikaria, the island famous for the healthy longevity of its residents. Satisfied with our decision — and the *gourounopoula* — we paid up and headed back to our apartment.

"I can't believe I'm saying this," Rich told me, as we strolled homeward. "But I actually think Kalamata is my favorite stop so far."

6. Lesbos Island / *What Color Is Your Mullet?*

Our cabin on the overnight ferry to Lesbos had a full-sized green bathtub. I was stunned by the extravagance of its size and weight, having naturally expected the usual miniscule space housing a toilet, a sink the size of a cereal bowl, and a hand-held hose with a showerhead guaranteed to drench the entire cabin. I pictured myself soaking luxuriously in that tub surrounded by bubbles. And then I pictured myself sloshing about in its slick, soapy confines on rough seas. I'd once ridden out a storm on the Adriatic gripping the side of my bunkbed all night to avoid being hurled to the floor. I decided I'd wait until landfall and shower at the hotel.

With the possible exception of that bathtub, most Mediterranean ferries haven't turned out to be nearly as romantic or comfortable as I'd imagined. The food, even on the Italian lines, is marginal at best, and we all know it isn't that easy to screw up spaghetti. I've learned the hard way that for overnight journeys it pays to book a cabin and pack road rations. My granola bars and trail mix were supplemented with the best the snack bar had to offer: cold beer and microwaved spinach pie. I slept fitfully, and rose with the first light of dawn.

As I was tying my shoes, the ship's loudspeaker began repeating, "Τώρα φθάνουμε στη Λέσβο." Which apparently means, "We are arriving in Lesbos."

Still half asleep, I slung on my shoulder bag, grabbed the handle of my suitcase, and threaded my way through the maze of corridors to the departure deck. Seconds later Rich and I were standing on the wharf of Mytilene, a city that had been welcoming seafarers for more than thirty centuries. The air was sweet and balmy, the light luminous. But first things first; I really needed a recombobulation coffee. Fortunately the Greeks are as deeply attached to their καφέ as any Starbucks addict so I spotted a café in less than a minute.

Seated at a tiny table within sight of the port, I sipped my coffee and ate the complimentary cookies a thoughtful barista had placed on my saucer. I soon learned this was a tradition on Lesbos and I, for one, thought it was splendid. When the caffeine and sugar had restored my wits sufficiently, I asked, "How far is the hotel?"

"About a half hour's walk."

It was closer to 45 minutes, with the last bit uphill, followed by three sets of stairs. But it was a wonderful walk, along the vast arc of the harbor where fishing boats bobbed, whistling young men pushed carts of supplies, ancient Vespas puttered by, women flung checkered cloths over tiny tables, and old men sat nursing thick ceramic mugs and hand-rolled cigarettes. Big, shaggy, loose-limbed dogs sprawled sleeping in café doorways. The buildings were a jumble of styles: Mediterranean, shapeless old stone, Western European, ornamental Byzantine, and a few boxy, 1960s-style concrete eyesores.

Our hotel added yet another style to the mix: a 1916 Victorian mansion. The austere lines of its grey exterior were softened by vines bearing masses of yellow flowers. The lobby was full of rich carpets and fussy gilt furniture like something out of an old English movie. I was charmed to discover we'd been given a tower room; it was perfectly round, like something in a fairy tale. Long red curtains were draped over the bed, and a little side table bore a red landline telephone, like a hotline from the Cold War era.

"There's not enough room in here to swing a cat," said Rich.

This was true. Despite the room's modest dimensions, they'd jammed in an entire suite of gold-and-white furniture: queen bed, two round side tables, a dressing table, a stool, a chair, and a cupboard holding a small refrigerator and TV. Even our minimal luggage was going to take up every inch of floorspace and then some. Rich knew that I'd always longed to live in a house with a round tower, and that this would be my first — possibly only — chance to sleep in one. He didn't protest further, just sighed and continued attempting to wedge his suitcase under the dressing table.

Setting out to explore, we soon found ourselves on narrow, colorful Ermou Street, which ran from the city's busy Southern Port, where the ferry had dropped us off, to the old Northern Port, now mostly occupied by fishing boats and seafood restaurants. Ermou Street itself was a delightful jumble of fishmongers, cobblers, confectioners, second-hand bookshops, and purveyors of such antiquated curiosities as Kodak film, DVDs, and little brass knickknacks for those who feel their homes lack sufficient surface clutter.

Presiding over the southern end was the magnificent nineteenth-century church of Saint Therapon the Wonderworker. A Palestinian mystic and ascetic who loved nothing more than suffering alone in the wilderness, Therapon was forced to flee to Cyprus during an uptick in Christian persecution. (Just to be clear, in this instance I'm talking about the Christians being persecuted, not the other way around.) In Cyprus, he found an equally uncomfortable little patch of desert and settled in. Word soon got around that if you didn't mind him preaching at you, he had a rare knack for curing the sick, and he was soon doing a brisk business in minor miracles.

For some reason the Cypriot authorities objected to this, so they roughed him up and lashed him to four stout wooden posts; these promptly became green trees later discovered to have their own miraculous healing properties. Eventually they killed him, and the saint continued to heal the sick from beyond the grave. Every year a piece of his forehead is paraded through the streets of Cypress, while the rest of him is buried in Istanbul, no doubt still performing miracles for the faithful. I was unable to discover whether any of his relics had found their way to his church on Lesbos Island; I hoped so, because he seemed like a handy saint to have around. I suspect he became extra popular in 2020.

By the time I reached the old Northern Harbor I had worked up quite an appetite for lunch. All the restaurants looked out over the water, and we chose one and settled at a wooden table covered with a blue checked cloth. I was still studying the menu when the waiter arrived and urged me to try the red mullet, a fish I'd never eaten.

Red mullet used to be known as bottom-feeding goatfish but was renamed when it became the darling of ancient Greece and Rome. Everyone praised the red mullet for its tender texture and delicate flavor; more ghoulishly, they were fascinated with the way it changed color as it died. Jaded old Romans used to invite their friends over for dinner and have a prime specimen brought in alive, in a glass jar, so everyone could witness the spectacle of its final moments.

"In the very struggle of its failing breath of life," wrote the Roman philosopher and statesman Seneca, "first a red, then a pale tint suffuses it, and its scales change hue, and between life and death there is a gradation of color into subtle shades ... See how the red becomes inflamed, more brilliant than any vermilion! Look at the veins which pulse along its sides! Look! You would think its belly were actual blood! What a bright kind of blue gleamed right under its brow! Now it is stretching out and going pale and is settling into a uniform hue." Such fun for the spectators! Obviously not so amusing for the fish.

As the fad grew and overfishing made red mullet ever rarer, top specimens were sold for their weight in silver, a trend satirized by the poet Marital in a story about a man who sells a slave and uses the entire proceeds so buy a four pound red mullet.

The wealthy had special ponds built for their red mullets and would come out to caress them, bragging to friends that they'd taught the fish to come to the sound of their voice or a bell. (Having owned goldfish, I can tell you that most fish will come to any signal associated with food, so this boast doesn't imply any special brilliance on the part of red mullets. Or their owners.) Pliny, Cicero, and other great thinkers of the day discoursed on the red mullet's charms, and artists were commissioned to add red mullet mosaics to the floors and walls of the great houses.

Things have calmed down considerably for the red mullet since those glory years. Now it's back to being the plain old bottom-feeding goatfish to its friends and is no longer worth its weight in silver. The four little red mullets I had for lunch that day were reasonably priced and prepared with traditional simplicity: dusted with flour and salt, fried in olive oil, and served with lemon. It was delicious, but not extraordinarily so. I could see why, back in the day, so many Roman satirists had fun mocking the craze.

Now, you may be wondering if the island's most famous wordsmith, the poet Sappho, ever wrote odes or satires about the red mullet. Sadly, we're unlikely ever to find out, as only a tiny fraction of her work survives. This is a terrible loss, as her talent was phenomenal. Sappho took the ancient world by storm, earning widespread popularity and the kind of critical acclaim that placed her among the literary giants of her day. She was the only women to earn a place in the pantheon known as the Nine Lyric Poets of Ancient Greece. Plato called her "the Tenth Muse," referring to the nine inspirational goddesses of the arts and sciences.

So Sappho was celebrated throughout the ancient world. But nowadays we know surprisingly little about her; we can't even be sure of her much-discussed sexual orientation. She was born in Mytilene to a wealthy Lesbos family, possibly around 630 BC. When she was perhaps thirty (the dates are a bit fuzzy) the family moved to Sicily; historians guess the family somehow got caught in the crossfire between warring political elites on the island and found it prudent to make themselves scarce. The move must have been wrenching, as many of her poems speak of love and loss.

I have had not one word from her

Frankly I wish I were dead.

When she left, she wept

a great deal; she said to me,

"This parting must be endured, Sappho. I go unwillingly."

I said, "Go, and be happy but remember (you know well)

who you leave shackled by love."

Writing such verses made Sappho an enduring symbol of love and desire between women. This was no big deal in ancient Greece, where gender fluidity was the norm, especially early in life. Lots of people fooled around with same-sex relationships during their school years, then later settled down to marriage and raising kids. It's possible, as some scholars insist, that Sappho was married, bore a child, and was (mostly) heterosexual, but the one scrap of information said to support this theory now provokes roars of derisive laughter if anyone tries to cite it.

Apparently scholars uncomfortable with Sappho's same-sex interests clung to the idea she must have been heterosexual because of references to a husband called Kerkylas of Andros. Eventually somebody realized this was probably a hoax based on an elaborate pun.

Kerkylas isn't a name but a word derived from *kerkos*, which can mean "penis." It's then linked with "Andros," a Greek island that's also a form of the Greek word *aner*, which means man. "Thus, the name may be a joke name," notes Wikipedia, with as much dignity as possible given the subject, "and as such could be rendered as 'Dick Allcock from the Isle of Man.'" You won't be surprised to hear that nowadays, the name Kerkylas of Andros is rarely invoked in scholarly debates about the poet's personal life, as the ensuing outburst of jeers, mockery, and ribald comments tends to permanently derail the discussion.

Was Sappho a lesbian? My uneducated guess would be yes. But at this point, it hardly matters, because to the vast majority of the world, she has come to represent female homosexuality. The term "sapphic love" refers to same-gender attraction, and the name of her home island gave rise to the term "lesbian."

As you can imagine, this has driven some conservative residents of Lesbos completely around the bend, especially with the rise of the LGBTQ movement in the twentieth and twenty-first centuries. In 2008 a group of Lesbos islanders tried to get a legal injunction banning gay women's groups from using the world lesbian in their names, claiming it violated the islanders' human rights by associating them with "disgraceful" practices. They were laughed out of court.

Now they are insisting everyone spell the island's name Lesvos, which to be fair is a more accurate transliteration of the Greek Λέσβο and one that has gained widespread use. I will attempt to remember to spell it this way for the remainder of the book, although to me, it will always be Lesbos. And despite vigorous resistance by a small group of hard-core conservatives, I'm pleased to report there's a modest but growing LGBTQ tourism trade on the island.

Apparently our hotel was part of that effort, for hanging on the dining room wall was a large Baroque painting of two women, clothes in partial disarray, engaged in romantic dalliance surrounded by cherubs and flower blossoms. When I came down to breakfast the first morning, I saw two gray-haired women sitting at the table beneath the painting, talking cozily with their heads close together. How sweet, I thought, wondering if they were here on a second (or perhaps tenth) honeymoon. Alas for my stereotypes, it turned out they were not lovers but sisters (siblings, that is, not nuns), and once we'd introduced ourselves, I learned they were on the island for an entirely different reason.

Ann and Linda were visiting the refugee camps. As you may recall, in 2015 tens of thousands of asylum seekers — many fleeing wars in Syria, Iraq, and Afghanistan — crossed the 3.4 mile gap between Turkey and Lesvos Island in a ragtag flotilla of scrounged-up boats, seeking sanctuary in the European Union. With true Greek *xenia*, the islanders went down to the beaches and welcomed them with water, blankets, and tarps. But the sheer numbers soon became overwhelming. "Refugees were sleeping everywhere, even on the sidewalks," one islander told me, shaking his head.

In the ensuing chaos, temporary camps were set up as a stepping stone to more permanent relocation. When I visited four years later, refugees were still arriving in droves, and fewer were getting moved on, as tougher EU policies kept reducing the places that could or would accept them. The results were horrific.

In Moria, the largest camp on Lesvos, "the overcrowding is so extreme," the *New York Times* had recently reported, "that asylum seekers spend as much as 12 hours a day waiting in line for food that is sometimes moldy. Last week, there were about 80 people for each shower, and around 70 per toilet." The filth, squalor, and violence had led to widespread disease, an atmosphere of fear and depression, and an epidemic of suicide attempts. The year after I was there, Covid-19 spread through the refugees like wildfire.

And these two nice American women were visiting the camps?

"We mostly spent time at Pikpa Camp, which is really well run,"

Linda told me. "It's where they send the most vulnerable refugees, the ones who simply can't survive at Moria."

Frankly, I wasn't sure how anyone could survive at Moria. Before coming to Lesvos, I'd read up on the camps and had struggled with the question of whether I should try to arrange a visit. Did I have an obligation to go, learn about conditions for myself, and then tell my readers what I'd seen and felt — as I had, some years earlier, with Auschwitz?

After seeing the horrific stories about the camps on Lesvos, I'd decided not to pursue it — partly from cowardice (or sensible caution, depending on how you look at it) and partly from conviction that top journalists were already covering this story and I wasn't sure how much more I could add to the conversation. On top of everything else, I had no idea how to go about arranging such a visit.

Linda and Ann explained it was actually quite simple. One of them had gone online and found an email address for Pipka Camp, then written to the staff explaining she and her sister wanted to make a small donation to support the work and hoped they could visit while they were on the island. I liked their approach. Obviously it would be more comfortable visiting as a donor (part of the solution) than as a random visitor (just one more bit of bother for the overworked staff to cope with) or a sightseer (some rubbernecking ghoul there for a sick thrill).

Checking online, I couldn't find contact details for the other two camps, but Pipka's website listed an email address, so I wrote to the staff and was invited to come over the following day.

Contrary to all my expectations, the visit was uplifting and inspiring. Staff members Derek and María showed us around the tidy wooden cabins, the communal garden, the "store" where donated clothing and supplies were given out, the tiny medical clinic. There was workshop space where refugees were learning to sew so they could transform the life jackets they'd worn on the crossing into tote bags to be sold in a local shop and online. In the large, spotless kitchen, Derek explained that the facility, designed for 150 residents, sometimes fed as many as 3000 people a day when sudden influxes of refugees overwhelmed other camps. As we walked past dogs dozing in the sun, he told me seven stray dogs had adopted the camp, keeping watch over the grounds and the residents at night.

This was a refugee camp done right — a bright contrast to the other two I visited that day. I knew I wouldn't be allowed past the gates of Kara Tepe or Moria without having made arrangements in advance, so I asked our cab driver to stop out front while Rich and I got out and spent a short while observing each camp from the road.

At Kara Tepe, people slept in metal shipping containers lined up behind cyclone fences topped with barbed wire. In a hut by the gate a couple of staff members kept a close eye on everyone passing through, but it was clear that residents could move in and out freely. I was pleased to see they were dressed in clean clothing and wearing shoes; after the reports I'd read I wouldn't have been surprised to find them barefoot, bloody, and wearing rags. Families moved about in tight little clusters, kids held close; mostly they walked slowly down the hill to a store where they could purchase supplies. The atmosphere was somber and subdued.

Next I asked the driver to take us to the infamous Moria, which had 13,000 people crammed into space intended for 3,000. The sea of pale grey tents, mostly made of plastic and scrap wood, had overflowed the original enclosure to sprawl up and down the bare hillside. A few lines of laundry provided the only color in the drab landscape. Some people walked about listlessly while others simply sat beside their tent staring at the ground. Thanks to inadequate plumbing, a noxious smell hung over the camp and wafted over to where I stood.

Everyone in those camps was trapped and waiting. The luckiest residents would eventually be sent to Athens, where living conditions were somewhat better but their fate would remain in doubt for a long time.

Navigating the Byzantine complexities of the processing system could take many frustrating, desperate years in which the refugees couldn't legally work or move on.

"I am counting my blessings," I said to Rich in the cab on the way back to Mytilene. "Remind me never, ever to complain about anything again. Ever."

All in all, It had been an emotionally challenging day. After lunch and a siesta, we packed our bags in preparation for the next day's ferry to the island of Ikaria. But before we bid farewell Lesvos, I had one more bit of research to do, and it couldn't have come at a better moment. It was time to check out the island's most popular product: ouzo.

This dry, anise-flavored aperitif was created by monks in the fourteenth century and was popular throughout Greece until the arrival of the teetotalling Ottomans in 1453. Production was put on hold for 400 years, then Greek distillers sprang back into action when independence was achieved in 1821. Today, Lesvos boasts seventeen ouzo factories, some quite large, others no bigger than a home kitchen; together they produce half the nation's supply.

There was an ouzo museum on the island, but I felt I owed it to my readers to perform more in-depth, first-person research. I'd read ouzo is traditionally drunk around sunset, with a plate of the small snacks called *mezes*, and that one of the best places for this civilized ritual was a bar near the Northern Harbor called Kastro Tavern, owned by a magician named Georgios.

Rich and I arrived at dusk to find Georgios — a grizzled man sporting a black bandana tied pirate-style around his head — playing backgammon with a couple of friends. There was no one else in the place. Glancing through the empty dining room into the kitchen, I could see a dog stretched out on the floor fast asleep. After Rich and I were comfortably settled at a table on the porch, Georgios ambled over to ask what we'd like.

"Ouzo," I said. Digging deep into my scanty store of knowledge on the subject, I produced the name of one popular brand. "*Kefi*?" I figured I couldn't go wrong with an alcoholic beverage named for the state of sublime, transformative contentment and fellowship.

"No," said Georgios. "It is turned off." He mimed closing a tap. "Two brothers made it, and they ..." He made fists and pantomimed punched them together. "No more *Kefi*." Well, that's one for the irony department, I thought.

I looked at the list and chose another brand at random. "Ice?" asked Georgios. "Yes, of course," I said.

I'd just read that ouzo, which I'd been taking neat, should always be served over ice or with a little cold water, which turns the clear liquid cloudy. Why is this important? Possibly because its alcohol content is between thirty-seven and fifty percent. No doubt that's why you're supposed to nibble some *mezes* with it as well.

I ordered white beans and our old friend the red mullet and sat sipping, nibbling, and listening to the clatter of dice and the low hum of talk and laughter from the backgammon players. Occasionally the dog wandered over so Rich could scratch behind its ears. When I eventually bestirred myself to ask for the bill, Georgios said, "Would you like to see magic?" Obviously, there's only one answer to that question.

Georgios proceeded to dazzle us with nifty bits of sleight of hand. "The bag is empty, yes? And now..." he flipped cards out of the bag onto the table. I gave the expected gasp and applauded. "Now," he said, "look closely..."

As Georgios performed his tricks, I reflected that this was the true magic of Greece: its age-old ability to welcome strangers who wash up on its shores. I thought of the refugees, stumbling off the boats, traumatized and terrified, being met on the beaches with blankets and bottles of water. My heart ached when I thought about all those who had arrived so hopefully, only to wind up trapped in those nightmarish overcrowded camps. Then I thought about Derek, María, and the rest of the staff at Pipka Camp, stubbornly fighting to help the most vulnerable newcomers survive, giving them shelter and tools to build a better life for themselves.

In my mind's eye, I kept seeing those stray dogs, finding their own way to the camp, standing guard over the huts, making sure that for this one night at least, the humans inside could rest, knowing they were sheltered and safe, even though their fate was uncertain and they were very far from home.

7. Ikaria Island / *The Longevity Diet*

"If time has no meaning on Ikaria," Rich said the next day, as our ferry pulled away from the island of Lesvos, "isn't it going to be a bit boring? What if nothing happens the whole time we're on the island?"

He had a point. Ikaria, which lay in the far eastern reaches of the Aegean Sea, was famous for ignoring the time pressures that propel so many of us through our day. I'd read that local shops posted signs reading "Clocks, Anxiety and Stress Have No Place On Ikaria," and that they lightheartedly referred to any time of day as *argamisi*, "late-thirty."

It was entirely possible the whole island would feel like the pot-fogged communes I'd known in the sixties, where people draped themselves over the furniture for large swaths of the day, thinking grand thoughts and hoping someone would come around with a plate of brownies. When I mentioned Ikaria to the young couple we had dinner with on the night we arrived in Crete, Alex had snorted with derision. "You know what I call Ikaria? Freakaria! Everybody there moves sooooo slooooooow."

Ikaria might be laid back, but I doubted it would be dull. For a start, this remote island was populated by non-conformists. Over many centuries, right up until the 1960s, it was the dumping ground for misfits, free thinkers, rebels, scofflaws, and political undesirables. Not unlike America, come to think of it.

"In remoteness and want, islanders learned to be self-reliant, independent of thought, and close-knit," wrote Ikarian-American chef Diane Kochilas. "To distain the pursuit of material acquisition and live simply and essentially, to pay little heed to the zeitgeist of the times, indeed to pay no heed to time at all."

Kochilas wasn't born on Ikaria but her parents and many of their New York neighbors were, and island attitudes were so woven into the texture of her life that she describes arriving for the first time at the age of twelve as a kind of homecoming.

"The adage 'man plans, God laughs' is really how life is," Kochilas writes of Ikaria. "Being tuned into life's ephemeral truths means being open to chance. It means being sent for coffee to the general store by your mother, as our friend Christos Kourdos once was, and coming back 3 months later, after having met a group of buddies on their way to a *panygyri* (local festival), hooking up with them, cavorting all night, heading with them all the way to Athens, landing a temporary job, and, finally, returning home, coffee, of course, long forgotten. At some point early on, he probably called home."

I was frankly staggered by the idea that anyone could live without being fixated on clocks or calendars. As a writer, I'd spent most of my adult life laboring mightily to meet one deadline after another, including the weekly blog I was producing during this trip. Oh sure, I allowed myself a little more flexibility these days, moving the publication date around to fit my travel schedule and wifi availability, but the blog had become the steady heartbeat of my writing life and it was a rare week that I didn't publish a post. Would I still be capable of doing the work I loved if I didn't give myself the structure of deadlines?

What would it be like, I wondered, to simply ... stop ... thinking ... about ... time? To live and write spontaneously? Could I do it, given the chance? Would I want to? How would that single change affect my life?

How it affects the lives of Ikaria's residents is clear: they live longer than nearly any other community on the planet.

One third of the island's residents live into their nineties. (In contrast, less than five percent of Americans over sixty-five are likely to earn a birthday cake with ninety candles.) Ikarians not only live longer, they age well, without any dementia and with vastly lower rates of heart disease, cancer, depression, and all the other ills that make the so-called golden years so miserable for millions. Aging well means the island's nonagenarians are fit enough to embrace many of life pleasures, including lovemaking. According to one study, eighty percent of Ikarian males between sixty-five and a hundred still enjoy an active sex life, and I'm fairly certain Viagra has nothing to do with it.

As you can imagine, researchers from around the world are trying to figure out how to replicate these conditions. Foremost among the researchers is Dan Buettner, a National Geographic Fellow and bestselling author who popularized the term Blue Zones as a shorthand for the longest-lived communities on Earth. The term came from the original demographers who marked clusters of extraordinary longevity by drawing blue circles on a map. Buettner identifies five Blue Zones around the world: Okinawa, Japan; Sardinia, Italy; Nicoya, Cost Rica; the Seventh-day Adventists in Loma Linda, California; and Ikaria, Greece.

"The brutal reality about aging," Buettner wrote, "is that it has only an accelerator pedal. We have yet to discover whether a brake exists for people. The name of the game is to keep from pushing the accelerator pedal so hard that we speed up the aging process. The average American, however, by living a fast and furious lifestyle, pushes that accelerator too hard and too much."

How are Ikarians keeping their foot off the accelerator pedal? In addition to a low-stress lifestyle, which includes sleeping late and taking a daily siesta, they eat a healthy yet pleasurable diet — which is why I was determined to include them in the Mediterranean Comfort Food Tour.

On Ikaria, meals center around plants grown at home or harvested from the mountain forests in the center of the island: olives, grapes, beans, wild greens, potatoes, fruit. The islanders consume hefty amounts of olive oil and two to four glasses of wine a day. That's right, I said two to four glasses of wine a day. (Note to self: I have some catching up to do.) Compared to Americans, they eat six times as many beans and a quarter as much refined sugar. Honey is the preferred sweetener and taken by the spoonful as a general aid to health. Coffee is popular, but they drink twice as much tea. Fish is on the table maybe twice a week, meat five times a month. They drink goat's milk from the lean, semi-wild animals roaming the island.

"We do eat better here than in America," Thea, an Ikarian who'd lived in Detroit, told Buettner. "But it's more about how we eat. Even if it's your lunch break from work, you relax and enjoy your meal. You enjoy the company of whoever you are with. Food here is always enjoyed in combination with conversation."

Dr. Ilias Leriadis, a vice mayor and one of the island's few physicians, told Buettner, "It's not a 'me' place. It's an 'us' place."

My head was so full of extraordinary images of Ikaria that it was almost a shock to arrive at Elvidos and find it looking so ordinary. Ordinary, that is, by the standards of Greek islands. Whitewashed houses, cafés, and shops were clustered around the harbor. Some fishing boats rocked in the surge caused by our ferry's arrival. A couple of cars and vespas puttered along the shore road, which rose steeply to wooded cliffs. There weren't many people about on the streets. I realized it was lunchtime on Sunday and wondered if that mattered to the islanders.

It definitely mattered to me; I was hungry and very curious to try some local food. As soon as we'd checked into our hotel, a modern, blue-and-white building a few blocks from the harbor, I went downstairs to consult Dimitris, the large, affable young man who staffed the hotel's front desk.

"Popi's," he said promptly. "It has the best food on the island, possibly all of Greece. And it is just ten minutes' walk up the coast road."

Twenty minutes later, as Rich and I staggered up yet another rise, I began to wonder if somehow we'd missed the place. Dimitris had said it was across from a playing field, and so far we'd seen nothing but rugged cliffs, a few scattered buildings, and the sea. Pulling out his phone, Rich was amazed to discover that Google had actually heard of Popi's and claimed it was just around the next bend, adding helpfully, "Closed. Opens again 1:00 AM."

"That can't be right," he said.

"Well, they say time operates differently here," I replied doubtfully. "But still, opening at 1:00 AM? Really?"

We soldiered on, passing a wire fence enclosing a section of hillside with deep grass and four or five grazing goats. One of them picked up her head and bleated a greeting; the others grew curious and ambled over for a closer look at these two strange humans wandering past. I noticed the goat pen was attached to a vegetable garden, which backed up on a vine-covered, two-story building. And to my joy and footsore relief, attached to that building was a sign reading "Popi's."

I climbed the steps to the flagstone terrace and chose one of the half a dozen small wooden tables in the dappled shade cast by overhead vines; it offered a splendid view of the cliffs and sea. Rich and I were the only customers, although later a few others trickled in.

A handsome, bearded youth came out to take our order. I soon learned his name was Zisis, and that his mother was the owner, Mrs. Popi. She'd operated the place as a bar until he was born in 1993, at which point she converted it into a restaurant. He stood, chatting casually, as if he had all the time the world. I asked if he'd lived on Ikaria his entire life.

"I went to work in Crete for a time," Zisis told me with a slight shudder. "Too much stress. It's better here."

He brought us bottles of the crisp local Ikariotissa Ale and went away again to prepare our order of spinach pie and grilled fish with herbed bean sauce. I settled back in my chair and gazed out at the Aegean Sea stretching away to the horizon. I had the delightful and all too rare sensation that for once there really was "nothing to do, no place to go," as one of my teachers, the Buddhist monk Thich Nhat Hanh, was fond of saying.

The food was every bit as delicious as Dimitris had suggested, and I soon began to wonder if the good-natured Zisis would be willing to let me into the kitchen to watch him cook. As with Yannis and the snails, I decided to wait and ask this after I'd returned a second time as a customer.

My plan worked perfectly. Rich and I came back the next day for lunch and ordered one of the island's specialties: wild goat. Cooked in its own juices and garnished with wild herbs, the lean meat tasted simply marvelous — succulent, rich, and comforting. I said as much to Zisis and asked if I could come back and learn how he him made it. He said sure, stop by the next morning before the restaurant opened. I was jubilant.

Now I know what some of you are thinking: How could I even consider eating one of those sweet little goats that had bleated such an endearing welcome as I approached Popi's? Well, as it happened, Ikaria was hideously overrun with goats, thanks to EU subsidies rewarding larger herds. On an island with just 8423 residents, there were currently 35,000 goats, most roaming free and wreaking havoc on the ecosystem. Islanders were desperate to cull the herds to protect the island's vegetation — the main food supply for the human residents — from these four-legged marauders.

I certainly didn't mind pitching in to help with the effort. Besides, I'd just learned that goat is a surprisingly healthy option, far leaner than lamb or beef, with forty percent less saturated fat than skinless chicken.

The next morning, I found Zisis in the kitchen holding a large metal tray filled with chunks of pale meat. "The goat is very fresh," he told me. "I butchered it this morning." I probably should have regretted missing out on this earthy part of the story, but I was relieved to be spared the necessity of witnessing the bloodshed. Once, long ago, I'd seen a baby goat casually grabbed and killed by a knife-wielding Greek villager, then skinned on the spot for the family's lunch. It wasn't pretty.

Zisis explained that he and his mother, like so many on the island, raise their own goats and occasionally, when the restaurant was extra busy, got more from relatives and friends. "Some goats are kept in pens, but many are free," he told me. "And then the people must go hunting."

With Zisis translating for her, Mrs. Popi explained that all cooking begins in the garden. She led the way outside, through her vegetable garden, to the lush, sloping field of knee-high grass and herbs where the small flock was grazing. The day was mild and overcast; the breeze blowing in from the sea was fresh and slightly salty. I scratched one of the goats behind the ears and thought this was one of the most tranquil places I'd ever been.

Back in the kitchen, Zisis was prepping the meat. Asked to pin down quantities, he estimated he starts with about two and a quarter kilos (five pounds) of goat. Because it's so lean, formal cuts such as loin and shoulder aren't practical; instead you make "village cuts," dividing the meat any way you can, so long as it winds up a size that's roughly suitable for cooking.

Then you add lots of salt, pepper, and about three quarters of a cup of olive oil. You cook the meat in a ceramic pot at 200 degrees Celsius (400 degrees Fahrenheit) for an hour and a half to two hours. The cooking brings out the meat's natural juices, but it's best to check it a few times, adding vegetable broth if it seems at all dry.

When the meat is tender and the smaller bones practically

liquified, you take it out of the oven and sprinkle it with fresh herbs. Often this includes the local oregano, which is full of vitamins, antioxidants, omega-3 fatty acids, and other beneficial elements. A study showed the variety grown on the island is three times more nutrient-rich and aromatic than the kinds raised in other parts of Greece. (How does this compare to the commercially produced oregano sold in the US? I probably don't want to know.)

When I'd finished taking notes and spent some time thanking Zisis and Mrs. Popi, I came out onto the terrace to find several customers had arrived. I fell into conversation with a cheerful young Australian named Diana who was staying with relatives in a nearby village.

"Are your relatives cooking amazing things for you?" I asked.

"The food's better here," she said.

A short while later, as Rich and I were walking back along the coast road to our hotel, Diana pulled up in her little rental car and offered us a lift. We accepted with pleasure and invited her to join us for a coffee.

As we settled in a café near the harbor, I asked if she was going to that night's *panygyri*, the all-night dance party we'd heard about from the ever-helpful Dimitris. Nominally a celebration of a saint's day, a *panygyri* was more about gathering as a community for food, wine, music, and dancing; we all agreed it wasn't to be missed. Diana offered to drive, and Rich promised to get the location details from Dimitris.

Diana, Rich, and I arrived in the village of Avlaki just before sunset, parking on the road and walking up a steepish incline to a large building that seemed to be a sort of community center. Musicians sat on a bench against one wall, playing lively folk tunes on guitar, violin, and lute while people gathered at long tables over enormous platters of food. When our turn came in the food line, Diana's ability to speak Greek enabled us to walk away with a huge tray filled with roast pork, *tzatziki* (yogurt with cucumber and garlic) dip, a loaf of bread, a slab of feta cheese, fried

90

potatoes, salad, and a carafe of the dark red local wine.

This wine had been famous since the sixth century BC. The god of party animals, Dionysus, who was born on this very island, used it in his ancient rituals. Odysseus stupefied the giant man-eating Cyclops with it in order to escape. And now we had a liter of it sitting in front of us. I took a sip; strong stuff! Clearly we were in for quite a night. Rich, tragically, is allergic to red wine, and there was no white, so he had to content himself with beer.

All around us people were chatting and laughing. There were perhaps two dozen foreigners and a hundred islanders, with more drifting in all the time. Several Ikarians were kind enough to strike up conversations with us. One fellow in particular, who spoke not a word of English, seemed to get a tremendous kick out of Rich, and pointed to himself then drew numbers on the tabletop to indicate his age: eighty-four. Rich didn't have to exaggerate his surprise; he'd have pegged the man as a decade younger at least.

As the music picked up in tempo, Rich's new friend excused himself and stood up. Moving to the middle of the floor he opened the dancing, swaying gracefully around the center of the room, arms held wide. After a while he reached out to a twenty-something woman and led her onto the dance floor. Pretty soon everybody was getting to their feet and joining in. When space got crowded, everyone threw their arms over one another's shoulders, moving in swaying circles.

Most of the foreigners got their dancing in early and were gone by midnight; the locals were now in the majority and the quality of the dancing improved significantly. I watched as Rich's new Ikarian friend, who had barely sat down all night, led yet another young woman onto the dance floor.

"You have to give the guy credit," I shouted over the music. "He's got a lot of energy for eighty-four."

A man sitting nearby laughed. "Eighty-four? He's ninety-three."

I regarded the dancer with even greater respect. He was the life and soul of the *panygyri* and seemed prepared, like the party itself, to go on until dawn. He certainly outlasted us; we wandered out somewhere around one. Or maybe two. By then things had gotten a bit blurry.

"Still worried there won't be enough to do on the island?" I asked Rich the next morning, as I sipped some much-needed coffee at a small café on the harbor front.

"Are you kidding? I'm exhausted. I can't keep up with these folks."

Lingering over breakfast, I watched islanders stroll about their business at a leisurely pace. Occasionally someone would drive in to do an errand, stopping their car in the middle of the street, leaving the door open and engine running while they stepped inside a shop to make a purchase. They'd return unhurriedly to their car and drive off, usually before any other motorists appeared. Anyone who did come along simply maneuvered around the stopped vehicle without any honking, fuss, road rage, or gun threats. I saw motorcycles left at the curb with the keys in the ignition and bicycles propped unsecured against lampposts. Ikarians don't sweat the small stuff … or the large stuff either.

Later, taking a walk around the village, I noticed I was moving more slowly than usual, adopting something closer to the pace used by the Ikarians. Was it last night's wine or the island's influence? Whatever the cause, Rich and I idled away an entire an hour sitting quietly on our favorite wharf-side bench, watching the world amble by.

Close to sunset, I noticed dozens of chairs being set out in the harbor's small plaza, and soon villagers began drifting in to take their places. A local election was coming up, and the community was gathering to listen to the candidates. Everyone sat in silence as one would-be representative spoke at length, no doubt outlining his vision for Ikaria's future in the most glowing possible terms. I saw no bunting, banners, lawn signs, pins, flyers, or protest posters. It was democracy in its most essential form, courteous and serious in its intent. A far cry from what I was used to in my own country.

It wasn't easy to leave this island, and when the time came, I found myself hoping I'd carry some of its relaxed attitude away with me. We'd booked passage on a ferry leaving from the island's southern port, Aghios Kirykos, and Dimitris arranged for "the best taxi driver on Ikaria" to take us there via a leisurely route that would allow us to drop in at various scenic locations.

The highlight was the Monastery of Osias Theoktisti, built to honor a female saint no one seems to know anything about. We were shown the cave where her remains were found, a church with an inscription referring to 1688, and another cave that had been turned into a chapel, tucked beneath a rock to size of a small spaceship. In the gift shop I bought a jar of the best honey I've ever tasted; the woman who sold it to me told me it would cure a host of ills.

During the hours it took to cross the island on narrow, winding roads, our driver regaled us with stories. The most famous, of course, was about young Icarus, who famously flew too close to the sun and met his doom just off the coast of this very island. It happened while he and his father Daedalus were trying to escape from Crete. King Minos had hired them to build the famous Minotaur's labyrinth at Knossos then imprisoned them there to make sure they could never reveal its secrets. After breaking out, Daedalus created wings of wax and feathers so he and his son could escape by flying over the sea. But in his youthful arrogance, Icarus soared too high and the sun melted his wings.

Poet Billy Collins writes of young Icarus' defining moment: "here we have the horrified face, contorted with regret not unlike the beady-eyed Wile E. Coyote, who pauses in mid-air to share with us his moment of fatal realization before beginning his long descent into a canyon."

Our driver then told about a man who'd returned to Ikaria to die — and was still living here decades later. Demetris had mentioned this same story, which had been reported in the local paper a few years earlier. But it wasn't until I came across the details of the tale in Buettner's book that I got the full story.

It seems that during World War II, a young Ikarian named Stamatis Moraitis was in a munitions accident that left one of his hands mangled. He went to the USA for treatment and stayed on, marrying a Greek-American woman and raising a family. At the age of sixty he learned he had lung cancer; the five doctors he consulted all gave him six to nine months to live. Eventually he decided to go back to the island so he could die among his own people, pointing out that on Ikaria funeral costs would only be about $200 instead of the $1200 they'd run in America, so he could leave a bit more for his wife. The couple moved in with Stamatis' parents, and he retired to bed to await the inevitable.

Old friends turned up at the house, bringing bottles of the island's red wine, which Stamatis sipped all day — because hey, why not? Occasionally he would get out of bed to sit quietly in the family garden and vineyard. One day, for old times' sake, he planted a few vegetables. He puttered around the vineyard, tidying up a little. Pretty soon he was building an addition on the family homestead.

"Today," wrote Buettner, "35 years later, he is 100 years old and cancer-free. He never went through chemotherapy, took drugs, or sought therapy of any sort. All he did was move to Ikaria." Buettner asked Stamatis if he had any idea how he'd recovered from lung cancer.

"It just went away," he said. "I actually went back to America about ten years after moving here to see if the doctors could explain it to me."

Buettner asked what happened.

"My doctors were all dead."

8. Athens / *The Rooster on the Roof*

Rolling into Athens on a warm May morning, I was feeling utterly relaxed and contented. Fresh off the ferry from Ikaria, I was ready to take life as it came, viewing every passerby as a potential friend, drinking companion, and dance partner.

That feeling lasted just about as long as it took to pull my bag out of the taxi's trunk and drag it to the sidewalk. Every one of the city's three and a half million residents seemed to be rushing furiously past, shouting into their phones against a backdrop of graffiti so virulent that I could almost hear it howling with fury.

I hovered on the sidewalk, buffeted by the crowd, feeling invisible.

And then someone behind me said, "Karen?"

I turned to find tall, dark-haired man smiling in welcome. He introduced himself as Nikos and explained he was there to escort us to the luncheon I'd arranged with his partner Michail through the private dining group EatWith.

"We are cooking on the roof today," Nikos said. He grabbed the handle of my suitcase and took off down the sidewalk, striding toward a high-rise apartment building.

Trotting along beside him, I reflected that this is one of the sensations I love best about travel: hurrying toward a situation about which

I know practically nothing. EatWith does a good job of vetting their hosts, but still, Rich and I were about to share a meal with two strange men in a foreign country. I felt the little tingle excitement that goes along with any small adventure.

In minutes I was shaking hands with stocky, bearded, genial Michail, and then Nikos stood back and invited me to admire the view.

It was breathtaking. All of Athens lay at my feet, presided over by the Acropolis, the enormous rock outcropping at the center of the city. Perched on top of it were the ruins of the Parthenon temple, an enduring symbol of civilization and humankind's capacity for artistic achievement and acts of spectacular stupidity, spite, and greed.

Built as a temple to Athena in 438 BC, the Parthenon had remained more or less perfectly intact for 2125 years. Over time it had served as a treasury, Christian church, and Ottoman mosque depending on the prevailing political winds, but every generation, and all who worshipped or worked there, had treated it with deep respect as one of the world's greatest cultural monuments. Until the catastrophic events of 1687.

It happened during the chaos of an attack on Athens. The city had been under Ottoman rule for centuries, and the Venetians decided it was time for the city to be in Christian hands again. They laid siege to the city, and the situation began careening out of control. Some genius in the city government thought it would be clever to hide gunpowder and high-ranking civilians inside the temple itself. Why? Because nobody would ever, ever do anything to damage the world's most beloved building.

I think you can see where this is going.

According to one eyewitness account, a Turkish deserter snuck over to the Venetian camp and told their commander, Francesco Morosini, what was hidden in the Parthenon. Others insist it wasn't insider knowledge, just a stray mortar that inexplicably shot 500 feet into the air and dropped down right on the temple. An unlucky accident. Yeah, right.

However it happened, the temple took a direct hit, the gunpowder inside it exploded, and three hundred people were killed. Large sections of the temple collapsed, and chunks of marble and flaming debris showered down on the city, killing countless more and setting so many houses on fire the neighborhood would still be burning the next day. Before the smoke and dust had begun to settle, a victorious Morosini rushed up to the Parthenon and had his men start hacking priceless carvings off the walls; in their haste and inexperience, they dropped and destroyed many of the best.

A year later the Ottomans were back in force, baying for blood, and the Venetians decided keeping Athens wasn't worth another fight. As they prepared to flee, a plan was made to blow up the remains of the Parthenon and other buildings on the Acropolis. The Venetians later claimed they believed the Acropolis might offer their enemies a military advantage in defending the city (although obviously it hadn't done the Ottomans much good). I suspect it was actually sheer spite. Luckily cooler heads prevailed and the plan was abandoned at the last minute.

For the next few centuries, the Parthenon sat around crumbling and being looted by all and sundry. Many consider Lord Elgin, the British Ambassador at Constantinople, to be the worst of all the vandals. From 1801 to 1812, his agents chiseled half the remaining sculptures off the Parthenon walls and sold them to the British government, who promptly donated them to the British Museum. Lord Elgin claimed he'd obtained permission from the Sultan, who as ruler of the Ottoman Empire was their legal owner, but the documentation is dubious, an English translation of an Italian transcription of the lost original.

Not surprisingly, the Greeks keep demanding the return of the Elgin Marbles, and the British Museum is clinging to them like an octopus wrapped around a big, juicy lobster. Government and museum officials maintain Britain has legal ownership, and even if it didn't, they owe it to the world to keep these treasures safe.

Archaeologist Dorothy King, author of *The Elgin Marbles*, summed it up this way: "We can't even think about returning the Elgin Marbles to Athens until the Greeks start caring for what they already have. I'm sure they'd take great care of the Parthenon sculptures if they were returned. But if you knew a woman was abusing her child, you wouldn't let her adopt another. And that's what the Greeks are asking for." What? No, it's not. In this scenario, the Greeks are the blameless mother demanding the return of her kidnapped child.

Please note my incredible self-restraint in not using the words "patronizing," "condescending", or "colonialist attitude" in the above paragraph.

As for who is better suited to care for these priceless works of art, I'll just point out that the Greeks kept them intact for more than 2000 years, while the British Museum has already done irreparable damage to them. In the 1930s, someone had the bright idea of cleaning them with wire brushes and copper chisels, removing much of the detail from the carvings. The gallery in which the Elgin Marbles are housed has a glass roof that sprang leaks in 2018 and 2021, although to be fair, so far this hasn't resulted in more damage. But if we're talking about responsible stewardship, I don't think the British Museum should be casting any stones.

In 2022 an Italian museum returned their fragment of the Parthenon sculptures, adding to the growing international demands that the UK follow suit. The British Museum has been exploring the idea of a "cultural exchange" that will "change the temperature of the debate." You can almost picture them dabbing beads of sweat off their beleaguered brows as they say it.

Meanwhile, in 1975 the Greek government finally began a serious effort to restore the Parthenon to its former glory. Most of the surviving sculptures were removed for safekeeping and are now on display at the new, gorgeously designed Acropolis Museum, where you can view them with the Parthenon visible in the background through a wall of glass. Space has been conspicuously left for the Elgin marbles, should they ever return home.

Sorry for the lengthy digression, but Athens is the sort of city that provokes grand thoughts and long-winded diatribes about historical misadventures. People have been living there for the better part of 12,000 years, and as you will have gathered, it's a city with a particularly checkered past. And present. But more about that later.

Dragging my eyes away from the Parthenon, I looked around at the rooftop, which was charmingly decorated with flowering vines and tropical plants, and shaded with a wooden lattice. A porch swing stood invitingly at one end, and at the other, a worktable and burners created a kitchen, with a sink tucked away in a corner.

The two men beamed as I admired the setting, and then Michail got to work. He would be showing me how to cook one of his signature dishes, *Pastitsada*, a rooster and pasta casserole traditionally served for Sunday lunch on the island of Corfu and beloved throughout Greece.

Cooking rooster properly is tricky business. Usually we're talking about tough old birds that have outlived their usefulness and only then are conscripted to make the ultimate sacrifice in the stewpot. Years of servicing hens, fighting off other roosters, breaking up fights over the pecking order, and defending the flock from the occasional hawk or lynx leaves the mature country rooster lean, mean, and leathery.

I've never had occasion to butcher a rooster, but one Georgia farmer who'd just dispatched six wrote this on the Many Fold Farm blog: "Their skin is tough to cut, requiring constant re-honing of the knives, and their cavities are impossible to open up: it took the full-strength of both my arms to pull them open enough to remove their innards. You can actually see the striations in the bands of muscle tissue, the thought of which made my jaws clench in fear of excessive mastication and the need for dental floss. To look at an old rooster carcass, one imagines a meat that has more in common with rubber bands than with actual food."

How do you deal with this kind of toughness? By slow-cooking the bird in lots of red wine, of course. The classic French *coq au vin* (rooster in wine) was invented as a way of breaking down the scrawny old birds into something soft, pliable, and flavorful. The process takes at least four hours in the oven, more if you can manage it, and is often enhanced by a glass of brandy (ideally with a second glass for the pot). I wondered exactly how Michail planned to cook his rooster in the timeframe of an afternoon luncheon. Perhaps, like the people of Ikaria, he was simply not going to fuss about time.

He began by massaging salt into pieces of rooster sitting in a large bowl. They looked remarkably plump to me, a far cry from the gaunt, elderly fowl I'd been expecting.

"How old is this rooster?" I asked him.

"He is about eight months old. Anything older is very tough. It takes a long time to cook."

I suppose a purist might have preferred something more aged and scraggly in accord with tradition, but this certainly seemed as if it would make easier cooking and better eating. Afterwards I looked up Julia Child's *Coq au Vin* recipe and discovered she used ordinary thighs and drumsticks from hens; apparently there's a certain amount of wiggle room with the ingredients of so-called rooster dishes.

I spent the next few hours on the flower-decked balcony watching Michail and pestering him with questions. Occasionally he let me chop up a vegetable or herb so I could feel more useful. Rich nobly volunteered for taste testing as required.

The recipe was simple country fare with more than a hint of Italian influence, which is common in the cuisine of Corfu Island, situated a mere 70 miles from the heel of Italy's boot. Michail began by browning the pieces of salted rooster in a frying pan then simmering them for an hour in a pot with tomatoes, onions, garlic, and spices that included cinnamon, cumin, oregano, nutmeg, and sweet red paprika. Meanwhile Michail made the traditional *bucatini*, fat, tube-shaped spaghetti. The pasta went into a ceramic pot along with grated, salt-dried *mizithra* cheese. When the rooster was done and several rounds of sampling had affirmed the sauce was perfect, Michail spooned the meat and sauce over the pasta and announced we were ready to eat.

Just then the sky, which had been steadily darkening, let loose with the first fat drops of rain, and the men hastily dragged the table into a covered alcove. Settling into our seats, Rich and I dug in.

"Magnificent," I mumbled around a succulent mouthful. "Truly magnificent."

"I have died and gone to heaven," said Rich.

In addition to the *Pastitsada*, salads, cheeses, fried vegetables, and other accompaniments were arranged on the table, and I sampled all of them with pleasure. When I'd eaten all I possibly could and then some, I bid a fond farewell to Nikos, Michail, and the remains of the rooster, and Rich and I took up our suitcases for the walk to our rental apartment.

The previous year, Rich and I had visited Athens, staying in a cozy neighborhood inconveniently located nearly an hour's hot, uphill walk from the city center. Every time I staggered up the stairs of that Airbnb apartment, after my breath and heartrate finally returned to normal and I regained the capacity for speech, I swore in future I'd stay someplace closer in on flatter ground.

So this time we'd rented an Airbnb downtown, in a neighborhood that was considerably less cozy. The morning after the rooster cookout,

Rich and I set off for a walk, passing building after building covered with lurid graffiti expressing the artists' sentiments about the rocky economy, the idiocy of politicians, and his or her personal love life (real or imagined). Rich had looked up the safety rating and kept reassuring me we were in a good neighborhood. I soldiered on.

Catching a glimpse of green up ahead, I dared to hope we might be approaching some sort of park. It turned out to be a strip of grass and a few desultory trees set between rows of modern apartment buildings covered in the usual virulent messages. The remains of a smashed-up, stripped-down, graffiti-covered car squatted at the curb, quietly rusting.

"I thought we only going to walk in the good neighborhood," I muttered to Rich.

"This is the good neighborhood."

I sighed and kept walking.

The choice of neighborhood had seemed so logical at the time. In addition to avoiding the strenuous hike up the hill, I'd wanted the convenience of being close to both the rooster lunch and our next activity: volunteering at the Caritas Athens Refugee Program.

Ann and Linda, the sisters who had helped me organize the visit to the refugee camps on Lesvos, had also volunteered in the Caritas Athens soup kitchen and had sent me the contact information. I'd emailed Caritas, explaining that Rich and I wanted to make a small donation and volunteer for a day at the soup kitchen. The Caritas administrators were happy to accommodate both requests.

People were already patiently waiting in clusters outside the slightly shabby, modern Caritas Athens headquarters when Rich and I arrived. Every day Caritas provided hundreds of people with their main (often only) meal of the day. I found the staff and volunteers — Greek, European, American, Australian, and others I couldn't identify —

astonishingly well-organized, efficient, and cheerful.

The clients were mostly refugees from Afghanistan, Iran, Iraq, and the drought-ridden Horn of Africa, plus some Greek families who had fallen on hard times, and a handful of other Europeans. The staff made sure everyone felt welcome and respected, and while many clients seemed too shell-shocked to talk much, lots of them — especially the families with kids — clearly knew each other and chatted like old friends.

The first one through the door was a young man missing several fingers on one hand. Using his good hand, he guided his two small children to the food line. He was courteous, making sure his kids ate everything and behaved themselves properly, but much of the time he simply sat giving the far wall a thousand-yard stare. When he had finished eating, he stood, collected his children, and made his way to my station to return his tray. He thanked me very politely for the meal, looking me in the eye and speaking softly in what I'm guessing was Greek; my grasp of the language being nonexistent, I could only smile and nod. I watched him leave and silently wished him luck. He seemed due.

I'd like to be able to say I connected on a deep personal level with lots of refugees, but most of the time I was far too busy flying through my chores. Having volunteered for years at a Cleveland soup kitchen, I thought I knew what to expect. Boy, was I wrong. I hadn't worked so hard in decades.

Before lunch I peeled endless heads of garlic for the stew, then I distributed pitchers of water to the tables and set up stacks of trays and plates. After that I was assigned to tray-cleaning, and one of the veteran volunteers showed me the routine: capture any uneaten bread to redistribute (I tried not to imagine what the U.S. Department of Public Health would say about that), scrape scraps into a compost bin, wipe the tray with a wet cloth, dry with another, stack just so for collection and reuse. Repeat a thousand times. No matter how frantically I worked, more and more trays kept piling up. If you've ever seen Disney's *The Sorcerer's*

Apprentice you'll have a pretty good idea what my job felt like.

As rushed as I was, I still managed to enjoy the background hubbub of talk and laughter. To me, that's one of the most comforting sounds in the world: people enjoying their meal and the simple, human pleasure of each other's company. These feel-good moments aren't just pleasurable; research shows they're good for our bodies, souls, and communities. Which is why it's so worrying — to social scientists, spiritual teachers, and me — that American families now eat together fewer than five times a week, and that in the UK, only twenty percent of families ever gather for meals, and they often do so in complete silence.

When the room quieted down and everyone had gone but the staff, someone handed me a bowl of stew, and I sat down gratefully to eat. After the first bite I marveled yet again at the Mediterranean knack for throwing together a few inexpensive ingredients and creating something delicious and nourishing. When this came to the attention of the world in the 1960s, corporations leapt on this concept like teenage boys at an all-you-can-eat buffet. Industrial food manufacturers have kept generations of scientists gainfully employed attempting to isolate the active ingredients and reproduce their effects in a laboratory so they can be synthesized, packaged, and sold at a profit. It can't be done.

The Mediterranean diet is neatly summed up by nutrition guru Michael Pollen in just seven words: eat food, not too much, mostly plants. And when he says food, he means real food, not hydrogenated compounds laced with chemicals and drizzled with guar gum. If your grandmother wouldn't recognize the ingredients, if you can't pronounce or spell them, or if they have so many preservatives they'll last through the next century, you really don't want to put them in your body.

"If it came from a plant, eat it," said Pollen. "If it was made in a plant, don't."

I'd like to report that I live by that motto, but I freely admit that I am not about to give up everything (yes, chocolate nut bars, I'm thinking of you) that comes in a package with a logo. But I am making an effort to eat as much real food as possible. Pollen also reminds us that it's not just what you eat, it's how you eat. "The shared meal elevates eating from a mechanical process of fueling the body to a ritual of family and community, from the mere animal biology to an act of culture."

And an act of comfort. On dark and shellshocked days, sometimes the only ray of light is holding a warm bowl of stew in your hands, listening to the hum of voices around you, knowing that in this moment, the only thing life demands from you is putting a spoonful of goodness in your mouth, and then another. In better times, the pleasure of eating is a reminder of just how much fun life can be, and why it's worth the effort to stay in the game.

9. Thessaloniki / *Freddos, Frappés & Fortunetellers*

"You know, at some point we're going to have to leave Greece and get on with the rest of the Mediterranean Comfort Food Tour." Rich took a leisurely sip of coffee and continued gazing contentedly out over the sea.

"Absolutely." I peered into the dregs at the bottom of my cup. Michail and Nikos had told me, during our rooster-cooking afternoon in Athens, that Greek fortunetellers used coffee grounds to see into the future. I had no idea what, if anything, my coffee grounds were trying to tell me, but I said, "I predict we're going on a long journey. Very soon. But not today."

We were lingering in the city of Thessaloniki in the far north of Greece, taking a ten-day breather before the big push into unknown territory: North Macedonia and Albania. Thessaloniki is a great place to linger; sitting on the shore of the Thermaic Gulf, the northernmost section of the Aegean Sea, it's Greece's second largest city and quite possibly its most cosmopolitan. It's my kind of town: ancient, mysterious, a crossroads of every culture known to humankind, small enough to navigate on foot, big enough to offer countless neighborhoods to explore, and famous for its vibrant street life, fueled by a truly astonishing amount of coffee.

I'm from America's West Coast, where coffee-drinking has achieved a near-cult status, but I soon realized that we were novices compared to the Thessalonikians. Of course, they had a big head start, as they'd been swilling it since the Ottomans took over the region in the early fifteenth century. It was clear the good citizens of this city had made good use of their time; I saw cafés everywhere, as many as five or six on a downtown block, doing brisk business at all hours of the day and night.

For the first time on this journey, I was no longer seeing the traditional all-male *cafeneons*. No doubt a few were tucked away in back streets, but in the city center men and women mingled freely in countless richly scented coffee houses and sidewalk cafés. Younger locals took their caffeine to the streets — a rare sight in Europe — sipping from go-cups as they walked, shopped, worked, and chatted on their cell phones. What was in all those go-cups? Mostly *frappés* and *freddos*, the brash, young, hipster descendants of the original Greek coffee.

The Ottomans brought to Greece a thick, Turkish-style boiled brew that's still quite popular throughout the country. The taste is rather like extra-bitter instant coffee, the texture's much grittier, and it's a challenge to get it down without swallowing the sludge at the bottom of the cup. I prefer my Greek coffee *sketos* (without sugar), but nearly everyone else takes it *metrios* (moderate, with one heaping teaspoon of sugar), *glykos* (sweet, two teaspoons), or *variglykos* (very sweet, four teaspoons, at which point it's more or less Red Bull).

And so matters stood for centuries. Then a single impulsive moment at a 1957 trade fair changed Greece's coffee culture forever. The Swiss manufacturer Nestlé had come to the trade fair in Thessaloniki in order to promote instant Nescafé and a short-lived product involving chocolate milk made in a shaker. One day a Nescafé employee called Dimitrios Vakondios was desperate for a jolt of caffeine but couldn't find any hot water. On impulse, he borrowed the shaker from the chocolate milk rep and mixed Nescafé instant coffee with cold water and ice. The idea of iced coffee was shockingly radical — yet irresistibly alluring in Greece's warm climate. Suddenly everybody in Thessaloniki wanted to try it, and soon iced instant coffee became the drink of choice for younger, trendier Greeks everywhere.

This revolutionary drink was dubbed the *frappé* (from the French "*frapper*," meaning to hit, referring to the ice smashing around in the shaker). It can be served with varying amounts of white or brown sugar, with or without condensed milk, and — if you really want to feel the love — a scoop of ice cream.

The *frappé* reigned supreme until the 1990s, when it was overtaken by the *freddo*, a similar iced drink made from the classier Italian espresso. It can of course be configured to any degree of sweetness, and if you want milk, you ask for a *freddo cappuccino*.

Which is better? I felt I owed it to my readers to conduct a rigorous taste test so that I could properly evaluate the contenders. A golden opportunity to do this came my very first morning in town.

Rich and I had set off in search of breakfast, wandering in the general direction of the seafront. Pausing at a pleasant-looking eatery called Θερμαϊκός Κήπος, I said, "Hey, isn't that our wallpaper?"

The enormous pink roses set against a bright turquoise background were unmistakable. They made an eyepopping statement in the bedroom of our bohemian rental apartment, a modest attic filled with quirky charm perched on top of a seven-story high-rise. As he handed me the keys, the young manager mentioned that the landlady's mother was Natasa Kalafatis, owner of Thessaloniki's historic yet hippest café-bar, Thermaikos.

"You must go to Thermaikos, it is great," he said. "She has a restaurant as well, Thermaikos Garden."

I figured this must be Thermaikos Garden. Because how many people in this city would decorate with giant pink roses on bright turquoise?

As I peered in through the open doorway, a lively, long-haired woman came out to explain they weren't open yet, and it didn't take me long to work out that this was the owner, Natasa Kalafatis. I introduced myself and told her how much I liked her daughter's apartment. As we chatted, I explained about the Mediterranean Comfort Food Tour and asked if she could recommend a place for us to learn more about *frappés* and *freddos*.

She nodded thoughtfully. "Yes, meet me in an hour at Thermaikos bar."

Presenting myself an hour later, I found Thermaikos to be a dimly lit homage to the decadence of times past. The walls were red, the floors black-and-white tile, the furnishings bohemian vintage, with glass lamps, old-fashioned sofas, and framed photos of long-ago movie stars. Pop hits from the fifties and sixties, mostly Elvis, played in the background. A few well-dressed, dissipated-looking older customers lounged in the outdoor chairs, giving the impression they'd been sitting there gazing out over the sea for years.

In the inner sanctum stood a long bar presided over by a barista called Athanasia, which means "immortal." I'm not saying she was an actual goddess; that's for future historians to decide. But she was tall and beautiful and wielded her coffee shaker with the poise and gravitas of a minor deity presiding over a ritual in her home temple.

I asked Athanasia and Natasa if they drank *frappes*. Both instantly said no.

"The quality of the coffee is not good," said Athanasia dismissively.

"It is bad for your stomach," added Natasa, wrinkling her nose.

"So why do people drink so much of it?"

Natasa said, "It's the symbol of coolness." Ah, that.

Athansasia kindly agreed to show me how to mix up a frappé: a little water, two teaspoons of Nescafé, and four teaspoons of sugar. She used a blender to beat it to a creamy consistency, added ice and a little condensed milk, stirred, then topped it up with a bit more water. Adding a straw, she handed it to me.

Even without the optional ice cream, it was practically a milkshake. I could feel synapses lighting up all over my brain. This stuff packed a wallop.

"Amazing," I told her. "Seriously, wow. OK, I'm ready for my *freddo*."

"Freddo, you broke my heart," said Rich, doing his best impression of Al Pacino in the famous scene from *Godfather II*. Corny, I know, but somebody had to say it.

No doubt the *freddo* broke a lot of hearts at Nescafé, which had reigned supreme among hipper coffee addicts until the new, classier drink muscled them out of the number one spot. Watching Athanasia make one, I saw it was essentially the same recipe but with brewed espresso in place of the instant coffee. I stood at the bar with both drinks, sipping from one straw and then the other. Both drinks were yummy, frothy, and packed with caffeine and sugar; I could see why they were so popular, especially among the young. But there was really no doubt; Athanasia and Natasa were right, *freddo* was the way to go.

Walking out of Thermaikos with a lovely caffeine buzz, I thought back to the long years during which I'd avoided coffee because I believed it was bad for you. I'd bought into all the myths: that coffee has no nutritive value, will make you a nervous wreck, and is likely to shorten your lifespan. In fact, I was so certain of all this that I decided to write an article on the perils of coffee. And that's when I discovered how utterly mistaken I'd been.

My research, and that of actual qualified scientists, revealed that coffee is full of antioxidants that fight cancer, liver disease, Parkinson's, and lots of other ills. Coffee drinkers bounce back more easily from injuries and infections, are generally more contented and alert, and suffer less from dementia, depression, and suicide. One study showed that sleep-deprived rats felt less stressed simply smelling coffee brewing. Well, don't we all?

Even more excitingly, people who drink four to five cups of coffee a day are likely to live longer — twelve percent longer for men and sixteen percent longer for women. Whenever I read studies like this, I vow to up my intake. Adding sixteen percent to your lifespan, with better physical and mental wellbeing? Now that's the kind of future we'd all like to foresee.

Scientists have plenty to say on the subject of longevity, but their findings are based on statistical analyses of large populations. When Thessalonikians want to know what their personal future holds, they consult a true expert: one of the local soothsayers operating out of the city's coffee houses. Tasseography — the art of interpreting patterns in tea leaves, coffee grounds, or wine sediment — dates back to Medieval times. Luckily for me, practitioners of the ancient art of divination are now listed online; it took less than five minutes for me to locate three within walking distance.

I confess I'm not a believer myself. But my grandmother, the silent film actress Ramona Langley, loved to consult psychics; in fact, my mother's name was chosen by the ghost of my great-aunt during a séance. While I was still trying to decide whether or not I was actually going to consult a local tasseography practitioner, I learned the next phase of my travel plans had been derailed, and I realized I could no longer be picky about where I was going to seek guidance.

According to the online schedule, there was supposed be a train the following Wednesday that would take us the hundred and forty-six miles north to Skopje, capital of North Macedonia. As a veteran of many obscure rail systems, I thought I was prepared for anything — trains

KAREN MCCANN

leaving at 3:30 AM, running once a week, or requiring awkwardly timed changes at obscure junctions that might no longer exist. But who (except possibly a good clairvoyant) could have foreseen the news that awaited me?

"Trains?" said the man at the railway station ticket counter, as if this were a foreign concept. He peered at my handwritten note, which read, in large block letters, "Thessaloniki —> Skopje Wednesday June 12." He shook his head. "No. No trains to Skopje. After June 15, is possible. Now, no."

"Looks like we'll be taking the bus," I said to Rich.

The lady at the nearby bus counter peered at my note and then shook her head. "Tomorrow. Next day. After that no."

"I want to go next week," I said, in case the words "Wednesday, June 12" were somehow open to misinterpretation.

"No. Tomorrow, next day, then is finished. No more buses."

"Ever?" I asked.

She shrugged.

By now I'd worked out that a transit strike was in the offing, leaving me in something of a quandary. Rich and I had agreed we'd complete the entire trip on public transit — trains, buses, ferries, the occasional taxi — without driving a car or taking a plane. What to do?

I returned to the railway counter. "Could we buy tickets now for June 15?" I asked. It would mean three extra days in Thessaloniki — not exactly a hardship.

"No. I have no tickets. Maybe June 15, maybe not." Seeing my puzzled look, he leaned forward and added, with the air of one clinching an argument, "They are Serbian trains."

112

I nodded as if that explained everything, thanked him, and walked away.

There was a time I might have been a trifle perturbed that a transit strike was placing seemingly insurmountable obstacles in my path. But like everyone else in Thessaloniki, I was floating along on such a powerful caffeine high that nothing really bothered me.

As I headed to the station's exit, I noticed a chapel which was, in keeping with my luck that day, closed and locked. However, for those in urgent need of a way to call upon heaven for travel assistance, the station had set up a brass tray full of devotional candles. I dropped in a coin and lit one for luck.

"In the unlikely event that candle doesn't do the trick, what about going to one of those coffee house psychics?" I said to Rich. "Sure, they're a bit sketchy. But what harm could it do? Maybe I'll learn something useful."

So the next morning I went to the café Ωκεανός (Ocean) for a reading with their resident soothsayer. Elena was a dark-haired, slightly heavyset woman, a second-generation psychic who was in such in demand I had to take a number and wait for over an hour while she did readings for the others — all women, I noticed — who'd arrived ahead of me.

Eventually Elena came over to my table, picked up my cup, swirled the cold dregs around, tossed the liquid into a bucket, and upended my cup to drain in the saucer. She went off to do another reading then came back, set the cup upright, and peered into my future.

I peered in, too. All I could see were splotches in a mostly even pattern, like spongeware, with a white area at the very bottom and one large mass of dark grounds on the left rim. A bad omen? A hopeful sign? Who could tell?

Elena studied the grounds and began to talk about a female relative who was giving me trouble. "A dark-haired women, a bit heavy." Five generations of my relatives passed before my mind's eye. Not only did no one match the description, but currently there was, by my family's standards, a remarkable lack of drama brewing. Elena soldiered on, talking about documents and papers and the hope that some money might be coming my way. That sounded promising. Was Elena suggesting the book I planned to write about the trip would become a bestseller? Somehow we never got around to the subject of travel arrangements.

Rich, who has little patience for psychics, had gone for a walk during these proceedings, and when he returned I said, "So much for that. What'll we try next?"

"Travel agencies. Somebody must go to Skopje."

The first travel agency confirmed that a transit strike was planned and no public or tourist buses were running to Skopje in the foreseeable future. As I emerged onto the street, a tiny, toothless old woman in black tried to shove a badly painted icon of the Virgin Mary into my arms. At my repeated refusals to buy it, she hurled a curse at me and stomped away. She and I had been through this same routine days earlier, just before our transit problems began. Hmmm, could there be a connection?

"Do you think I need to buy some of her horrible art to get our karma back on track?" I asked Rich.

He shuddered. "Let's hope not."

I kept checking back with the travel agencies, and eventually I heard that bus service had been extended for some days while negotiations continued. Rich and I raced to the railway station and secured bus tickets to North Macedonia for the following week. Whew! Perhaps the stars were beginning to align.

The next few days were spent strolling around the city, sampling the food, and listening to live music. On one happy occasion we had lunch with Diana, the Australian woman we'd met on the island of Ikaria, who happened to be passing through town. The three of us shared a delicious meal of spiced lamb dumplings known as *manti*, mussels, and *samphire*, a succulent green found in salt-sprayed coastal marshes; it was delicious cooked and served in a salad with feta cheese and tomatoes. We agreed it was nearly as fabulous as the cooking at Popi's on Ikaria.

Another day I found myself standing in front of the former Bank of Athens, a handsome building constructed in 1904 and one of the rare downtown survivors of the Great Fire of 1917, the event that reshaped the city.

It all began one Saturday afternoon when a spark from a kitchen fireplace landed on a wisp of straw and began to smolder. Before anyone realized what was happening, fire filled the room, then leapt to the house next door, and soon engulfed an entire square kilometer of the city center, which blazed away for thirty-two hours.

It was a disaster of Biblical proportions, especially for the city's Jews. For four hundred years they had made up the majority of the city's population — the only major European city where this ever happened — and now they made up the vast majority of the city's homeless. They had also lost the majority of downtown businesses. Eventually half the city's Jewish population would leave Greece as a result of the fire. The bank had become a museum telling their story, and I went inside to find out more.

As you'll recall, many Sephardic Jews were fleeing the Spanish Inquisition at the end of the fifteenth century, and those that found their way to Thessaloniki could hardly believe their luck; the city welcomed them with open arms. The ruling Ottomans were keenly aware of the benefits of having skilled merchants, bankers, craftspeople, and tradespeople in town and gave them the status of *dhimmis*, protected persons. Word soon got around, and more Jews began arriving from Italy and France. By 1519 the Jewish community formed fifty-eight percent of the city's population, earning Thessaloniki the nickname "mother of

Israel."

Fast forward to 1912 when the Greeks won their independence from the Ottomans and the Jews lost their protected *dhimmis* status. Their legal position under the new regime was still being sorted out when the Great Fire of 1917 devastated the community.

The museum had wonderful photos of the glory years showing big, prosperous families, graceful synagogues, charming shops, proud firefighters, thriving wool merchants, and beaming schoolchildren. There were quaint housewares, rare books, stones from the old cemetery, newspaper reports of the destruction of the Great Fire, snapshots of emigrating families, and finally, heartbreakingly, photos of Nazis rounding up the remaining Jews and sending them to Auschwitz.

I was glad I'd gone to the Jewish Museum to learn about this vivid chapter in the city's history, and I was equally glad to get back out into the bright sunlight and head to the nearest café for a restorative coffee. The days were getting hotter, and I was becoming ever more appreciative of the invigorating effect of iced *freddos*.

It was June, and Europe was really beginning to feel the effects of the summer heat that would soon break all historic records. Winds from the Sahara Desert were blowing across the continent, causing triple digit temperatures, scorching the earth, and leaving 321 million people sweaty and grumpy, including me. My adorable little bohemian attic wasn't air conditioned, and tragically, the ceiling fan died a few days into my stay. The manager had scrounged up a small table fan, an incredibly scarce commodity at the time, but all it did was stir the air listlessly around the room.

And the days kept getting hotter. Morning walks started earlier and earlier, when temperatures were slightly cooler, and tended to get shorter and shorter. One day, Rich and I climbed the hill to Ano Poli, the sleepy old upper section that had escaped the Great Fire. After hours of rambling past faded wooden buildings and catching sparkling glimpses of the distant sea, I was only too ready to start heading downhill again.

"I have a place in mind for lunch," Rich said, checking an app on his phone.

"Where?" I demanded suspiciously. I was hot, tired, and determined not to take any detours that would require extra walking or uphill climbs.

"It's right around the corner."

"I love it already."

Arriving at Taverna Giannoula, I observed with pleasure the simple wooden tables with their cheerful red checkered cloths. It was nearly 2:00 pm, still on the early side for lunch by local standards, and we soon learned that everyone in the place was a member of the family: Stavros the owner, his wife Katerina who was chief cook, his brother Nikos who helped out, his mother-in-law, ensconced by the window sipping her soup and keeping a discrete eye on everything, and his two young sons, who were in the back corner playing a computer game with friends that sparked plenty of muffled laughter.

As I sank gratefully into a chair at one of the three sidewalk tables, Rich wandered inside to poke around. Stavros instantly invited him into the kitchen, where Rich peered into pots and eventually chose *kolokithakia gemista*, zucchini stuffed with pork and drizzled with *avoglemono*, the classic Greek egg-lemon sauce. Perusing the menu, I settled on smoky grilled eggplant topped with crumbled feta cheese. The meal was heavenly, and when I felt fully "reanimated" (as the Spanish like to put it), I went inside to pay my compliments to the cooks. I mentioned the Mediterranean Comfort Food Tour, and Stavros and Katerina promptly invited me to come back on Monday to learn how to make proper Greek moussaka.

Arriving for my lesson, I marveled at how much they'd managed to cram into the modest kitchen. It had begun life as a room about ten feet square, but now, fitted out for cooking and storage, the available floorspace was half that. Stavros, whose parents had bought the restaurant when he was three years old, was an old hand at working in its cramped confines, and as the moussaka got underway, he and Katerina wove back and forth across the room, handing off tasks to one another with the practiced ease of circus acrobats. Even having to dodge around me as I peered over their shoulders didn't throw them off their stride.

Stavros spoke English, so it was he who explained each step, but it was clear that Katerina was in charge of the kitchen and that she took great pride and delight in her work. The moussaka recipe was her own creation, and as she pivoted from stovetop to sink to fryer, leaping up on her little stool to check the eggplant sizzling on the high burner, dashing over to layer potatoes in the pan, she soon dispelled my foolish assumption that making moussaka was roughly akin to whipping up a batch of lasagna. This was serious cookery, performed by a serious chef.

"In China, robots are making moussaka," Stavros told me. "They freeze it and send it all over the world. Even some islands in Greece are serving such things. But this—" He nodded toward Katerina, who was now laying slices of fried eggplant tenderly in the pan. "This is made with love."

It was also made with fresh vegetables from the nearby farmer's market and lavish quantities of olive oil, ground beef, potatoes, eggplant, butter, white flour, and whole milk. The moussaka at the Giannoula family restaurant was all-out, no-ingredients-barred, hedonistic indulgence, the kind of old-fashioned comfort food people ate before corporations, calories, and chemicals invaded the kitchen.

One of the hardest things about making moussaka is resisting the urge to cut into it the instant it comes out of the oven, but as Katerina explained with her husband's help, the top layer, a creamy béchamel sauce, needs time to cool and set.

Now, I know what you're thinking: béchamel sauce? That doesn't sound very Greek. That's because it's French, and you can thank Nikolaos Tselementes, the Jamie Oliver of 1920s Greece, for the upgrade.

Tselementes was born on the Aegean island of Sifnos, trained as a chef in Austria, and worked for embassies and top restaurants in Europe and America. His skill was legendary, and he soon became one of the most influential Greek cookbook writers of his own or any other era. He reinvented moussaka — which originally had no topping or maybe just a little custard — by creating a thick, creamy layer of béchamel oozing with continental flair. His moussaka recipe became an instant hit and has inspired chefs around the world for a hundred years.

I spent hours at Taverna Giannoula enjoying the whirlwind pace of the cooking and the easy ebb and flow of family life. Uncle Nikos picked the kids up from school and brought them to the restaurant for lunch. Another uncle stopped by to eat. The butcher on the corner brought Katerina a particularly fine piece of beef, and Rich and I were called into the kitchen to admire it. Katerina's mother observed everything with a twinkle in her eye, and I sat with her for a while, showing her photos and videos I'd taken of her daughter at work. We might not share a language, but we easily pantomimed our common admiration for her daughter's wizardry in the kitchen, heads bent together over my phone's screen.

It made me wonder, not for the first time, what it would have been like to grow up in such close family circumstances. In my childhood, lunchtime meant Dad at the office, Mom feeding the baby with one hand while clutching her own sandwich with the other, and us older kids eating off trays in Catholic school cafeterias. As an adult I'd spent decades working in various offices and studios, and I couldn't imagine trying to navigate my day — every day — under the eyes of three generations of my relatives and in-laws. Would it have made me nuts? Or perhaps added an element of love to the labor? A bit of both?

Life would never be lonely. Whatever the pros and cons of this kind of family business, everyone belonged, found a place for themselves in the work, and never had to eat alone. How many people around the world, especially those struggling with isolation, would give anything to be able to say that about their own lives?

As I took my first, glorious forkful of Katerina's moussaka, rich with vegetables, beef, and warm, creamy béchamel sauce, I thought about Chinese robots shipping their flash-frozen food products around the world. It made me deeply grateful that at least in this little corner of Greece, the old ways were still honored. Food was grown on nearby farms, sold in the shop on the corner, prepared in a kitchen surrounded by family, and served with kindness and ice cold local beer.

It doesn't get better than this, I thought. The world seems to be moving faster and growing crazier all the time now, which makes it extra comforting to know that there is still delicious slow-cooked food on the menu somewhere, if we just take time to look for it.

NORTH MACEDONIA & KOSOVO

10. Skopje, North Macedonia / *Red Pepper Caviar*

Arriving in Skopje, the capital of North Macedonia, it was abundantly clear I'd left behind the cozy hospitality of Greece and was plunging into a far more bracing environment. The advertising was brasher, the walking pace sped up, and the air felt grittier; I later learned it was the most polluted in Europe.

But where this city really jumped up to smack me in the face was the just-completed, ultra-garish downtown makeover. Everywhere I looked were fake baroque buildings, poorly executed pseudo-classical statues, and plenty of ye olde decorative elements covered in gold spray paint. Sculptures of warriors, goddesses, rearing horses, massive lions, torchbearers, heroic mothers with children, and modern men with briefcases jostled for space among the arches, pillars, temples, and fountains.

"Call Las Vegas," I said to Rich. "See if anything is missing."

This eye-popping excess was foisted upon the city by one Nikola Gruevski, then prime minister, now a fugitive from justice hiding out in Hungary — with half the $700 million in public funds allocated for the project, according to just about everyone in the country except Gruevski and his lawyers. No doubt you could have a pretty nice retirement in Hungary with a nest egg of $350 million.

The gussy-up-the-capital project, known as Skopje 2014, was widely viewed as a shameless boondoggle, a blatantly nationalist move designed to promote a largely fictitious historical narrative about Macedonia's glorious past and a megalomaniac's fantasies about its bright future. But the main goal, according to popular opinion, was to create opportunities for politicians to line their own pockets.

It wasn't hard to understand why Gruevski thought he had to do something, however rash and ill-considered, to change the national conversation. For decades Macedonia had been embroiled in bitter fight with Greece about borders and national identity. A couple of thousand years ago the kingdom of Macedon was a superpower, its core kingdom including both the nation currently known as North Macedonia and twice again as much land in what's now northern Greece. When Macedonia declared independence from a crumbling Yugoslavia in 1991, Greece grew alarmed that its northern neighbor might try to re-establish the old borders by taking Greek territory, so it decided to keep Macedonia busy, broke, and off balance by vigorously blocking its entry into the EU and NATO.

The UN caused yet more hard feelings by admitting the newly independent nation under the awkward, temporary moniker "former Yugoslav Republic of Macedonia." The UN's insistence on a lower-case "f" in "former," which was designed to show the provisional nature of the name, drove the world's proofreaders insane and caused mapmakers to throw up their collective hands and label it FYRM, adding yet more confusion and annoyance to the mix.

Meanwhile, to boost self-esteem (and pave the way for any future land-grab plans, just in case), Macedonia continued to proclaim, as loudly as possible, the magnificence of its Macedon heritage. In particular it was trotting out such major historical figures as Phillip of Macedon (the name says it all, folks) and his son, Alexander the Great. You'll remember Alexander as the guy who overthrew the Persian empire in 331 BC and created an empire of his own stretching east from Macedon through Asia Minor, Israel, Mesopotamia, and Babylon to northwest India, and south into Egypt and North Africa. Not bad for a guy who only lived to the age of thirty-two.

Greece hotly protested that Phillip and Alexander were their heroes, dammit, and Macedonia should keep their grubby hands off. Upping the ante, Skopje politicians installed, in the city's central square, a gigantic, eight-million-euro bronze statue of Alexander the Great on horseback, brandishing his sword. Standing 38 feet tall, mounted on a 33-foot pillar, the statue is a can't-miss landmark.

"This is our way of saying [up yours] to them," said Antonio Milososki, North Macedonia's former foreign minister, in case anybody missed the point.

News reports said locals "wept for joy" as they watched the statue go up; I suspect they were weeping for the eight million euros. Greece responded with outrage and demands that the statue be removed. The Macedonians pointed out that the statue was officially named "Equestrian Warrior" and could be anybody, blithely ignoring the fact that everyone on the planet who wasn't Greek called him "Alexander the Great."

The international community, heartily sick of the whole kerfuffle, eventually pressured both sides into a compromise. In 2018, Macedonia/fYRM/FYRM officially changed its name to North Macedonia, symbolically giving up claim to being ancient Macedon 2.0 and leaving every one of its citizens bitter and upset. Greece grudgingly withdrew its objections, allowing the EU and NATO to accept North Macedonia's applications for membership. And despite constant rumors that he's about to be removed at yet more enormous expense to the taxpayers, Alexander — sorry, I mean the Equestrian Warrior — is still brandishing his sword in the center of Skopje.

As for the rest of the cityscape, it suffered a double tragedy: first, losing 80% of its buildings in the catastrophic earthquake of 1968, and second, rebuilding during an era of cookie-cutter blandness, soulless utility, and the kind of shoddy concrete that manages to look shabby five minutes after it's been poured — and then goes downhill from there.

Only two old-fashioned, heavily restored sections remained: the Bohemian quarter, where Rich and I dined in quaint, crowded old restaurants with live folk music, and the Old Bazaar, one of the biggest and most historic markets in the Balkans. When I heard there was a guided food tour in and around the Old Bazaar, I immediately signed us up.

The day of the tour dawned hot and humid, and I was already damp and breathless by the time Rich and I arrived at the ten o'clock rendezvous. Our engaging young guide, Elena, steered us through the market's labyrinthine streets and alleyways, past old wooden storefronts shaded with striped awnings, and into a rustic restaurant, chatting as she went.

"I have a travel blog," she confided. "Since it is impossible for me to travel 365 days a year, I chose a job where the world is coming to me."

We discussed the blogosphere over breakfast, which consisted of *ćevapi*, delicious little meat patties in the shape of sausages, and *flia,* ultra-thin layers of bread and cream stuffed into a sesame-seed bun — a sort of bread sandwich. Topped off with a large, cold glass of yogurt, this was filling fare.

Elena then led the way through the outdoor produce stands and a vast covered market jammed with low-budget clothing stalls. I love these kinds of markets and promised myself I'd return later for a more leisurely exploration. She led the way in and out of courtyards covered with flowering vines, showed off ancient mosques and churches, and stopped at a confectionery where we sampled marvelous little hand-made chocolates.

Pausing in front of a jeweler's display window, Elena pointed out a tray of filigree earrings and pendants featuring the famous Macedonian ruby, a raspberry pink stone found only in a single mine near the town of Prilep forty-six miles away. Various online articles quoted "crystal experts" (qualifications unspecified) asserting the Macedonian ruby has the strongest energy emanations of any stone on the planet and can powerfully affect the heart's energy — a sort of cosmic defibrillator. I made a mental note of the jeweler's location in case this might be needed at any point during my stay.

When Elena suggested stopping for a coffee, I was more than ready. By now we'd been walking for hours, and the temperature had soared into the low nineties. Were hot beverages supposed to cool you off on hot days or not? No matter, I sat down gratefully and took deep gulps of the steaming brew.

"And now," announced Elena, with the air of one producing a special treat, "we visit the Kale Fortress." For a moment I pictured a castle constructed entirely of the curly cabbage known as kale, and realized I might possibly be getting a bit light-headed from the heat and the carbs. I downed the last of my coffee, hauled myself to my feet, and followed her up the long, steep slope.

Passing through the fortress gates, I noticed a small crowd gathered around a woman who had apparently collapsed and was stretched out on some grass in a small patch of shade under a tree. I wondered if anyone had been sent to fetch a Macedonian ruby to revive her.

Trudging on, I learned that "*Kale*" is from the Turkish word for fortress, so the place was called Fortress Fortress, a name sadly lacking in the poetry such a venerable site deserved. People began living there 6000 years ago, during the final years of the Stone Age when farming was just coming into fashion. Parts of the current structure dated back to the sixth century, but you'd never know it. A major reconstruction project had just been completed, leaving the fortress looking crisp and new, which I found disconcerting as well as disappointing.

The battlements offered a splendid view of the city's high-rise apartment buildings, huge shopping malls, and distant hills, hazy with heat and smog. Elena pointed out a large modern sports complex with an undulating shape. "That is Toše Proeski National Arena. He was our most famous singer." I nodded as if he was a household name in my country, too. And maybe he was; I'm about the least musical person on the planet.

Elena explained that over its long history, Fortress Fortress had been destroyed and rebuilt many times, most recently due to the 1968 earthquake. During the latest round of reconstruction, massive numbers of artifacts had turned up, keeping the archeologists happily occupied for years. They'd discovered 5000-year-old musical instruments, a huge stash of Byzantine coins, the ruins of a thirteenth-century church, and many other noteworthy treasures. After taking decades to sort through it all properly, officials finally gave reconstruction a green light at the end of 2006.

Everything was going along swimmingly until the ethnic Albanians (who make up twenty percent of the city and are a bit touchy about their minority status) demanded a halt, claiming the site belonged to them. They insisted that underneath the sixth-century section of the fortress lay older remains, dating back thousands of years to the powerful Illyrians, ancestors of modern-day Albanians.

The Macedonians said this was nonsense, pointing out that everyone could see for themselves that all the objects removed from the site were clearly labeled as being Macedonian in origin — which by the way, just happened to support their claim to the historic Macedon heritage.

The ethnic Albanians said, "Yes, because you labeled them that way, you бесрамни лажговци (shameless liars). You're falsely labeling Illyrian artifacts as Macedonian to suit your own political games." They demanded reconstruction halt immediately so the site could be turned over to its proper owners (themselves).

The government loftily ignored these claims. A hundred ethnic Albanians showed up at the site in the middle of the night, found fifty construction workers laboring there, and the fight was on. There followed several lively days of physical clashes interspersed with heated exchanges of opinions, personal and political, leading to yet more physical clashes. It was a miracle only ten people wound up in the hospital and none were taken to the morgue. As is so often the case, the side with more guns eventually won the day, and Fortress Fortress remained in the hands of the national government.

After our tour of the fortress, Elena led us back down to the Old Bazaar for lunch. Left to my own devices, I'd have cheerfully traded another meal for a large cold drink of any kind, but I felt I owed it to my readers to sample the national dish, *tavče-gravče*, fresh butter beans cooked in a clay pot. The secret was repeatedly soaking and draining the beans to soften them and release indigestible sugars; after that they would be baked slowly in an earthenware pot with chunks of onion and a handful of sweet paprika. The beans were rich and filling; I could see why many North Macedonian households served them every Friday, when lots of Orthodox families still honored the tradition of fasting from meat, as I had done during my Catholic childhood.

Lunch also included my favorite Balkan salad, *shopska*, a mix of cucumbers, tomatoes, onions, peppers, and *sirene,* a white brine cheese much like feta (although I'd learned not to voice this comparison, given the friction with Greece). The star of the show was a dish of *ajvar*, a mix of red peppers and oil that's popular throughout the Balkans. The name comes from the Turkish *havyar*, meaning caviar, as it was invented in the twentieth century as a substitute for real caviar, which had become hopelessly expensive due to the dwindling number of sturgeon. The North Macedonians claim they invented *ajva*, although that's hotly contested by Serbia and Slovenia, and I'm not getting into the middle of that squabble.

Wherever it came from, red pepper caviar is elaborate to make —

peeling all those peppers apparently takes forever — but is still traditionally prepared in just about every home in North Macedonia every autumn. Thrifty housewives are meant to make enough to last until the next year's crop of peppers shows up in the spring, but most homes run out long before that, and I could see why. It was delicious and would be a real treat during the long winter months when fresh vegetables were scarce.

"And for dessert…" Elena said. I managed not to groan. It was way too hot to eat so much, but (again, selflessly thinking of my readers) I gamely followed Elena to a bakery. There she handed around parachute cookies, apparently named for their lighter-than-air texture. I was profoundly glad that this marked the end of the tour. Elena had done a terrific job, but I was feeling the heat and the exertion, to say nothing of the staggering amount of food I'd consumed, so I was more than ready to head back to the apartment.

I said to Rich "Taxi back?"

"You bet."

We ducked into a nearby hotel, and while Rich spoke with the desk clerk about calling a cab, I went into the ladies' room. The sight of my face in the mirror — bright red, puffy, and surrounded by sodden tendrils of hair — made me reel back in alarm. Dear God, I looked positively demented. If this was the US, members of the staff would even now be calling 911 while their co-workers staged a mini intervention, asking tactfully if I had stopped taking my meds and were there any in my purse. I should have bought one of those re-energizing Macedonian rubies when I had the chance.

As I splashed cold water on my face, I realized I was no longer as heat-tolerant as I'd been twenty years earlier, when I thought nothing of spending whole days tramping around Costa Rica's steamy jungles or India's teeming cities. Ah well, I could take it easy for the next several days. And having learned our lesson in Thessaloniki, we'd rented a modern place with excellent air conditioning.

The remaining days in Skopje passed at a slower pace, exploring the streets in the cooler parts of the day and taking long afternoon siestas. Rich discovered a candy shop selling what he assured me was excellent *rahat-lokum*, known as Turkish delight, a sort of rubbery gel dusted with powdered sugar. (As you may have guessed, I'm not a fan.) I was delighted to discover a health food shop selling oatmeal, which I prepared in a frying pan, the only cookware in the Airbnb's poorly stocked kitchen.

One morning we walked around the massive sports stadium Elena had pointed out from Fortress Fortress. I'd looked up the singer Tоše Proeski, whose name now graced the stadium, and learned he was an iconic — make that insanely popular — pop star, known as the Elvis Presley of the Balkans. From the age of fifteen he'd been a tireless performer and self-promoter, raising lots of money for charity along the way. Early one morning in 2007, he was asleep in the passenger seat of a car when the driver smashed into the back of a truck and Proeski was killed instantly. He was twenty-six.

The entire nation went into mourning. It's a testament to the depths of public sentiment that the powers that be were willing to re-re-name the stadium, which just ten years before had started calling itself Phillip II National Arena as part of the whole heritage-claiming effort. The Tоše Proeski National Arena was just another in a long line of honors the singer had received during his short life, including being named a Regional UNICEF Goodwill Ambassador and receiving the Mother Teresa Humanitarian Award for his many benefit concerts.

The humanitarian award was highly prestigious, as was anything bearing Mother Teresa's name. As everyone was quick to tell me, she was born and raised right there in Skopje. And while her family home was gone, the city had built a memorial to her on the site of the old Sacred Heart of Jesus church where she was baptized. I went to see Mother Teresa

Memorial House and found it had been designed in a disconcertingly asymmetrical modernist style that struck me as wildly inappropriate as an homage to the world's famously forthright nun.

I wasn't the only one to feel that way. Architecture professor Divna Pencić called the building "a tactless and tasteless homage to Mother Teresa" and "a depressing example of political meddling." And she didn't stop there. "It is like someone tastelessly dressed, arrayed in gumboots, lace stockings, a brocade skirt and a Chinese silk shirt, all heavily accented with bling and what appears to be a cosmonaut's helmet … If it weren't designed to commemorate such an important figure, this building might have gotten away with its inoffensive zaniness. But, as it turns out, it is hugely offensive. It offends with its skewed selection procedure, with its pretentiousness, with its arrogance, with its tastelessness. But, most of all, it offends by totally ignoring any architectural correlation with the life and work of Mother Teresa."

You won't be surprised to hear this architectural disaster was the brainchild of our old friend, then-prime-minister-now-fugitive-from-justice Nikola Gruevski. He'd spent the equivalent of two million dollars creating this blot on the landscape, which opened with great fanfare in 2009 as a sort of warmup act for the Skopje 2014 project.

Gruevski himself inaugurated the site, announcing it housed some of the saint's relics, which he personally had obtained by special arrangement with the Catholic Church. I felt it was probably best not to enquire too closely into the nature of those special arrangements — or whether Gruevski had taken half the relics (and half the building fund) with him when he'd gone into exile.

Skopje proved consistently entertaining, but as you no doubt have gathered, I didn't exactly fall in love with the city. So when Rich proposed a side trip, I was only too happy to consider a day or two in Kosovo.

11. Pristina, Kosovo / *Yogurt-Baked Lamb*

When Rich first mentioned Kosovo, I thought he was just tossing out fun facts.

"There's a brand-new freeway between Skopje and Kosovo," he said.

I was too busy making notes for my blog to look up from my screen. "Huh? Really? That's cool."

"You can take the bus there in just two hours."

"Oh, yeah?"

"We could do an overnight trip. Let's go tomorrow."

Now he had my full attention. "Kosovo? Tomorrow?"

"Yes, the bus goes right to the capital, Pristina."

I considered the idea for a moment.

He added persuasively, "It's a whole new country that we've never visited."

Well, if he put it like that ... "OK, I'm in."

"We can be there by lunchtime tomorrow. And let's go luggage-free. Just take our toothbrushes and passports."

If this suggestion sounds bizarre to you, you're not alone. Twenty-five years ago, when Rich first brought up the idea of skipping-the-suitcase travel, I could hardly believe my ears.

"Why in God's name would we EVER want to travel without luggage?" I'd asked incredulously. Up until that moment I'd always considered him reasonably sane.

"Freedom," Rich said. "Mobility." And now he began to get a little starry-eyed. "Imagine getting on a plane or train carrying nothing but a toothbrush and a passport!"

"That toothbrush isn't going to do you much good without toothpaste," I pointed out. "And what about sunscreen? A change of underwear? Something to read on the plane?" From every standpoint, the whole idea was ludicrous. And I said so, every time it came up, for the next couple of decades.

But then, a few years ago, a friend sent me an article about a woman named Clara Bensen who spent three weeks on the road without a suitcase. "She did take a purse to hold electronics and toiletries," I told Rich as I skimmed the article. That didn't sound nearly as harebrained as the nothing-but-a-toothbrush scenario. And then, before my rational mind could stop me, I found myself blurting out, "OK. I'll do it. But only for a weekend!"

Rich was overjoyed. He instantly began nailing down details before I could change my mind. "Where shall we go?"

I wanted someplace fun to write about, and my research turned up the tiny French village of Rennes-le-Chateau, a place that contained enough mysteries and secrets to give the Bermuda Triangle a run for its money. The village had everything: buried treasure, occult conspiracies, secret codes embedded in ancient parchments, weirdly demonic church art, mysterious tombs, a dodgy priest, the dodgy priest's dodgy "housekeeper," Knights Templar, and the last of the Merovingian dynasty — that's right, the French royals some claim were descended from Jesus

Christ and Mary Magdalene. Starting to sound familiar? Yep, Rennes-le-Chateau is where Dan Brown got his ideas for *The DaVinci Code*.

Now, I know some of my more sensitive and civilized readers will be wondering how I managed about hygiene on a luggage-free journey lasting several days. In fact, whenever I write about this kind of travel, I get lots of emails and social media comments containing surprisingly personal questions about how often I shower on these trips (daily) and about the depths of sordid squalor to which I degenerate (not nearly as low as everyone apparently thinks). I wear fast-drying shirts and undergarments which I launder every night in the bathroom sink; if they're still a trifle damp in the morning, the hotel's hair drier soon makes them fully roadworthy for another day.

I can assure you it's possible to maintain decent hygiene standards without luggage just about anywhere. Including, of course, Kosovo. The next morning I threw my nightdress, sunscreen, toothbrush, and a few other odds and ends into my purse and was ready to go.

And I had to admit, Rich was right; the chance to visit Kosovo wasn't something to pass up. It's a tiny country, about half the size of New Jersey, with a hugely complicated and blood-stained history, even by Balkan standards. The more I learned about it the less I understood, and I soon realized that trying to come to grips with even the bare essentials of its backstory was akin to attempting to summarize the plot of *Game of Thrones* in ten words or less.

I'll fill you in on the little I know. Kosovo sits right in the center of the Balkans, sharing borders with Serbia, Montenegro, Albania, and North Macedonia. Naturally it's been conquered, occupied, annexed, or "assisted" by every major player in the region, including the Roman, Byzantine, Bulgarian, Serbian, and Ottoman Empires and the communists.

Kosovo's closest friend? Albania, which shares the same language, religion, food, folklore, and general culture; nowadays the two refer to themselves as "one nation, two states." Left to their own devices, the majority of ethnic Albanians in both nations would like to erase the border they share and become one country.

Kosovo's worst nightmare? Serbia, which grabbed Kosovo for a few centuries in medieval times and has occupied it off and on since. When Yugoslavia broke up in the late 1990s, Serbia made a grab for Kosovo, justifying the move on the principle that, to put it in prison movie lingo, Kosovo's role in life was to be Serbia's bitch, and everyone should just accept that and move on.

But the Kosovars had other ideas. They loudly declared their independence, rallied the Kosovo Liberation Army, and began shouting their war cry "*Bac u kry*," which means "Uncle, it's over." Apparently the sentiment is more rousing in the original Albanian.

The Kosovo War was a shockingly nasty and brutal conflict. Serbian president Slobodan Milošević, a big fan of ethnic cleansing, directed his troops to chase Kosovo's ethnic-Albanian families out of their homes, their cities, and their country while engaging in as much looting, pillage, and rape as they could squeeze into their work schedules. At the height of the war, terrified Kosovars were fleeing over the border into Albania at the rate of 4000 an hour. Not surprisingly, the Kosovo Liberation Army didn't hold back when it came to reprisals. It was a horror show all around.

NATO bombings halted the conflict in 1999, and the UN stepped in. Kosovo was now a partially recognized state that remained embroiled in territorial disputes, but at least the ethnic cleansing, shooting, looting, and raping had stopped.

What would Kosovo be like now, twenty years after the ceasefire? Only one way to find out for sure.

Rich and I abandoned our suitcases to the tender mercies of the Skopje bus station's left-luggage department and headed off to the departure bays. And here was my first surprise. When they said there was a bus to Pristina, somehow — call me crazy — I expected an actual bus. But apparently the Skopje-Kosovo run isn't in high demand (hard to believe, I know) so we'd be riding in a crowded van, with the passenger door left open to allow slightly fresher air into the steamy interior, and Albanian pop music blasting from tinny speakers.

It was a wonderful ride. The van threaded its way sedately through Skopje's teaming ethnic-Albanian street market, picked up speed on a flat stretch of green countryside, and slowed to a crawl over winding mountain roads. The two border crossings (leaving North Macedonia and entering Kosovo) were surprisingly efficient, and then we were tooling along past cultivated fields and villages with red tiled roofs until we finally arrived at the capital city, Pristina.

Even those who love it best will admit that Pristina is not a city with storybook charm. Most of the buildings are modern, thanks to Yugoslavia's post-WWII philosophy "destroy the old, build the new" and of course, all the war damage. Much of the city had been rebuilt, mostly with forgettable but functional modern structures, and people were busy getting on with their lives.

The Kosovars faced huge challenges, including how to grow the economy and deal with fairly desperate water shortages, but they were making headway. Although the citizens were ninety-five percent Muslim, Kosovo was a secular state with a constitution that guaranteed freedom of belief, conscience, religion, and atheism; that year they were ranked as having the highest religious tolerance in Southern Europe .

Another thing Kosovo had going for it was outstanding food. Travel blogger Jackie Nourse wrote, "Looking back at my nine-month trip around the world, I can honestly say that besides Italy (obviously), Kosovo cuisine was my favorite." Why is this little corner of the world so blessed? As one cab driver explained it to me, "This is where the Mediterranean meets the Orient." It's a match made in foodie heaven.

I could hardly wait to try the local fare, and luckily the van got in right around lunchtime. After checking into our hotel, Rich and I walked to an old-school restaurant called Liburnia that specialized in traditional Albanian dishes. Once an old Turkish-style home, Liburnia had a cozy, romantic interior with dim lighting, dark wood, and gorgeously patterned cushions. Rich and I settled in the leafy garden courtyard, where overhead vines created dappled shade, and ordered Kosovo's version of the Albanian classic *tavë kosi*, baked lamb in yogurt sauce.

You probably won't be surprised to hear that in true Balkan style, *tavë kosi* was born in the midst of a war. It happened back in 1452, when Ottoman Sultan Mehmet II was laying siege to Kruja, Albania, the current hideout of the rebel leader Skanderbeg. Naturally, a sultan can't lower his culinary standards just because he's at war, and on this occasion his servants prepared a lovely dish of marinated lamb in oregano-spiced yogurt. After serving the dish to their master, they thriftily reused the yogurt and leftover lamb, plus a handful of rice, to create this casserole, which has been a regional favorite ever since.

And if, like me, you have a soft spot for rebels, you'll be glad to hear Skanderbeg got away and continued his twenty-five year resistance campaign, which slowed the Ottoman Empire's advance into Europe; to this day he's honored as a hero.

As I waited for my *tavë kosi* to arrive, I idly watched a waiter bring over a step ladder, climb up, and pour water into one of the irrigation tubes running through the vines overhead. Moments later water began drizzling down all over our table. I waited for someone to rush over, apologize, and move us to a drier spot, but apparently this was standard procedure. Possibly it was the restaurant's clever method for cooling down customers on a hot day.

Eventually the drizzle stopped, and wine and salad were placed on the soggy tablecloth. Not long after that the waiter returned triumphantly bearing a large earthenware dish containing sizzling yogurt sauce over

136

chunks of lamb on a bed of rice. The lamb was so tender it fell apart under my fork and melted in my mouth. I took my time, savoring every bite. When I'd spooned up the last, heavenly mouthful, the waiter removed the plates and reappeared with complimentary glasses of *rakia* (fruit brandy), which he placed tenderly before us.

"For the digestion," he murmured.

"Oh, well, if it's medicinal..." said Rich, reaching for the little glass.

Rakia is not only good for the digestion, it keeps you cheerful on the walk back to your lodgings and encourages a long, deep siesta. By the time I woke from mine, it was growing dark. Venturing out into the streets again, I discovered the area was filled with shops and restaurants, mostly modern, none with anything like the romantic charm of Liburnia. Rich and I strolled around a while then chose a place, ate a light meal, and called it a day.

As I dressed the next morning in my freshly washed blouse, the bright sunlight streaming in through the hotel window made the pale green gauze fabric look nearly translucent. When I remarked on this, Rich glanced over and said, "Nonsense. It's fine."

Setting out in search of breakfast, or at least coffee, we couldn't find a single café in the vicinity of our hotel. Eventually Rich stepped into a chocolate shop to ask for advice. The two young women who worked there, giggling hysterically over the need to summon their scant English, walked outside, pointed down the street, and gestured to the right. "*Furra Labi,*" they kept repeating. That could have meant anything: *turn right, get lost,* or possibly *furry laboratory.* I thanked them (sparking more giggles), and Rich and I walked to the corner and turned right .

And there it was, a narrow storefront with a huge sign reading *Furra Labi* (which I later learned meant Labi's Oven). Underneath that it said, *"Pizzeri."*

"A pizza parlor?" I said. "For breakfast?"

"Hey, it's food." Rich ducked under the low overhang to peer into the window.

Big silver trays held a promising collection of fluffy pastries. Moments later we were inside, inhaling the heavenly scent of baking. Standing behind the counter were Leonard, a slender goateed youth whose family owned the pizzeria, and his even younger assistant, Hana, who'd worked there for just one week but seemed to know her stuff. Hana spoke excellent English and was delighted to help by recommending *byrek* and *flia.*

These were great, classic choices. *Byrek* is a flaky pastry stuffed with fillings such as spinach and cheese, much like the Greek *spanakopita* (although obviously I wasn't tactless enough to mention the resemblance to Leonard or Hana). *Flia,* which I'd had for breakfast during the Skopje food tour, consisted of very thin layers of pastry interspersed with equally thin layers of yogurt and cream.

The Ottomans, who knew a good thing when they tasted it, introduced these flaky pastries throughout their empire. Each region tweaked the recipe and the spelling of the name. Here in Pristina they used the Albanian *byrek;* the Turks called it *börek,* and it became *burek* in the former Yugoslavia, *buurek* in Bulgaria, *brik* in Tunisia, and *burekas* in Israel. As for *flia,* it eventually became known around the world as phyllo dough.

Having ordered *byrek* and *flia,* I took a chance and asked if they happened to serve coffee. I wasn't surprised when I got blank looks. In the Balkans, coffee is almost never taken with meals; it's a stand-alone drink served in dedicated coffee houses, and only a barbarian — or a loony American — would consider combining coffee with food. Luckily the deeply engrained tradition of hospitality carried the moment.

"No problem," said Leonard. "I will go get you coffee.

Macchiato?"

"Of course," I replied, having just read this is what everyone in Kosovo drinks

The pastries were delicious, warm, flaky, and gorgeous on the tongue. Leonard returned bearing two paper cups of coffee with a splash of milk, and after a single sip I had a pretty good idea why Kosovo's macchiato is considered a hot contender for best on the planet. I had it several more times, and it never disappointed. I left Leonard and Hana with a flurry of thanks for their kindness, and they invited me back to try more delicious pastries whenever I was in town.

Next on the agenda was wandering the streets of Pristina. The larger boulevards were lined with low-budget modern chain stores, but the alleys and side streets held tiny storefronts where people worked at such old-fashioned tasks as sewing clothes, mending shoes, even — and when was the last time you saw this? — repairing vacuum cleaners and other appliances. There were supermarkets, but I also saw plenty of people buying their groceries at little fruit stands and in the marvelously labyrinthine farmers' market, where next to the egg stalls I watched a small gaggle of hens pecking in the dirt and sitting on nests, producing more inventory.

I was curious to see the newly consecrated Cathedral of Saint Mother Teresa. Its giant bell tower was one of the tallest buildings in the city, and in fact, the entire cathedral was absurdly large for a country where less than one percent of the population was Roman Catholic. But this wasn't so much a house of worship as a monument to one of the few ethnic Albanians whose name is a household word everywhere. She may have been born in Skopje, but all ethnic Albanians, including those in Pristina, claimed her as their own.

The vast, ice-white cathedral contained a modest statue of the nun and a stained glass window with her image, but all the other art venerated steely-eyed patriarchal male saints. Equally stern-looking eagles glared from the end of each carved pew, a reminder that Albania considers its true name to be *Shqipëri* (Land of Eagles). The cathedral's designers might have been commissioned to build a landmark honoring a woman, but they made it clear this was still very much a man's world.

How macho is the culture? The city seemed very modern in its attitudes, but I've heard in some remote Albanian villages, it's still traditional for the father of the bride to present his new son-in-law with the gift of a single bullet, representing his permission to shoot his daughter if she fails him as a wife. This made me wonder what the mothers of those young women gave their daughters on eve of their wedding; a well-honed shiv, maybe, passed down through the generations? Whatever it was, they wisely refrained from posting anything about it on social media, so I'll probably never know.

A few minutes after leaving the cathedral, I caught my first glimpse of the city's most unnerving building, the Kosovo National Library. Built in the early 1980s by a Croatian architect who had obviously watched way too much dystopian sci-fi, it was grimly colossal, with ninety-nine geometric domes and an exterior wrapped tight in what appeared to be a giant metal fishnet. In a movie, you'd know instantly this was the place where you'd be taken so robots could wipe your brain, evildoers could perform unspeakable scientific experiments, or the authorities that caught you spitting on the sidewalk could sentence you to twenty years hard labor in the asteroid belt. Clearly nobody would ever dare to return a book past its due date to that library.

The interior was classic outdated modern, the materials and styling being the architectural equivalent of the early eighties' velour tracksuits, crop tops, and *Dallas*-style big hair. I was surprised to see a room labeled "American Corner" and displaying a large US flag and a picture of Lady Liberty. I struck up a conversation with one of the young people sitting inside reading books (a welcome sight in these digital times), and she explained the American Corner was part of a long-standing education and outreach program of the US Embassy.

This wasn't the first American presence I'd seen in Pristina. There was a replica of the Statue of Liberty presiding over the freeway, the stars and stripes were flying (well, drooping) in my hotel's lobby, and US flags had been offered for sale at the farmers' market. But the biggest red-white-and-blue lovefest was reserved for the monument to Bill Clinton.

Why?

"If it wasn't for Bill Clinton," a Kosovar shop owner told me, "we would still be fighting the war."

As you may remember, Bill Clinton was president in 1999, when the Kosovo War was entering its second nightmarish year, and he pushed hard to get the US and NATO involved in order to put a stop to the conflict. Over the next three months, NATO aircraft flew 38,000 combat missions attacking the Federal Republic of Yugoslavia (aka Serbia and Montenegro). The bombing forced everyone to the negotiating table, where Milošević — no doubt with gritted teeth and steam coming out of his ears —signed the international peace plan.

I'd missed Bill Clinton by just a week; he'd been in town to mark the 20th anniversary of the conflict's end. At a speech in Skanderbeg Square (named for the fifteenth-century Albanian resistance leader who fought off the Ottoman Empire), Kosovar President Hashim Thaci called Clinton a "hero of Kosovo" and presented him with the Freedom Order award.

No doubt Bill Clinton — a man who adores being adored— was in his glory that day, surrounded by cheering fans, riding down the *Bulevardi Bill Klinton*, and revisiting the larger-than-life-sized statue of himself that he had personally unveiled when it went up in 2009. Nearby a huge billboard praising Hillary Clinton stood next a women's clothing store called Hillary, its display window showing a row of mannequins in pants suits.

I was taking a picture of Hillary (the shop, not the former Secretary of State) when Rich suddenly blurted out, "Karen, I know I said it was fine but it's not." I stared at him blankly. "Your blouse. I can see right through it. And so can everyone else."

Yikes! Apparently the repeated washings had proved too much for the delicate gauze, which was disintegrating before my eyes — and the eyes of everyone in the city, to say nothing of President Clinton on his pedestal across the street.

And now I became keenly aware of the one glaring disadvantage of luggage-free travel. Ordinarily I'd just return to the hotel and grab something else from my suitcase, but instead, I began a frantic shopping effort that even now I shudder to recall.

Having seen hundreds of attractive summer shirts in shop windows all through Greece and North Macedonia, those now confronting me were, without exception, hideously unacceptable. Later, I discovered that the average age of Kosovars is 29.5, the youngest in Europe, and it was clear the shops were catering to a very different demographic. I rejected bare-midriff tank tops, t-shirts sporting large "Hello, Kitty" logos, skinny camouflage-patterned gear, and other unsuitable options. After visiting three or four hopelessly discouraging shops, I finally purchased the ugliest turquoise t-shirt ever manufactured. But as Rich pointed out, at least I no longer risked creating an international incident by getting myself arrested for indecent exposure.

Aside from the wardrobe malfunction, I'd thoroughly enjoyed my time in Pristina. Heading back to the bus station for the return journey to Skopje, I felt a pang of regret that the time had come to leave. I'd found Kosovo hospitable, entertaining, affordable, and delightfully free of tourists. It didn't have the gorgeous monuments I'd visited in Greece, or the overwrought glitz of its neighbor Skopje, but Pristina was a city brimming with energy, fueled on marvelous food and endless cups of macchiato. With or without luggage, I hoped to visit Kosovo again. Only this time, I promised myself, I'd be wearing a shirt that could go the distance.

12. Dihovo Village, North Macedonia / *Beehive Therapy*

"No taxis?" I exclaimed incredulously. "How can there be no taxis — at a railway station — in the second largest city in the country?"

We'd taken a train out of Skopje that morning, heading to a rural guesthouse outside of Bitola, a city in southwest North Macedonia not far from the borders of Greece and Albania. Online, it was constantly referred to as the "transportation hub of the region." Where was all this alleged transportation?.

"To be fair," Rich pointed out, "there is a taxi. There's just nobody in it."

I gazed hard at the empty yellow cab at the curb, willing a driver to materialize. Because that always works. Then I looked back at the silent railway station, helpfully marked "Bitola," confirming that this was, in fact, Bitola. I glanced at the handful of men quietly sipping Turkish coffee at the station café, eyeing us discreetly but with interest and no small amount of amusement. I gazed at the taxi again.

As usual in such situations, I felt decisive action was called for. So I departed in search of the ladies' room. I eventually located it at the far end of the station, and by the time I returned, Rich was standing beside our bags with a stranger and a bemused expression.

"This guy will drive us out there," he said.

"Is he a taxi driver?"

"I don't know. He was walking by, and I thought he might belong to the yellow cab, so I said, 'Taxi?' And he said, 'OK.' Apparently he has a car and is willing to provide transport. He seems like a nice guy."

"Famous last words."

The stranger, a robust middle-aged man with massive shoulders, smiled pleasantly, grabbed my suitcase, and took off in the direction of a battered blue sedan. He wrestled with the latch on the car's trunk, muttered what I assumed were a few choice Macedonian curse words, gave up, and tossed my bag into the back seat. He then grabbed Rich's bag and tossed that in after mine. I climbed in after them, saying a quick prayer to St. Christopher, patron saint of travelers who are about to do foolish things. Yes, I knew St. Christopher had been thoroughly debunked by the Church, but after a lifetime of appealing to him in tight spots on the road, I wasn't about to stop now.

The stranger's car sped past an enormous park (called, with more accuracy than originality, City Park), threaded its way through some lesser urban streets, and headed into the open countryside.

Afterwards, when I described this car ride on my blog, a long-time reader wrote in to say she was appalled that we'd taken such a chance and that we should stick to "real" and "reputable" taxi services. And she had a point, so I'll advise everyone reading this to play it safe and hire the most reliable transport available. In other words — kids, don't try this at home … or abroad.

However in my defense I should point out that the two most terrifying rides I've ever taken were under the auspices of mainstream cab companies. One was in Madrid, where the driver was apparently on drugs, weaving erratically and spitting constantly into something (I tried not to think what) on the seat beside him. I had the impression his eyes were actually spinning in their sockets like pinwheels.

The other horror ride was in San Francisco, where we happened to pass Bill Clinton (in town for a conference) and his security detail walking near Fisherman's Wharf. Our cabby began shouting such furious invective I was sure we would all be hauled off to Guantanamo Bay without further ado. The timing was particularly awkward as five minutes earlier Rich had mistaken one of the President's Secret Service vehicles for the Uber he was trying to summon, and the steely eyed agent in the driver's seat was not amused by the mix-up. We'd fled that embarrassing scene by leaping into a passing cab, only to run across Mr. Clinton a few blocks later, triggering our cabby's wrathful rant. Luckily, this was San Francisco, where screwball behavior is the norm, and we managed not to get arrested. Or shot.

Meanwhile, back in North Macedonia, our randomly hired, unauthorized non-taxi drove sedately along increasingly narrow lanes and rolled to a smooth stop in front Vila Dihovo's front gate. You see why I still invoke St. Christopher in these situations.

I couldn't know it then, of course, but our non-cabby was only the first of many Bitola residents who would reach out to us with kindness in the days to come. In this case, there was a small fee at stake, but mostly, people just seemed to want to connect for a few minutes, welcome us to their town, maybe practice their English or perform some small service, and wander away again. It was my kind of low-key, open-ended friendliness.

Vila Dihovo's host, Petar, came hurrying out to greet us. He was a tall, robust man, a professional footballer turned farmer with the perpetually preoccupied air common to innkeepers. He gave our driver a friendly wave, hoisted our suitcases, and took off through the wide front gate. I followed him up a stone path through lush grass dotted with shrubs, flowerbeds, and a scattering of tables and chairs. A big, white, shaggy dog raised his head but evidently decided (much like Bill Clinton's security detail had done) that we were harmless; he laid his muzzle back down on the grass and closed his eyes.

Petar's place had acquired mild fame for its quirky pricing structure — you paid whatever you thought was right for lodging and food — and for being part of North Macedonia's burgeoning slow food, farm-to-fork movement. I was a bit skeptical, as I'd learned those terms could refer to anything from a few fresh herbs in the salad to snail-like service with no discernable difference in the quality or sophistication of the fare. Still, there was a vegetable patch at the far end of the lawn, homemade beer and wine were mentioned, and there was plenty of fresh air and sunshine, so I was prepared to give the whole enterprise the benefit of the doubt.

I followed Petar into a stone building and up a set of wooden stairs that were, frankly, terrifying. The steps were festooned with a colorful striped runner that had long since come loose from its moorings and was now a tumble of rucked-up fabric and scattered iron rods. I picked my way carefully along the bare wooden edges, wondering how many guests per week broke a leg on these stairs and hoping I wouldn't be one of them.

On the upper landing, Petar flung open a door and gestured for me to precede him into the room. The modest chamber was entirely filled with three massive, rough-hewn wooden beds.

"Are we sharing the room with another family?" I whispered to Rich.

A modern shower stall, unable to squeeze into the minuscule bathroom, had inserted itself into the corner beside the largest bed, which was festively attired in purple and gold checked seersucker with a yellow cotton canopy drooping so low it nearly brushed the bedspread. When Petar had gone, I pulled gently on the canopy to adjust it, sending clouds of dust billowing into the air.

Tossing my suitcase onto one of the extra beds (there being no spare floorspace whatsoever), I made myself at home — that is, I put my Kindle and reading glasses on the miniature bedside table and managed to find a nail in the bathroom sturdy enough to hold my toiletry kit.

Rich settled in by choosing a spot on which to set our travel photos. These are a pair of silly pictures taken at our wedding, one snapshot of each of us sporting cheerful, unguarded, slightly goofy expressions. After more than three decades of accompanying us everywhere, these photos were still in their original cloth-covered folding frame, which by now has become lightly stained, thoroughly shabby, and liberally festooned with small talismans picked up around the world. The simple act of setting out this grubby but beloved object always defined any place as home.

These modest domestic tasks completed, Rich and I went downstairs just in time to join the other guests for dinner. Meals, I soon learned, were one of the true perks of the place. What they lacked in gourmet flourishes they made up for with ample portions bristling with fresh vegetables, served on a porch overlooking the lawn and the garden where the produce was grown.

Every morning and evening I would find myself sitting with eight or ten well-traveled fellow guests — British, Dutch, German, and American — all content to linger at the table holding long conversations about travel, food, the new puppies they'd seen near Petar's front gate, and the rival merits of various local trails.

Everyone else, it seemed, was there for serious hiking. Vila Dihovo was nestled in the foothills of Baba Mountain in scenic Pelister National Park, sixty-six square miles of pine woods and rugged mountain tops, inhabited by bear, deer, wolves, wild boars, eagles, trout, and trekkers. I heard talk of a distant waterfall, the stunning view from the top of Mount Pelister, and a couple of glacier lakes. The German couple announced they would leave at six in the morning in order to get in a decent day's exercise.

"To leave later, there is no point," one said austerely.

The rest of us politely suppressed our shudders and showed up for breakfast the next morning at a more civilized hour. I love eating in community like this, with the easy ebb and flow of conversation all around me. People who found their way to a spot this remote were usually seasoned travelers with interesting perspectives on the world and a knack for researching destinations. Often they alerted me to aspects of the culture and beauty around me that I might otherwise miss, and I appreciated being clued in.

After breakfast, as the others pulled on their hiking boots and clomped off to their cars so they could drive deeper into the wilderness, Rich and I set off on foot to explore the village. The white dog, whose collar read "Leon," got up and shambled after us as we passed through the gate. An enormous, shaggy gray hound appeared, seemingly from nowhere, and fell into step with our little group. Then a skittish little black-and-white dog sidled up and began dancing around us on tiptoe. It was quite an entourage.

The black-and-white dog was clearly female, and judging by the state of her undercarriage, the mother of the puppies everyone was talking about. She was eager to please, tightly wound, and foolish beyond belief. I have never seen an animal sidestep the grim reaper so narrowly and often on a simple country walk. Maybe she was suffering from post-partum depression, or simply deaf and daft, but despite the scarcity of traffic, she nearly lost her life under car wheels on several exciting occasions, even with my shouted warnings and efforts to snatch her bodily out of harm's way.

Our rag-tag little gang meandered through Dihovo Village's winding country lanes, charmingly lined with stone and wood houses set in gardens just coming into the full bloom of late June. The landscape wasn't marred by a single commercial establishment, unless you counted the beekeeper, whom we'd arranged to visit later that day with Petar. After a while, the peaceful setting began to seem a little too quiet. Used to the hubbub of vibrant cities, I felt strange walking for over an hour without catching sight of another human besides the few drivers speeding past. I was glad Rich and I had the dogs for company.

After a late lunch and long siesta, Rich and I joined Petar and a couple of other guests for the visit to the beekeeper. Somehow I'd expected a gnarled, grizzled fellow like something out of an old woodcut in a vintage edition of Grimm's fairy tales, but Naco turned out to be a pleasant young man of about thirty. He spoke not a word of English, so Petar served as translator, explaining how to put on the wide-brimmed, veiled hats and zip them into the collars of special protective shirts in cheery yellow, white, and pink. The fabric's smooth finish and light colors were designed to reassure the hives' inhabitants; apparently if you show up in dark, shaggy clothing they grow alarmed thinking you're a bear seeking a snack of honey with a side of protein-rich bees.

Naco pumped smoke into one of the hives to make the bees drowsy and pulled out a honeycombed frame to point out the queen amid the busy workers. As he chatted about life in the hive, worker bees kept climbing up the frame and over his bare hands.

"How often do you get stung?" I asked.

"About ten times a day," Naco said. He poked at one of the bees, which promptly stung him. He laughed at my expression. "During the busy season, forty times a day."

If was true what they said about bee venom's anti-inflammatory properties, Naco would never have to worry about rheumatoid arthritis. And apparently his bees had even more medicinal benefits to offer. After we'd sufficiently admired the boxy wooden hives, Naco led us into the inhaling hut, a simple wooden building fitted out with large windows, long benches, and several tubes attached to inhaler masks.

"You breathe the air of the hive," Petar explained. "It is very good for the lungs, for the health."

Beehive air breathing is common throughout Europe as a remedy for allergies, asthma, bronchitis, weakened immune systems, and depression. It has failed to catch on in the USA, even as alternative medicine. In fact, it's so far out in left field that afterwards, I couldn't even find an article debunking the practice, let alone supporting it.

"How long do sessions last?" I asked Naco.

"About twenty minutes."

I breathed some beehive air for a few minutes but didn't sense any change in my physical or mental wellbeing. On the other hand, sitting in the wooden hut, gazing out the window at the hives as worker bees droned about their business in the sun, was pretty therapeutic in itself.

But of course, the real highlight of the tour was tasting the honey. Like so many Americans, I grew up squeezing honey out of plastic bears and buying jars of whatever was on sale at the supermarket. A few years ago, I was appalled to learn that what I'd been drizzling on my English muffins was a Chinese knock-off. Such honey as it contained was low-quality and diluted with cheaper sweeteners such as genetically modified high-fructose corn syrup; the mixture was then over-processed to the point of eliminating all the vitamins, amino acids, antioxidants, and cholesterol-reducing properties that make real honey so healthy. As if that wasn't bad enough, these fake sweeteners were often laced with antibiotics, lead, and other stuff it's best not to dwell on.

When all this was revealed some years ago, the US banned the import of Chinese honey. Enterprising entrepreneurs got around that pesky little technicality by sending boatloads of adulterated honey from China to neighboring countries for repackaging and shipping to the US under false labels — a process known as "honey laundering."

The FDA issued non-binding regulations about the labeling of honey and honey products, which proved about a useless as you might imagine. "Laundered" honey continues to show up on supermarket shelves, in those individual packets you get at chain restaurants, and as ingredients in processed food. Now that I know this, I'm a lot more careful to check labels and try to buy pure, local stuff whenever possible.

Now, as Nico handed me a spoon, I had the rare pleasure of scraping honey right out of the honeycomb into my mouth. I carefully avoided the stray bees that wandered, dazed and confused, over the wreckage of their former workplace. The flavor was luscious. Alas, as a minimalist packer, I could only justify buying one small jar, and even then, as I walked back to the guest house, I wondered if I'd have to jettison something to fit it in my suitcase. (I didn't, but it wasn't easy getting the zipper closed.)

Before dinner, Petar suggested a trip down into his cellar, which turned out to be lined with more than a thousand of bottles of homemade wine and beer. How he found time to add winemaking and beer brewing to all his other chores was a mystery to me. At the moment he was extra busy, he explained, making preparations to leave the next morning on long-overdue vacation with his wife and young child. The border of Greece was just a dozen miles away and they planned to take off at dawn.

"By eleven-thirty, I expect to be lying on a Greek beach," Petar said, his face alight with anticipation.

Rich and I were also departing the next morning. I'd enjoyed the brief country sojourn, with its farm-fresh food, hive-fresh honey, and the companionship of humans and dogs. But now I felt ready to embrace the more cosmopolitan pleasures of North Macedonia's second largest city, Bitloa.

13. Bitola, North Macedonia / *Zelnik & Turli Tava*

It may have been the second largest city in North Macedonia, but I soon discovered that Bitola, blessed with a population 75,000 souls, had a pleasantly small town feel. Everything centered around a single broad pedestrian street called Širok Sokak (meaning "Wide Alley"), which was lined with a shops, coffee houses, and a dozen restaurants, nearly all of which sported large, excitedly lettered signs saying "Pizza!"

I suspect the thrilling news about all the available pizza was a way of demonstrating just how modern the metropolis had become. For generations the city's most iconic fare had been *chkembe corba* (tripe stew), earning residents of Bitola the nickname *chkembari*. The stew was so popular people ate it all day, starting with the midmorning snack and moving right though all the other meals. This was appalling news for me. Dedicated as I was to sampling all sorts of outlandish local fare so I could tell my readers about it, I knew I wouldn't be able to force down a bowl of *chkembe corba*.

On the other hand, I sincerely hoped I wouldn't be reduced to a diet consisting entirely of pizza. Strolling along Širok Sokak for the first time, I spotted an old-fashioned eatery with a handful of wooden tables jammed tightly together in the shade of a low awning. Nobody was eating pizza nor — as far as I could tell — *chkembe corba*.

"I think we've found our lunch place," I said to Rich.

Wriggling into a chair wedged between the wall and a table full of chattering men, I picked up the menu and was relieved to discover it had English translations. "Kebabs, burgers, *loveka* — that's minced meat with yellow cheese," I read aloud. "*Ustipec*, minced meat with cheese and garlic. Also there's *raznic*, chicken on a stick. Ribs, homemade sausage. I think we can eliminate the liver …"

A comfortably middle-aged man at the next table leaned over and said, in heavily accented English, "Try the *ustipec*. It is good."

His friendly advice settled that decision and led to a few minutes' conversation. It turned out our new friend had lived in the US for a while and was happy for the opportunity to exercise his English skills and help a couple of clueless visitors come to grips with the local fare. That done, he cheerfully returned to the conversation with his mates. I was beginning to warm to the easygoing *chkembari* social style.

The *ustipec* was delicious, as was the other dish I ordered, *sopska*, the region's favorite salad made from tomatoes, cucumbers, and parsley topped with shredded *belo sirenje*, a white cheese that was North Macedonia's answer to feta. A green pepper had been placed on one side of my plate. I eyed it with suspicion.

"What do you recon?" I said to Rich. "Is it killer hot or should I give it a try?"

My new friend leaned over from the next table and said, "No, do not worry, not at all hot."

The instant that pepper hit my mouth I knew I'd been well and truly had. All the men roared with laughter, and I made a bit of drama out of spitting out the fiery remains, then I grinned and joined in. Their laughter wasn't unkind; in fact, I suspected I'd just participated in a local rite of passage and was being welcomed, however obliquely, into a tiny corner of *chkembari* culture.

The men departed soon after that, and I waved them off like old pals. This was clearly the most sociable eatery in the city, for when we lunched there again some days later, another Good Samaritan volunteered to help us with the menu and parlayed that into a half hour's chat. He, too, had lived in America, and had a long, woebegone tale of a good job, a series of demotions, divorce, and a forced retirement on slender means, necessitating a return to Bitola, where he had a family house. "But no family," he added sadly.

His melancholy was not uncommon in North Macedonia. By most objective measurements, people had enjoyed a much better life as part of communist Yugoslavia. Back then, everyone had a job, a place to live, free medical care, a pension, and far fewer worries about the future. Now people had to fend for themselves under bewildering new rules, in a stagnant economy with 21% unemployment and an average household income of $2000 a year. I began to share the slow-burning, deep-seated outrage expressed by every Macedonian I talked to about the ex-prime minister spending $700 million on gaudy statues in the capital and (allegedly) his own cozy Hungarian retirement-in-exile.

Our landlords, Victoria and Mladen, maintained a philosophical attitude. They lived on the ground floor of a house with two apartments above; the other was occupied by a young Peace Corps worker I rarely saw. Rich and I often sat with our hosts on the tiny back porch in the shade of the cherry tree, talking about the old days and idly watching the new litter of kittens exploring the brave new world into which they'd been born. Victoria, who worked in a government office charged with preserving old buildings, spoke sadly of the budget cuts that left her department helpless to do much more than sit around watching the buildings crumble.

One night at dusk Mladen invited us to join him on a walk through a neighborhood filled with historic mansions from the final years of the Ottoman era, which ended in 1912. The once bright paint had faded to a mere whisper, and gaps in the plaster and trim spoke volumes about decades of neglect. A few had been renovated and occupied, but most of the old houses loomed overhead as dark, deserted husks silhouetted against the twilight sky. I wondered how much longer they could hold out against the twin ravages of time and a sagging economy.

North Macedonia allocated fractionally more of its slender means to preserving archeological sites, and I was eager to see the one sitting just a mile and a quarter south of Bitola. Built in the fourth century BC by our old friend Philip II of Macedon (father to Alexander the Great), the city was called Heraclea Lyncestis — an homage to Hercules and to the ancient kingdom of Lynkestis, which had flourished in the region until Philip conquered it. Apparently the city had enjoyed a lively heyday, and one morning, Rich and I set out to discover what was left of it now.

Bitola's lovely parks, bustling squares, and historic architecture were soon left behind, and I found myself slogging on through the rising heat past gas stations and tire stores that seemed to go on forever. I'm never good at estimating distances, but surely we'd walked more than a mile and a quarter? I wouldn't have been surprised to find we'd overshot and were well into Albania.

I paused to take a swig from my water bottle, and a man riding by on a bicycle stopped and began to speak. Was it English? Albanian? Macedonian? I couldn't make out a single word, but I guessed he was offering to help us find our way, although for all I knew he could have been trying to sell me the bicycle, buy Rich's hat, or get directions back to the mothership.

"Heraclea Lyncestis?" I asked. "Ancient city? Archeological ruins?"

He beamed, nodded, and beckoned for me to follow him. Here, in the hour of need, was yet another Good Samaritan wanting to practice his English (or whatever language he was speaking) and help out a couple of hapless foreigners.

He led us a short distance up the road and through a pair of gates.

I spotted a tiny ticket booth up ahead, but my new friend craftily veered off to the right and started making a wide loop up a steep, rough hillside, a stratagem that enabled us to avoid paying the entrance fee. (I later learned this was a modest forty-eight North Macedonian *denars*, or about eighty cents). By now I was huffing and puffing, but he seemed unaffected, keeping up the flow of chatter as he pushed his bicycle uphill. I still couldn't grasp a single word.

So it wasn't until I reached the top that I realized there had been a slight miscommunication. Our new friend had led us into the Bitola Zoo.

If you've not had the dubious pleasure of visiting this particular establishment, it's the kind of small, cramped, old-fashioned zoo that many countries have outlawed on grounds of animal cruelty. The Bitola Zoo claims to have two hundred prisoners — the website calls them "guest animals" — from forty species. I saw less than half that number, most of them sitting alone, dejected, in small, dark, barren cages without food or water.

"This is really the saddest zoo we've ever seen," wrote one Trip Advisor reviewer. "We know Macedonia is a poor country, but that doesn't mean you have to treat your animals this bad." Another wrote, "100% regret going to this zoo, the conditions of the living environment are very, very poor, even plastic rubbish in the cages. All the animals looked miserable, especially the bears :("

Our self-appointed guide proudly showed off each of the listless monkeys and resentful felines, and it took us some time to thank him properly and extricate ourselves from his hospitality. Eventually he rolled his bike away down the hill, and as soon as we figured the coast was clear, we made a beeline for the exit, feeling as miserable as the bears.

"What do you say we come back late tonight a free them all?" I asked Rich. "Like in *Turtle Diary*."

"I'll bring the bolt cutters."

Fortunately, Heraclea Lyncestis was just up the road and a world apart in terms of atmosphere. Yes, it too was desperately in need of some serious funding and maintenance, but despite the missing tiles, the mosaic floors were charming, the largest sporting whimsical ducks and elegant geometric borders. There was an impressive theater, built so men and beasts could slaughter each other in order to provide a little zippy public entertainment. Eventually the Christians put a stop to it — possibly due to all-too-vivid recollections of how many of their fellows had become lunch for the lions in similar arenas.

The city of Heraclea Lyncestis prospered for nearly a thousand years. Its location on the main route between Greece and Rome gave it tremendous strategic importance, first under the Greeks, then under the Romans, and later as an Episcopal seat during the early Christian era. With some of the world's richest and most powerful men passing through, no doubt the city went all out to provide top notch gladiatorial contests and other entertainments. I could only imagine all the fabulous meals and serious drinking that went on over those delightful ducks on the floor tiles.

The ancient Greeks, in particular, were legendary ζώα κόμματος (party animals). They liked to assemble a congenial gang for a "symposium," which sounds downright upright until you learn the word actually means "gathering of drinkers." After even a relatively simple meal, servants would haul in a sort of urn known as a *krater*, from which you kept refilling your cup with wine while you indulged in drinking games.

One game included tossing the dregs of your wine at a target while shouting the name of your mistress. (Apparently this is more amusing than it sounds, especially after a couple of *kraters*.) The Greek poet and statesman Eubulus gave what seems very sound advice, suggesting that a prudent guest would take care to depart after the third *krater* of wine. The fifth *krater*, he noted, leads to yelling, the sixth "to prancing about, and the seventh to black eyes. The eighth brings the police, the ninth vomiting, the tenth insanity and hurling the furniture." Yes, I'd definitely advise going home before the tenth *krater*, unless of course you're already in police custody.

I wandered around Heraclea Lyncestis imagining all the wild parties and gladiatorial games that had once taken place there. No wonder they'd named the city after Hercules; you'd need incredible stamina to keep up the pace. Did the later occupants, the Romans and early Christians, carry on the carousing traditions? I suspect they did, in their own ways.

After the long walk home, Rich and I found our hosts waiting on the porch to invite us to lunch the following Monday.

"I would like to show you how we make two of our Macedonian dishes," said Victoria. "*Zelnik*, it is a kind of spinach pie, and *turli tava*, our vegetable stew." As you can imagine, I accepted her generous offer with thanks.

At the appointed hour on Monday morning, I was in Victoria's kitchen, watching her mix flour, olive oil, salt, water, and a few drops of vinegar — all by hand and eye, no messing around with measuring cups, whisks, or spoons, let alone a mixer or food processor. Her fingers made quick work of combining the ingredients into a ball of dough, but she decided there was still too much air in it and began whacking the dough vigorously on the countertop, again and again. (Note to self: remember this therapeutic recipe next time I have a bad day.)

Eventually Victoria divided the dough into two balls and placed it in a bowl where it could rest up after its ordeal. Nothing much would happen now for about forty-five minutes, so when she asked Mladen to go out and buy some spinach, Rich and I offered to keep him company.

Their house was just off the broad pedestrian boulevard Širok Sokak, which led to the marvelous Old Bazaar. Along the way we passed a modern supermarket, which didn't earn so much as a glance from

Mladen. Further on we came upon the stone clocktower, which Mladen told me was built in 1664 using mortar fortified by 60,000 eggs collected from the populace. (In olden times, eggs were believed to make building materials stronger, due to their binding properties. Bitola's clocktower had to be rebuilt in the 1830s, so possibly the eggs didn't prove quite as binding as they'd hoped.) Next came the narrow river Dragor, which in the winter of 2012 had frozen for the first time in history — something I certainly didn't need to worry about on that sweltering June morning, but a worrying sign of climate weirding all the same.

Just as I thought Mladen was about to plunge into the rabbit warren of tiny shops surrounding the Old Bazaar, he veered off into a large, blockish building known as Bezisten, the Covered Bazaar (or to give it a more contemporary translation, the Shopping Mall). Built in the fifteenth century by Grand Vizier Kodzha Daut Pasha Uzuncarsili, and no doubt reconfigured many times since then, the building was surprisingly bland, utilitarian, and deserted. Only a handful of the eighty-six stores remained open, and our footsteps echoed in the empty hallway as we made our way to a small shop selling parts.

Why were we there? Because a few days earlier, while doing a load of laundry in our apartment, I'd somehow managed to break off the control knob on the washing machine. I'm still not sure how it happened. But as anyone who has stayed in an Airbnb will attest, there are few problem-solving exercises as stimulating as wrestling with unfamiliar household appliances, especially those labeled in a foreign language. Forget Sudoku, crossword puzzles, Lumosity, and all the other brain boosters they recommend these days. My efforts to master various washing machines, shower controls, and coffee makers was keeping my synapses firing at lightning speed. Unfortunately, these epic struggles sometimes resulted in collateral damage, like that broken control knob.

Mladen showed the knob to the person behind the counter, and she, thank heaven, was nodding and checking her books to work out how long it would take to arrive.

Meanwhile Rich stood transfixed, gazing about in openmouthed delight. His father being a handy sort of man about the house, Rich had grown up learning how to fix things. It was one of the great regrets of his life that, in the US at least, nearly all appliances were now created with so much tech wizardry and planned obsolescence that attempting repairs was futile. Here, however, money for new purchases was scarce, older and simpler models were still in use, and plenty of people were willing to spend hours tinkering with gadgets on the fritz.

The parts shop was filled from floor to ceiling with shelves, bins, and hooks holding a dizzying variety of oddly shaped pieces of metal and plastic. If I'd stumbled over them on the street I'd have assumed they were junk, but here, if Rich's expression was anything to go by, they were treasure. I had to drag him back out the door when Mladen had finished placing the order.

And now, at last, we entered the Old Bazaar. This was my favorite kind of market, a warren of small shops, booths, and tables, some set beneath solid roofs, other tucked under awnings, tarps, umbrellas, bits of plywood, and sheets of corrugated tin. A brawny, bearded man walked by pulling a cart laden with sacks of potatoes. Housewives bent over tables displaying an astonishing assortment of shoes, clothes, kitchenware, knives, honey, herbs, fruits, and vegetables.

"It is all locally grown," said Mladen, threading his way through the tarp-covered aisles of the produce section. "Well, some few things are imported, such as bananas. But most of this is raised here and so it is sold only in season. Lettuce is reaching the end of its time now and will soon become tasteless. Cherries are just coming into season. They are still a little expensive, but they taste very good. I do not know if we will find spinach."

As he carefully inspected the heaps of greens offered at various stalls, I looked around, enjoying the bustle of everyday commerce that had been taking place on this very spot since the sixteenth century. Eventually Mladen turned back, saying, "No, spinach is not here. I will buy some *blitva*." Found throughout the Balkans, *blitva* is kale's delicate, tastier cousin; Mladen bought a couple of large bunches and we started for home.

Somehow our expedition had run well past the expected forty-five minutes, and when we returned to the house, we found Victoria had moved ahead with the preparations. When the two balls of *zelnik* dough had risen sufficiently, she'd rolled each one out into a large circle and coated it with butter. Then she cut a smaller circle in the middle, and sliced the outer ring into wedges like the rays of the sun. The whole thing was then folded in on itself and returned to the bowl to continue rising.

By the time I was back in the kitchen, Victoria was starting on the *zelnik's* filling, mixing egg, cheese, and — once Mladen had handed it over — *blitva*. She then took the first ball of dough from the fridge and flattened it using the kind of rolling pin favored in the region: a wooden dowel about a yard long and an inch thick. She laid the dough neatly on the bottom and sides of a large square pan and spread the filling on top.

And this is when things got interesting.

The top layer of dough was rolled out on the flour-covered counter, thinner and thinner, larger and larger. Still not satisfied, Victoria then grabbed one side and began dragging it over the counter's edge to stretch it still further. By now it was easily three times the size of the pan and so thin it was nearly translucent. When she was finally satisfied, Victoria draped this giant sheet of dough over the rolling pin, held it above the pan, and began unrolling it slowly, bit by bit, over the filling, draping it into fluttery folds. She finished it off by pinching the edges into a decorative little twist. It was a lovely work of art that spoke of a lifetime's practice.

Placing the *zelnik* carefully inside the oven, Victoria got to work on the *turli tava* (vegetable stew), sautéing chunks of eggplant, zucchini, onions, and carrots in a large skillet. She then put the vegetables into a large roasting pan, topping the mixture with thick slices of tomato sprinkled with minced garlic, splashes of olive oil, and chopped parsley.

By now the *zelnik* had finished baking, so Victoria set it on the counter to rest under a damp cloth. She eased the *turli tava* into the oven, and while it cooked, she charred some mild green peppers directly over one of the stove's gas burners and tossed together a green salad, taking advantage of the last good days of lettuce season. It was clearly a labor of love and more than three solid hours of work. I was beginning to understand why people were abandoning traditional fare in favor of takeout pizza.

The other tenant, the young Peace Core worker, had come down to watch the cooking, and now we all sat down to eat. Following local tradition, the meal began with *rakia* (fruit brandy), which Mladen assured me was the best way to wake up the stomach and prepare it for the pleasures that lay ahead. I don't think it was just the *rakia* talking when everybody exclaimed that the *zelnik* was absolutely marvelous, the rich filling perfectly complemented by the delicate, rippling crust. Conversation flowed lazily over topics ranging from food and wine to the future of North Macedonia to the antics of the kittens underfoot.

Now the *turli tava* emerged from the oven, and it too was eaten and much admired, along with the crisp green salad. A bottle of wine went around. Eventually Victoria brought out her signature cake, made with cherries she'd picked from the tree shading the back garden. We gave a round of applause for her efforts, and she looked shyly pleased.

I would be sorry to leave this warm little circle of friendship and the cozy town of Bitola. Rich and I were getting ready to head across the border into Albania, which I suspected would be the most unpredictable and challenging part of our journey.

Our first stop in Albania would be Korçë, some sixty miles away, which Victoria and Mladen recommended for its historic charm. I still had no idea how we'd be getting there. Having been isolated from its neighbors for decades under a paranoid dictator, Albania had no international rail service and few buses crossing its borders. Would we need to take a boat across Lake Ohrid, which formed part of the border?

Over lunch, Rich and Mladen began discussing logistics, and the next thing I knew, Mladen had offered to drive us to Korçë. In keeping with Bitola's strong tradition of hospitality, he seemed genuinely to want to complete our stay with this final act of service. Yes, we did pay him something for his trouble, and no doubt the money came in handy. But as far as I could tell, he sincerely wanted to provide this final measure of courtesy to which guests in that part of the world are naturally entitled. Rich and I accepted the generous offer with suitable expressions of gratitude.

"Korçë is lovely," Victoria told me. "Be sure to visit the icon museum." I nodded and thanked her for the suggestion, all the while wondering what could possibly be so special about a collection of small religious paintings.

At last Rich and I rose from the table, said our farewells, and stumbled upstairs to our apartment for a much-needed siesta. As I closed my eyes, I remembered Victoria beating the dough against the countertop to get the air out, frowning, and beating it some more. At which point I said to her, "As I always remind my readers, perfection is not a requirement." She'd laughed and set the dough down with a gentle pat. No, I thought drowsily as I slid toward sleep, perfection isn't a requirement. In fact, it's never really possible. But some days, like this one, come very, very close.

ALBANIA

14. Korçë / *Dragon Pie*

My first impression of Albania, coming over the mountains from North Macedonia, was one of breathtaking storybook charm. Mladen's car descended slowly into a broad valley filled with green fields and tidy little family farms. A few ancient tractors puttered by, but mostly I saw sturdy workhorses pulling ploughs across fields and drawing wooden carts along the roadway. Flocks of sheep and goats ambled in front of the car, and Mladen calmly stopped to let them pass. They surged around us, bleating companionably. Men and women stood waist-deep in fields of purple and orange flowers, harvesting blossoms and spreading them out to dry. Haystacks stood beside cottages that looked like illustrations from medieval fairy tales.

"Did we just go back in time?" asked Rich.

I could hardly contain my astonishment. This was not the Albania I'd expected. Those who love it best describe it as beautiful but rough around the edges; detractors call it grim, dangerous, and dull. When I mentioned to friends, relatives, and readers that I was heading to Albania this trip, nearly everyone asked "Why?" Followed by, "No, really, why?" And finally, "Are you nuts?"

Part of the reason I wanted to visit was because the whole time I was growing up Albania was completely cut off from the outside world. This was due to the hyper-paranoid communist dictator, Enver Hoxha. A former grammar school teacher who rose to power as a resistance leader during World War II, he was such a hardliner that he broke ties with the USSR and later China because they were too namby-pamby about communism (!). Unable to find allies who met his exacting standards, he decided to circle the wagons, isolate his country, and build a modern utopia, starting with secret police, forced labor camps, and political assassinations. Because nothing says utopia like unmarked mass graves.

Hoxha's maniacal obsession with security inspired one of the world's loonier defense systems: he installed nearly 175,000 hideous concrete bunkers (popular mythology places the number at 700,000) throughout the realm. Everyone over the age of twelve was encouraged to join the citizen militia and be prepared to rush to the closest bunker and repel a foreign invasion — which never came.

Nearly all of the bunkers remain standing, and while a few have been repurposed as dog kennels, children's playground equipment, and storage, most are derelict and abandoned. They're too heavy to remove, too expensive to demolish, too cramped to house humans or animals for long, too damp for most storage — in short, utterly useless for nearly all peacetime activities. Except one. As *Lonely Planet*'s Tony Wheeler put it, "Albanian virginity is lost in a Hoxha bunker as often as American virginity was once lost in the back seats of cars."

Today, the backseats of cars are giving those bunkers a run for their money. Cars were scarce back in Hoxha's day; when communism finally fell in 1990, there were just 6000 in the entire nation. Before the political dust had even begun to settle, Albania was rushing to construct its first highway and lift the long-standing ban on private car ownership. Soon every month saw 1500 automobiles rolling into the country, many (allegedly) stolen from Italy and brought over on the ferry.

Since then, road construction projects had sprung up everywhere, but due to skimpy planning and (it was rumored) excessive corruption, the resulting highways are not as glorious as everyone hoped. "They are badly configured," notes Wikipedia, "contain unfinished overpasses, uncontrolled access points, lack of fencing and either misplaced or missing road signs, inadequate entry and exit ramps, and are indiscriminately used by animals, mopeds, agricultural vehicles, and pedestrians."

Were the roads really that bad, I wondered? I consulted Gillian Gloyer's *Albania*, one of the few guidebooks available and a laudably unflinching report on conditions. "The greatest risk most people in Albania face is on the roads, where traffic accidents are very frequent and the fatality rate is one of the highest in Europe," she said. "Until a few years ago, Albanian roads were so bad that it was difficult to drive fast enough to kill anyone. Now, though, cars zip along newly upgraded highways that are also used by villagers and their livestock. There is no stigma attached to drink-driving and practically no attempt is made to check it."

As for other safety concerns, Gloyer said, "In general, violent crime in Albania happens either within the underworld of organized crime or in the context of a blood feud." In a typical year, some 3000 Albanians were involved in active vendettas, operating under the *koka për kokë* (head for a head) tradition that had led to the deaths of 10,000 people since the demise of communism. I made a big mental note not to fall afoul of anyone in the mafia — or indeed, anyone with a family — while I was in country.

As far as I could determine, all of the above facts were absolutely true, and yet they gave a very false picture of the country. For a start, Albanians turned out to be among the friendliest people I'd ever met. No one seemed inclined to shoot me, rob me, or embroil me in a nefarious underworld vendetta. In fact, pretty much everyone seemed prepared to go miles out of their way to help me navigate their country, sample its remarkable cuisine, and enjoy my visit as fully as possible.

Mladen's car rolled quietly through the countryside and into the city of Korçë, where the sleepy, old-world atmosphere gave way to the noise and bustle of a lively metropolis. Korçë had a vivid past, including serving as headquarters for the anti-Axis resistance of WWII, which was led by the communists under Enver Hoxha. When Hoxha's forty-year dictatorship ended, one of the ways Korçë shifted from communism to capitalism was by sprucing itself up in hopes of enticing tourists. Everyone began painting buildings, refurbishing the old bazaar, expanding parks, adding daring new architecture, and opening shops, bars, and coffee houses galore.

All this plus low prices made Korçë a popular vacation destination for nearby Europeans. But so far there were practically no British or American visitors, so naturally almost nobody in the service industry had gotten around to learning English. This became only too apparent when we arrived at our hotel, the Villa Parku Rinia, and met our congenial hosts, Elena and George. Our arrangements had all been made online and in English, no doubt with the assistance of a multilingual friend or relative, but there was nobody to help us now. Mladen tried speaking to them in Macedonian, but they simply smiled and shook their heads.

Still, everyone managed pretty well at first. My family is big on charades, and I easily pantomimed my pleasure at finding our room spacious, sunny, and blessed with a balcony overlooking the tree-lined boulevard out front. Then Rich produced a credit card, and George — who must have been pretty good at charades himself — managed to convey his profound personal regret at having to inform us that the hotel only took cash. We had been in the country less than an hour and had not acquired any Albanian lek, a currency worth (confusingly) 0.009 to the US dollar.

"Bank?" inquired Rich.

George and Elena nodded their understanding of the concept but pantomimed that they were utterly flummoxed as to where one might be found. They took us outside and flagged down various passing strangers, who looked equally dumbfounded by the question. A man in a nearby shop stepped out to add his two cents worth, and in no time there were eleven (I counted) people working on the problem. Eventually a group of women cut us out of the herd and escorted us to an ATM five blocks away.

Having acquired a sufficient quantity of leks for our immediate needs, Rich and I enjoyed a leisurely lunch with Mladen in the beer garden of the city's popular Birra Korça, Albania's first brewery, which opened in 1928. Afterwards the three of us wandered about the city a while, and then Mladen took his leave. So it wasn't until late afternoon that I was back in the hotel and had a chance to check out the accommodations more thoroughly. And that's when I discovered the death trap that was our shower.

The bathroom was newly renovated and sparkling clean but not overly large; sink, toilet, bidet, and shower jostled for space. To add a sense of drama, and give the user enough room to open the shower's glass door, some genius had placed the shower stall three feet above floor level, at the top of a polished marble staircase. Naturally there was no handrail to detract from the sleek line of the tiled wall. With hideous clarity, I pictured myself attempting to descend those slick steps with damp, soapy feet and toppling to my doom. Stark naked, soaking wet, and crashing head first onto a bidet was not the way I wanted to go out.

I conveyed this sentiment to Rich, who incredibly didn't seem share my view of the shower as a clear and present danger to life and limb. But he knew better than to scoff at my fears.

"If you're really concerned, we can always move to another hotel," he said. "I know of one near here; we'll go check it out."

After a short rest, we walked over to Bujtina Sidheri, a marvelously atmospheric old hotel and restaurant with beamed ceilings, rough stone walls, and antique furniture displaying lovely vintage tea sets, cameras, sewing machines, tools, farm implements, and knickknacks. The bedrooms were utterly charming but very small and dark. I could tell Rich wasn't keen to move there because he swiftly came up with a plan for emailing our current hotel, so that whoever handled their English communications could let Elena and George know we'd like another room with a more conventional shower.

"Great," I said. "I don't want to cause offence. We can mention my vertigo as the reason."

Every once in a while I suffer from momentary dizziness, which various doctors have diagnosed, with impressive professional precision, as "just one of those things; I wouldn't worry about it."

"I'll take care of it," Rich said. "But what do you say we come back here to eat tomorrow night? The online reviews say the food is great." The manager, who spoke some basic English, seemed pleased to take our reservation for eight o'clock the next evening.

In the morning there was a knock on the door and when I opened it, I found Elena, George, and an enormous tray laden with breakfast foods: homemade pastries, store-bought pastries, hard boiled eggs, and tall glasses of ice-cold liquid yoghurt. It was a classic Balkan breakfast, which meant it was hearty, delicious, and utterly lacking in coffee.

While George arranged the tray on our balcony's table, Elena led me across the hall to another guest room. It was clean but looked as if it hadn't been slept in since the fall of communism; the furniture was sparse and outdated, the fabrics faded and limp. But the bathroom had a nice, normal, floor-level shower, and Elena showed me that she was leaving the key in the lock of the outer door. It was all mine, any time I wanted it. I pantomimed my gratitude. Beaming, she and George slipped away upstairs.

It dawned on me that we were the only guests in the hotel. I was fairly sure Elena and George lived on the top floor — one of the emails mentioned there was staff on the premises twenty-four hours a day — but they crept around as invisibly as elves in the old fairy tales, slipping in to clean the room while we were out and showing up every morning with armloads of delicious food. Other than that brief daily contact, the entire hotel was eerily silent at all times.

As was Bujtina Sidheri when we returned to it that evening for dinner. There was no one at the front desk or in any of the public rooms on the ground floor, and we wandered all the way back to the kitchen before I finally spotted Griselda, a young woman who had been with the manager the day before. Hastily concealing her surprise at seeing actual dinner guests, she escorted us to a table. The three of us proceeded to engage in an elaborate interchange via pantomime, Google Translate, and her smartphone photos of various dishes, after which Griselda disappeared in the direction of the kitchen.

"What did we just order?" I asked.

"Who knows? I'm sure it will be wonderful," Rich said.

It was. First came the salad, elegant slivers of apple, cantaloupe, strawberry, kiwi, and orange, a handful of cherries, and a chunk of magnificent Gorgonzola, all drizzled with a balsamic vinaigrette.

We'd just begun tucking into the salads when two musicians arrived with guitars. After a bit of banter with Griselda and cheerful nods to us, they sat down and began to play. The lighthearted folk music danced through the rooms, the perfect accompaniment to the meal.

Griselda whisked away our salads and brought Rich pork topped with avocado, pomegranate, and fresh dill. For me she had a plate of chicken rollups that were tender and perfectly sauced with a creamy chicken broth, a scattering of pomegranate seeds, a dusting of poppy seeds, and a small, edible pansy.

A few other people trickled in, nodding polite hellos to us. Apparently they knew (or had hired) the musicians, who now joined them at the biggest table, keeping up the delightful tunes.

After the dessert of spice cake with brandied pear, I used Google Translate to tell Griselda I was a travel writer and asked her if I could return to learn more about the magic happening in the kitchen. She nodded enthusiastically and we agreed to meet two days later. The conversation then floundered over the question of what would be prepared. The only word I clearly recognized in Google's English translation was "cheeks." After a few attempts to elicit more information, I gave up, nodded, and the matter was settled.

"You think she meant pork cheeks?" I asked Rich as we strolled back to our hotel.

"You mean like the *carrillada* we eat in Seville? Who knows? Who cares? Whoever is doing the cooking is an artist."

The next morning, Rich and I discussed, with a distinct lack of enthusiasm, a visit to the icon museum recommended by Mladen and Victoria. I like a good icon as much as the next woman, but an entire museum of small, gold-encrusted religious paintings? Really? I figured I'd last about fifteen minutes, if Rich didn't drag me away after ten. Still, once I'd found it on the map, I saw it would make a nice destination for the morning walk, and if it was no good, I could always have fun making snarky remarks about it on my blog.

The National Museum of Medieval Art, as the icon museum was officially called, didn't look anything like I'd expected. I stood gazing in surprise at the blocky modernist building, part grey stone and part matte black sheetrock with a few bits of brick. There were several extremely skinny windows, which I decided were an homage to the arrowslits (also known as loopholes) built into castles so archers could shoot at approaching enemies. The concrete walkway sloping up toward a porch might have been a hybrid between a drawbridge and a wheelchair ramp. Rich didn't look at all impressed and I couldn't blame him.

"Five minutes," I said. "Then if it's no good, we're out of there."

Inside, the museum was dazzling. An award-winning German architectural firm had recently been given free rein to transform the original, staid 1980 museum, and they'd used the 6,500 icons, rich with gold leaf and the jewel-toned robes of saints, to eyepopping effect.

First came the Gold Room, painted the deep yellow of old-fashioned Number 2 pencils and hung, floor to ceiling, with icons. The effect was dazzling, the saturation of color — the tomato-red robes of the male saints and gorgeous royal blue of Our Lady's cloak — so rich I could hardly take my eyes off it. This was followed by a series of smaller rooms with equally intense walls — pomegranate red, stark white, matte black — that showcased the paintings of various eras, with a few statues and textiles thrown in for contrast. One side room was equipped with an old wooden floor that creaked loudly with every step. The designers were clearly trying to startle me at every turn and they did.

It's not a large museum, but Rich and I lingered for nearly an hour. As we headed out, discussing our favorite exhibits, a group of visitors was coming in, and one woman exclaimed to me, with surprise and pleasure, "Hey, did I hear you speaking English?"

English-speaking visitors were such a rarity in Korçë that she was just the first of several fellow Americans who stopped me for the sheer novelty of exchanging a few words in our common language. In addition to the woman at the museum, I met a couple of young Peace Corps workers and then an Albanian-American who'd come to town for a wedding.

It was the wedding guest who told me about the local mafia. "They have all the money around here," he said. "You see all the Volvos on the street? They steal them in Italy and bring them over on the ferry to sell them. That huge new park just north of here, Parku Rinia? You think the government has that kind of money? The mafia paid for it." Actually, I was rather impressed to learn that some of the mob's ill-gotten gains were going to civic improvements. Somehow I hadn't realized their mission statement had a benevolent side.

The following morning, as arranged, Rich and I returned to Bujtina Sidheri and found Griselda in the kitchen with two other cooks, Julia and Vida. As they laid out the flour, oil, cheese, and spinach, Griselda used Google Translate to explain, with many false starts and confusing digressions, what she'd be making: not, as I'd thought, pig cheeks or anything like it, but spinach pie.

I was a trifle dismayed, as I'd just watched Victoria making spinach pie in Bitola, and I hadn't intended to do any repeats. But hey, too late to do anything about that now. And as it turned out, while the ingredients were much the same, Griselda's technique was far more streamlined. No more than half an hour elapsed between picking up the first handful of flour and popping the assembled pie into the oven. Even with two helpers, it was an impressive show of speed.

The pie baked for just five minutes, then was hauled out and set on the stove's gas burner. While Griselda slathered the top with butter, the stoves flames browned bottom crust, and the whole pie swelled to gigantic proportions and began hissing steam like an outraged dragon. When it subsided, Griselda shoved it back in the oven for one minute more, then pulled it out again. Finished! She cut it up with kitchen shears and handed me a piece.

As I sighed blissfully over mouthfuls of the hot, flaky pastry with its lush filling, I reflected that Albania was rather like Griselda's Dragon Pie. It wasn't at all what I'd originally expected, but it turned out to be absolutely wonderful — deeply traditional yet wholly original, surprising yet comforting. Our entire visit to Korçë had proved to be safe, fun, friendly, filled with quirky moments, and blessed with great food. I began to wonder why I'd ever been at all nervous about visiting Albania.

15. Divjakë / *So This Fish Comes In on Horseback*

And now, after four years of eager anticipation, Rich was just days away from accomplishing his single most essential goal for the entire trip: having lunch at Ali Kali, where the owner delivers your meal on horseback. All Rich had to do was figure out how to get us halfway across the country to the railway station, and from there to the coast, and finally out to the middle of nowhere where Ali and his horse plied their trade.

From the first mention of Ali Kali as a destination eatery, I'd been just a teensy bit concerned about how we were going to navigate this part of the journey. Having read about the country's risky roads, drunk drivers, and high death tolls, I'd pinned my hopes on the railway system. Then I'd learned Albania's railways were in the process of being dismantled bit by bit so the nation could devote more of its transportation resources to the new superhighways. Were the old trains still running in any direction we wanted to go?

Rich sat down on the balcony of our hotel room in Korçë, rolled up his sleeves, and opened his laptop with an air of resolute purpose.

After half an hour's furious labor he said, "OK. There's still one Albanian railway line in operation. It leaves at 1:30 every day from a town called Elbasan, just seventy-seven miles from here. The train will take us to the port of Durrës, where the ferry from Italy docks, and then we'll be just a taxi ride away from Ali Kali."

"How do we get to Elbasan?"

But here, it seemed, was the snag. "We can go by *furgon*, a kind of unofficial minivan," he said doubtfully. "Apparently you ask around and someone will point out the right vehicle. Once you're on the *furgon*, you have to wait; they won't leave until all the seats are filled, so the timing is unpredictable."

The departure point listed for Korçë's *furgons* wasn't too far from the hotel, so we walked over to reconnoiter. The sight that met my eyes was not reassuring. Various white vans were parked seemingly at random on an unmarked strip of asphalt. All their doors were open, giving me a good view of the passengers sitting inside, sweating stoically in the mounting heat, waiting for the remaining seats to fill. I pictured myself spending many hours in one of those sweltering minivans, eventually arriving at Elbasan only to find we'd missed the train, and then spending several more hours wandering around town seeking lodgings on a day when — Google informed me — temperatures in Elbasan would hover around 100 degrees Fahrenheit.

"Or," said Rich, "we could hire a car and a driver."

Call us wimps, but in the end, that's what we decided to do.

At the appointed hour, Elena and George escorted us to the curb and prepared to hand us over to the next Albanian who would be responsible for our safety and wellbeing. I was beginning to admire the Albanian commitment to hospitality, the cornerstone of the code of honor known as *besa*, which was embedded in a set of fifteenth-century moral and social laws called the *Kanun* that defined the national character. To be fair, some of the Kanun's concepts seem outdated now — the sections on how to conduct a blood feud come to mind, as do the limits to women's freedom — but the authors' attitude towards the care and feeding of guests was very sound.

"The house of an Albanian belongs to God and the guest," says the *Kanun*. "The guest must be honored with bread and salt and heart."

Elena and George had given us bread and salt and a safe shower; now they spoke for a few minutes with our driver to reassure themselves that he was reliable enough to hold up his end of the social contract and transfer us safely to Elbasan. Apparently Reoland passed muster. Elena and George handed us tenderly into the back of his comfortable, air-conditioned sedan and stood on the sidewalk, smiling and waving goodbye, as the car pulled away from the curb.

Reoland was a cheerful, round-faced young man of about thirty, immaculately dressed, fluent in English, and, most importantly, a careful and competent driver. After everything I'd read about the perils of Albanian highways, I kept anxious eyes glued to the windows, the better to see rampaging vehicles hurtling toward me at ramming speed. But nothing dramatic appeared to be happening on the road that day. Traffic was light, and while there was some mildly aggressive overtaking, the prevailing style was no more alarming that you'd find, say, on the New Jersey turnpike at rush hour.

Reoland pointed out various landmarks as we passed and asked if this was our first time in the country. Rich explained it was actually the second. A year earlier, during a visit to the Greek island of Corfu, I'd discovered there was daily hovercraft service to the Albanian port of Sarandë, just 8.7 miles across the Ionian Sea, and we'd impulsively booked tickets for a day trip.

Sarandë had once been a peaceful little fishing village, but it now formed part of the new — and still largely theoretical — Albanian Riviera. Almost overnight Sarandë's population had mushroomed from a hundred and ten souls to 20,227 or possibly 41,173, depending on whose figures you believed. The skyline had become a series of unfortunate high-rises, bland yet intimidating and of dubious construction quality. Cafés and palm trees softened the shore, which had lovely white sand beaches, deep blue water, and more than 300 days of sun a year. Best of all, from my point of view, there were absolutely no tourists except for ourselves and one rather bewildered-looking Italian couple.

Despite the high-rises and a few trendy cafés, Sarandë was still a village at heart. I saw fishermen selling the morning's catch to their neighbors, spoke with an old fellow who wanted to know if Rich and I were married (I'm not sure why this was of interest), and poked my head into the dank interior one of Hoxha's famous concrete defensive bunkers. Rich got a haircut for 300 lev (about $3.70) and was nearly run down by one of the kamikaze drivers the guidebook had warned us about. But aside from that one driver and the cranky, hungover waiter at the coffee bar, everybody was warm and welcoming, laying before us such modest treasures as the city possessed, urging us to come back whenever we felt in need of a haircut, fresh fish, or a chat.

And now we were back in Albania, and everyone was exhibiting the same friendly attitude. I gradually stopped staring out the window worrying about fatal car accidents and began to relax. The landscape was unremarkable, mostly bare land and low hills dotted with shrubs and trees, with occasional gas stations marking side roads that headed off to (presumably) more populated areas. The ribbon of highway unspooled endlessly before my eyes. As Rich and Reoland talked in the front seat, I was gradually lulled into the kind of mindless contentment that's defined as "midding" in *The Dictionary of Obscure Sorrows*:

"Midding: feeling the tranquil pleasure of being near a gathering but not quite in it — hovering on the perimeter of a campfire, chatting outside a party while others dance inside, resting your head in the backseat of a car listening to your friends chatting up front — feeling blissfully invisible yet still fully included, safe in the knowledge that everyone is together and everyone is okay, with all the thrill of being there without the burden of having to be."

For the next twenty-five miles I drifted along in a lovely little bubble of midding — which burst abruptly when we pulled up in front of the Elbasan railway station. The low, grubby orange building was closed, locked, dark, and deserted. I stared at the station's closed door, hardly able to believe my eyes. And then the ever-resourceful Reoland switched off the ignition and climbed out to talk to some men in a nearby café.

Moments later he was back. "Today's train has been cancelled. They say that today there were not enough passengers to justify the petrol."

Well, that was a first. And now what? Luckily, my immediate course of action was clear, as I have a long-standing policy in cases like this: "Never chase a missed train. Have a pasty and wait for the next one." Here in Elbasan, it seemed likely the next train might be days away or never appear at all. Still, the principle held true; when travel arrangements fall apart, taking a few minutes to recombobulate over refreshments is always a sensible idea. Rich, Reoland, and I repaired to a blandly modern, blissfully air conditioned café to take stock of the situation and our options.

As we sipped restorative espressos, Reoland offered to drive us all the way to Durrës, forty-seven miles away. It was no trouble at all, he said, as he lived in Tirana, the nation's capital, which lay in the same general direction. After accepting his generous offer with suitable thanks, Rich tactfully inquired about the cost, making it clear he was happy to pay. Reoland refused to take more money, although in the end he accepted something to cover the cost of the extra gas. I was really beginning to like this guy. And the whole *besa* concept.

On the road again, I passed the time telling Reoland about our Mediterranean Comfort Food Tour. He was enthusiastic about the idea but dismayed to learn we didn't plan to visit Tirana. As tactfully as I could, I explained that everything I'd read suggested it was dreary, crime-ridden, and dangerous; utilitarian at best, life-threatening at worst. There was a political demonstration coming up in a few days which many online pundits feared would turn into an ugly riot; they all advised avoiding the capital city this week.

Reoland managed not to roll his eyes but made it clear he thought this was a bunch of Internet nonsense. He lived in Tirana with his wife and new baby, and yes, it was a city with the usual urban issues, but it wasn't particularly unsafe. And it was certainly not dull but rather a vibrant metropolis with much to offer, especially when it came to cuisine. He waxed eloquent about Tirana's restaurants and was in the middle of describing the exquisite roast lamb served at one of them when he broke off to gesture toward an upcoming overpass.

"My mother helped build that bridge," he said.

Taken off guard, I groped for the proper response. I fell back on the comparatively safe remark, "It looks like a fine bridge."

He gave a small sigh. "She was a schoolteacher, and she was forced to leave her job and come here for many weeks, to work doing hard physical labor." Ah, a complaint, then. As I commiserated with him over the unfairness of it all, I imagined myself as a young schoolmarm, yanked from my family, home, and career to put in twelve-hour days of strenuous manual labor followed by nights sleeping in a hut crowded with other disgruntled comrades. From the sound of things she was still bitter about it, and who could blame her? Hoxha's communist regime had a lot to answer for on every level.

Inevitably the conversation turned to the restaurant Ali Kali, and Rich could hardly contain his excitement when Reoland mentioned he'd actually been there. Yes, he'd seen Ali ride in on horseback, brandishing grilled meat for his guests.

"It was years ago," he said. "But I do not think it has changed much."

"Did you enjoy it?" I asked, holding my breath for fear he would make disparaging remarks and crush Rich's hopes.

"It was a lot of fun," he said with a grin. I sighed with relief.

By now the car's GPS was showing the fastest route involved

passing right through Tirana before turning west to the port of Durrës some twenty miles distant. As the car rolled into the nation's capital, I had to admit that Reoland might have a point; Tirana didn't seem nearly as dire as I'd expected.

In fact, the streets looked quiet, orderly, and rather inviting. There were lots of smart cafés, upscale bars, and colorful shops at ground level, although above them, the multi-storied apartment buildings tended to be quite scruffy, with faded paint, stained concrete, and sagging curtains. One section held several blocks of gleaming high-rise office buildings that would have looked at home in any major city in the world.

The last stretch of the day's journey, a broad highway running between Tirana and the port of Durrës, was very impressive indeed. It was lined with massive, glittering buildings displaying logos of international corporations, many of them household names in my own country. Somebody was clearly dumping a lot of money into this town. Whether it would pay off in the long run was anybody's guess, but it seemed a sounder investment than the gaudy statues and pseudo-classical facades of Skopje, North Macedonia. Admittedly a low bar, but still.

By the time we got to Durrës, Rich had invited Reoland and his wife, Irmira, to join us for lunch at Ali Kali in two days' time. As they were settling the details of the excursion, I caught my first sight of our hotel, a fairly unconvincing imitation of an Italian palace. As the car rolled to a stop, a uniformed staff member emerged to take our bags, and after exchanging a few words with the fellow to make sure he was equal to the task of safeguarding us, Reoland wished us well and took off for home.

Glancing around, I noticed several other flashy hotels that looked as if they'd gotten lost on their way to Las Vegas. As I soon discovered, the ancient port of Durrës had reinvented itself as a glitzy, low-cost vacation destination for Italians, who arrived on the overnight ferry to spend days sunning themselves on the beach and nights at the upmarket bars and hotels. I could never quite decide whether becoming a resort tragically diminished a once-vital and historic port or was a smart, realistic adaptation to modern economics.

In a way, Durrës has always been about offering visitors a little fun in the sun. In Roman times it served as the base for an extension of the famous Appian Way, which ran from Rome to Brindisi on Italy's coast. Roman legions could sail across the Adriatic and march on paved roads on all the way to Byzantium (modern Istanbul). But not before stopping for a bit of leave in Durrës. To entertain the troops, the city built the largest amphitheater in the Balkans, a showpiece seating 20,000 spectators. Today, after centuries of neglect and a few underfunded excavations, it's shortlisted as one of the most endangered cultural heritage sites in Europe.

The upside was that I could spend all the time I wanted roaming freely around the amphitheater, unencumbered by any pesky restrictions, never running into crowds of visitors. It's a lovely place to spend a morning, and I suggest if you ever get to Durrës you visit it immediately, while it's still standing.

And then, the next day, it was finally time to set off for our much-anticipated lunch at Ali Kali in a rural area known as Divjakë.

Reoland arrived and ushered me into the car's back seat next to his charming young wife, Irmira. Using her modest English and dozens of photos on her phone, Irmira explained she'd just had her first baby, who was currently with Irmira's mother. This being the first time mother and baby had been parted, it took a steady stream of text messages and real time photos to keep her acute separation anxiety at bay.

Reoland drove confidently along the shore, past a few farms, and into the forest. But after that, even his memory and the car's GPS couldn't properly pinpoint our destination. Small dirt roads, utterly signpost free, ran seemingly at random through the trees. The frazzled GPS pin kept jumping about, as if making random, Hail Mary guesses. Try this? Or maybe this?

At one point we bypassed a tree with a simple, wooden cutout of a white horse nailed to it. A little way down the road Reoland stopped, reversed, went back to the cutout, then turned down the narrow lane beside it. The car bumped slowly along the rutted track for quite a distance, and then suddenly I saw a horse corral and some parked cars. We'd found Ali Kali.

Climbing out of the car, our little band set off down the footpath, passing stands of trees and lush pink oleanders, eventually discovering a dozen or so rustic wooden tables, set beneath thatched roofs, arranged in a rough square around a cleared patch of ground. Every table was filled with Albanians, all seemingly talking at once; the atmosphere was buzzing with pleased anticipation. Irmira's preoccupied air gave way to bright-eyed interest, and soon she was going minutes without checking her phone.

Reoland stepped aside for a quiet word with a member of the staff. I suspect the magic phrase "American travel writer" made its way from Reoland's lips to Ali's ear, because I certainly got the red carpet treatment from that moment onward.

After settling at a table and agreeing that yes, beer would be lovely, I told our companions I wanted a quick look around. Rich and I followed our noses to the kitchen, where I discovered a series of open fireplaces in which whole fish were being grilled in wire baskets, scales glistening with reflections of the dancing flames, drops of fat sizzling fragrantly on the hearthstones.

Beyond the kitchen lay the winter dining room, a large, rambling space decorated with old-fashioned leather saddles, colorful horse blankets, and blackened cookware. Hundreds of visitors had scrawled their names on the rough pine walls.

"Got your pen handy?" Rich asked.

I dug it out of my shoulder bag and handed it to him. He began scribbling on the wall, and moments later he was beaming with delight and pointing to our names, now a permanent fixture in Ali Kali.

Back at the table, I found ice cold beer, bread, fried potatoes, salad, and *tarator* (a yogurt dip similar to Greek *tzatziki*). As soon as I sat down, Ali rode in. He was a wiry middle-aged man wearing Hugo Boss shorts, a sporty T-shirt, and an unsmiling countenance. It was an expression I'd often seen on the faces of Seville's flamenco dancers. As serious artists they would never lower themselves to pander to the crowd by grinning and waving. Ali had apparently adopted the same attitude.

Sitting bareback on a chestnut horse, he threaded his way through the tables and into the center area. A small pinto trotted along behind, presumably an apprentice learning the act. At some signal from Ali, the chestnut knelt, then lay down in the dirt, and Ali leapt off its back carrying a small vase of flowers, which he strode over and set down in front of me.

Fortunately, I had learned a word of Albanian for just such occasions, so I was able to say *"Faleminderit"* (thank you). As my companions clapped and laughed, Ali ran back to the horse, straddled it, and trotted off.

A few minutes later Ali rode back in, brandishing a flat grilling basket filled with fire-roasted whole fish. Down went the horse, off leapt Ali, and then he was at our table again, distributing the fish to our plates with his usual rapid-fire efficiency and serious demeanor. Everyone around us was grinning and snapping photos.

"Gëzojnë," Ali said.

"It means 'enjoy,'" said Reoland, smiling as he picked up his fork.

"Faleminderit," I replied. *"Faleminderit."*

An assistant handed Ali a metal basket of shrimp, and he swiftly added those to our plates. And then it was time for his grand exit. He ran back into the center where the chestnut horse stood waiting patiently. Ali gave the horse a slap on the cheek. It ignored him. He slapped it again.

Nothing happened. He leaned in and kissed its cheek. Immediately the horse dropped to its knees and lay in the dirt for Ali to mount. It was a lovely bit of theater, and everyone laughed some more and shot photos and videos with their phones. Ali and the horses threaded their way through the tables and disappeared in the direction of the corral.

I was still chuckling as I turned my attention to the food, which was simple and delicious, as fire-roasted meals tend to be. The fish proved to be hot, flaky and tender, with crusty skin drizzled with olive oil and dusted with coarse salt. I have no idea what kind it was, but I can tell you one thing for sure: it had a lot of bones. One of them lodged itself in my throat with a painful jab.

Fish bones are a fact of life, and I'd certainly dealt with my share over the years. Without any real concern, I swallowed a piece of bread. And some beer. And then some more bread. And then a lot more beer. The pain abated a little, as if perhaps part of the bone had broken off and now only a smaller splinter remained in place.

I swallowed yet more bread and considered my options: A) ignore it and hope it goes away, or B) seek medical assistance. No doubt Reoland could get me to a doctor. In fact, he seemed so competent and well-trained that I suspected he could perform an emergency tracheotomy with butter knife and a ball point pen if required. But I was rather hoping it wouldn't come to that.

And while I had every confidence in Reoland's skills, I wasn't eager to test those of the local clinic. "In small towns and rural areas, healthcare can be a problem," Gillian Gloyer's *Albania* had warned. "State hospitals are often short-staffed and their equipment is old and sometimes does not work at all; many rural clinics have closed altogether." I imagined someone — a local veterinarian, perhaps, or Ali himself — poking around in my throat with old tweezers and a flashlight. I shuddered and decided to take my chances with the fish bone.

I ate my meal very, very carefully, and managed to ignore the discomfort sufficiently to enjoy both the food and Rich's absolute delight at finally being here, in the place he'd dreamed of for so long. Toward the end of the meal, I whispered to him, "By the way, I seem to have a fish bone stuck in my throat." To which he replied, "Me, too." Good Lord, was everyone in the same boat? Well, if so, I certainly wasn't going to be the first to kick up a fuss.

(And not to keep you in suspense, ignoring the problem proved to be the right decision. By morning the bone had either broken free or dissolved away into nothing. At any rate, it never bothered me again. Rich said his had ceased being a problem within hours of leaving Ali Kali. Whew! Bullets officially dodged.)

After everyone had eaten and drunk to a state of stupefied satisfaction, Ali appeared one final time at our table. He carried a towel over one shoulder and held a metal pitcher and basin in his hands; it was time for post-lunch ablutions. He held the basin out with his left hand, poured the water with his right, then leaned his right shoulder forward to place the towel in more convenient reach.

"Boy, this guy really goes the extra mile," I murmured to Rich as I dried my fingers on the towel and smiled at Ali.

With clean hands, full tummy, and eyes still crinkled in merriment, I ignored the fish bone and sat back to enjoy the moment. This was convivial dining at its finest, surrounded by a dozens of people enjoying the simple pleasures of a trick horse, delicious food, and bit of silly fun. Voices rose in commentaries and jests, sending spurts of laughter ringing through the forest.

"Well?" I said to Rich, "What do you think of Ali Kali?"

"Even better than I'd hoped," he replied happily. And with that, I was well satisfied.

16. Tirana / *The Sword in the Lamb*

You won't be surprised to hear that Reoland convinced us to spend some time in Tirana, Albania's capital city. Obviously the article and guidebooks I'd read didn't tell the whole story, and I was curious to find out more. Besides, I wanted to see for myself the famous painted buildings that had caused so much fuss.

It's the sort of thing that can only happen when you have an art teacher as your mayor. Edi Rama was an artist, basketball player, and art teacher who was appointed as Minister of Culture, Youth and Sports in 1998. Two years later he was elected mayor of the notoriously dreary and troubled city of Tirana.

"With little money to repair the city's rundown infrastructure," wrote the *Guardian,* "Rama undertook a rough-and-ready makeover, ordering its drab, communist-era apartment buildings to be repainted in bright, bold colours. Blue and white stripes cascade down tower blocks; green squares punctuate coral-coloured facades. There's a palpable energy when you walk the streets of Tirana unlike anywhere else in the Balkans: the city's young, multiethnic, and literally multicoloured."

"The colors of the buildings were not art for me. It was a political action, with colors," explained Rama, who is now prime minister of the country. "Because we didn't have money to make big construction projects. People needed everything: water supply, roads, lighting. When I became mayor of Tirana, there were only seventy-eight lights functioning in the streets." As the city's landscape improved, so did residents' attitudes. "It had a chain effect I didn't imagine," said Rama. "Once the buildings were colored, people started to get rid of the heavy fences of their shops. In the painted roads, we had one hundred percent tax collection from the people, while tax collection was normally four percent. People accepted to pay their share for the city, because they realized through the colors that the city exists."

My Albanian guidebook, which always managed to find a dark cloud for every silver lining, noted that the paint project wasn't universally popular. "The colours and patterns became livelier and livelier, until even the more progressive of Tirana's citizens began to complain that their city was starting to look like a circus." Oh, come on. Did they really like it better when it looked like the Gulag? I doubt it.

As for me, the moment I saw Tirana's vibrant buildings, I fell in love with the whole wacky concept — even the most amateurish and garish efforts. One of my personal favorites was the freshly painted Ministry of Agriculture building, a vibrant persimmon red crisscrossed with a gold diamond pattern. Yowzer! To me — and I suspect to many residents — the flamboyant buildings are a shining symbol of the city's exuberant energy and determination to transform itself into a modern city, with a lifestyle that twenty years earlier its citizens had been forbidden even to dream about.

I like to imagine the late dictator Enver Hoxha turning in his grave over the metamorphosis of the nation's capital. He'd be apoplectic at the sight of everyone partying in the streets, consorting with international corporations, and painting the town persimmon. During his forty-four years in power, Hoxha fought tooth and nail against the pernicious influence of popular Western culture. He denounced the "spread of certain vulgar, alien tastes in music and art" which ran "contrary to socialist ethics and the positive traditions of our people," including "degenerate importations such as long hair, extravagant dress, screaming jungle music, coarse language, shameless behavior, and so on."

Needless to say, the moment Hoxha and his communist regime were gone, everyone — especially the younger generation — rushed to embrace the clothing, hair, music, language, and behavior that defined the modern world.

By the time I arrived, Tirana's downtown streets had become a hotbed of decadence, especially after dark, when the sidewalks filled with slickly dressed young people pouring in and out of an endless series of glitzy nightclubs throbbing to the beat of music that shook the windows and rattled the walls. The relentless trendiness extended to the restaurants, offering such world food as hamburgers and pizza in venues with glossy black interiors and amusing logos. Upmarket coffee bars were the latest craze, and Albanians took pride in the fact their country had the most coffee houses per capita in the world.

Tirana's makeover included new and refurbished museums designed to attract tourists and underscore how much better things were now than in the bad old days. The displays weren't always polished, but they were powerful. On our first day in town, Rich and I wandered into the Natural History Museum, and after considerable confusion over why it included information about fascism, communism, and Mother Theresa, we finally realized we'd misread the sign and were actually in the *National* History Museum. It was well worth a visit, although we didn't learn much about the local flora and fauna.

One of the most surprising exhibits dealt with the run-up to World War II and the rise of quirky King Zog, the only Muslim king in modern Europe. He had no royal blood, but his family was wealthy and powerful. At sixteen he assumed the governorship of Shkodër County when his father died in office, and by the age of twenty-seven, he was Albania's prime minister. In those days, Albania was a feudal system with an illiterate population, and Zog, who'd spent time in Vienna, was determined to drag his country into at least the nineteenth century, if the twentieth was

189

asking too much. There was plenty of resistance, and in 1928 he declared himself king to make it easier to get on with the job.

Like Rana's paint project, King Zog wasn't universally popular. There were 600 blood feuds against him, he survived at least 55 assassination attempts — including once being shot in Parliament — and his mother had to oversee the royal kitchen to make sure he wasn't poisoned.

He didn't get much respect abroad, either. "The European press portrayed Zog as a charming, exotic oddity," wrote Jeffrey Shucard in *Geist*. "In formal photographs we see him decked out in the full despot regalia of the epoch: chest laden with outsized medals and ribbons, shoulders replete with gold-braided, tasselled epaulettes. He looks for all the world like Errol Flynn playing Chaplin's Great Dictator, right down to the pencil-thin moustache, the insouciant smile and the rakish tilt of the visor cap."

In the 1930s, before Mussolini's fascists overran his country and forced him into exile, King Zog, leader of a nation that was three-quarters Muslim, quietly let it be known that the entire population of Albania stood ready to help European Jews fleeing Nazis persecution. Why? Because sheltering neighbors in need is a key concept of *besa*. To abandon those Jewish refugees to their fate without lifting a finger to help would have been unthinkable.

"Jews, who had escaped from other countries and who had literally been branded on the forehead with a J, were astonished to learn that the local population was jostling amongst themselves for the honour of sheltering them, for the honour of saving their lives," wrote the publication *Diplomat*. "Neighbours even shared the privilege, based on their ability to contribute to the welfare of their 'guest.' In one case, a rich neighbour fed the people in their care, while a poor neighbour gave them a bed to sleep in each night. No threats of punishment or death could cause these people to waver in their commitment." Albania was the only country in Europe whose Jewish population grew tenfold during World War II.

While those rescued Jews certainly had much to be thankful for, life in post-war Albania was no picnic. In fact, it was a grim and brutal business, as was vividly depicted in the Museum of National History's next exhibit area, the Pavilion of Communist Terror. I was peering at faded photos in the first glass case when a woman materialized at my elbow — presumably a docent or guard, although for all I know she could have been someone who'd wandered in off the street and just wanted to talk. She spent the next forty minutes describing, in heavily accented but intelligible English, Hoxha's stranglehold on the nation and ruthless determination to squash any hint of dissent.

I am still haunted by those photos: the secret police, the forced labor camps, the gaunt faces of prisoners. Among all the heartbreaking photos, the one I can still see most vividly is that of Simon Mirakaj. He was born in an Albanian concentration camp in 1945 and lived there until the communist regime ended in 1989. In the picture, taken some time in the 1980s, he looked like an ordinary, mild-mannered, middle-aged guy.

"Forty-five years in a cell," I said to Rich. "Can you imagine what that must have been like?"

"You can see for yourself what it was like," said our self-appointed guide. She led us to a corner where the museum had brought in an entire cell, to give us the real flavor of prison life (because who wouldn't want that?). "This housed three prisoners." I stared at the six by eight-foot room covered in filth and bloodstains, with chains hanging from the wall.

"Shoot me now," I muttered to Rich.

Eventually we thanked our guide and left behind the horrors of the museum, returning to bright sunshine and a bustling plaza in a free nation.

"Beer?" suggested Rich.

"God, yes."

We found a little bistro and restored our flagging spirits, then spent the rest of the day strolling the streets, finding examples, old and new, of the cheerful painting project begun by Rama in 2000. I saw rainbows, zig zags, stripes, and wilder patterns. Many were faded now, but others were freshly done and truly eyepopping. This was a city of contrasts, grim Hoxha-era administrative buildings enlivened with fresh paint, shabby apartment buildings with smart shops and discos on the ground floor, old people in somber grays while youngsters sported T-shirts emblazoned with fancy international logos.

The next morning, rested and refreshed, I felt strong enough to take another stroll down the dark side of Tirana's memory lane, so I suggested a visit to the House of Leaves. This was a graceful, vine-covered brick building originally constructed to house an obstetrics clinic. It later served as Gestapo headquarters before being taken over by the Sigurimi, Hoxha's secret police. Today it's officially known as the Museum of Secret Surveillance, "dedicated to the innocent people who were spied on, arrested, prosecuted, convicted and executed during the communist regime."

There were rooms displaying spy gadgets that looked almost ludicrously outdated, like something out of the old TV shows *Get Smart* and *The Man from U.N.C.L.E.* A tongue-in-cheek sign on the wall read "Attention dear guests! This room is bugged." But most of it was deadly serious, displaying harsh reminders of an era during which citizens were constantly spied on, and the smallest infraction, such as listening to an Italian song on the radio, could land you in a prison or concentration camp. Whispers, rumors, and lies scurried around the city like rustling leaves.

And then, in 1967, Hoxha outlawed God, making Albania the first officially atheist country in the world. More than 2,000 houses of worship were blown up with dynamite and 300,000 works of religious art and books were burned in the street. In 1974, he widened his scope still further, declaring that everything taking place outside the nation's borders — including all of twentieth century art and culture — was degenerate, corrupt, and strictly prohibited; violators would be prosecuted in unspeakable ways.

As a teenager at Tirana's art academy, Rama recalls the last slide in his introductory art history class showed a painting from 1854. "After that, it was just a white wall. The art history professor would tell us how bad things turned out. Some spoiled petit bourgeois kids who called themselves impressionists abandoned the working classes and transformed painting into an illusion. And then the schizophrenic Vincent van Gogh, and then the antisocial Paul Gauguin and the diabolical Pablo Picasso. All just words. Images were forbidden."

Travel to the outside world was, of course, prohibited, but Rama, who happened to be quite tall, joined the national basketball team and was eventually sent to play in Germany. Sneaking out of the hotel in Bremen, he went to a museum. "I still remember the unique perfume of the parquet and the sound of silence. It was morning. Nobody was there. First was Rodin, and then I was in front of Picasso. I couldn't believe it."

Today, Tirana enthusiastically embraces Western art and culture, capitalist ideas, and as many tourists as it can attract. Remaking itself as a vacation destination is very much a work in progress. Officials have adopted the slogan "Tirana: the Place Beyond Belief," which strikes me as the sort of ambiguous phrase that could easily come back to haunt them in later years. No matter, the city's economy is in growth mode now, and residents and an increasing number of business visitors and vacationers are flocking to the glamorous bars and restaurants springing up along the main boulevards.

One evening, as we were strolling about downtown and just beginning to think about dinner, Rich and I happened upon the demonstration I'd heard all those warnings about. There was a large crowd — a couple of thousand, at a guess — but it seemed peaceful enough. A speaker was droning on and on. Those nearby listened respectfully, but at the edges of the crowd, people were talking quietly among themselves, sounding more as if they were discussing where to go for a beer afterwards than plotting violent regime change.

I decided Reoalnd was right about this demonstration; it didn't seem to pose a serious threat, at least to the casual passer-by at this early hour of the evening. Maybe they'd build up steam and rampage through the streets later? (Afterwards I read things got a little boisterous as the night wore on, but nothing as wild as the riots I recall from my student days at the University of California Berkeley.) Just to be on the safe side, Rich and I slipped away from the demonstration and dined close to our hotel, where all remained serene. The food was fine, but nothing like the culinary delight that would come the following evening.

Reoland and Irmira had proved such entertaining companions that after our lunch at Ali Kali, we'd invited them to join us for dinner at a place Reoland had recommended: Ceren Ismet Shehu. It was one of the area's hottest new venues, he said, and offered spectacular views from tables perched on a hillside overlooking the city. Best of all, they were famous for tender, succulent lamb cooked in an outdoor kitchen. It all sounded marvelous.

Arriving at Ceren Ismet Shehu, I followed our Albanian friends up a long flight of stone steps under leafy arbors. As we drew closer to the top, I began seeing low wooden tables surrounded with bales of hay covered in the traditional manner with sheepskins and colorful blankets. Off to one side I glimpsed the outdoor kitchen and beside that, out on the open hillside, a bed of coals where chunks of lamb and whole potatoes were slowly roasting. Perhaps two dozen tables were scattered about, some tucked under trees, others on the bare hillside, with unobstructed views of the city far below. There was a cozy indoor dining room as well, but on this lovely warm evening, everyone was outside, settling in to enjoy the fresh country air and delicious food.

The owner and chef, Ismet Shehu, stopped by our table and introduced himself; he was an apple-cheeked man with thinning hair and a friendly grin. "I went to the UK and started as a dishwasher," he told me. "I worked my way up to chef. Then two years ago I came home and made this restaurant for my family. I didn't tell my mother until it was ready; I brought her here as a surprise." I can only imagine how dazzled she must have been. I thought: here was another Albanian who had managed to seize the moment, parlaying a very modest opportunity into a shining career.

Shehu was one terrific cook. Our meal began with ground goat meat stuffed with quail eggs, spinach *burek*, layered *flia* pastry, cheese with blueberries, fig rounds, pink pasta stuffed with green cheese, yogurt dip, tomato salad, and more.

Just when I thought I couldn't possibly eat another bite, a wooden platter arrived bearing a gorgeous portion of lamb with a carving knife embedded dramatically upright in the middle of it, like Excalibur in the Arthurian legend. "I'm calling this one 'The Sword in the Lamb,'" I whispered to Rich.

Reoland explained the lamb had been simmered in milk inside a clay pot which explained why it was so incredibly tender, succulent, and melting off the bone. Yes, of course, I managed to find room for it. Somehow. It seemed the least I could do for my readers.

Sitting, replete, at that table, I looked around at all the Albanians who were lucky enough to be living in this era and engaging in one of life's most essential pleasures: gathering outdoors on a warm summer night to enjoy great food in congenial company. Sipping my wine in the deepening twilight, I thought about all I'd learned in the past few days about the people of this city, who had lived with horrors I could scarcely imagine and had come through it all with enough strength and optimism to believe a better future was within their grasp.

As we started down the stone steps at the end of the meal, I turned to Rich and said, "Well?"

"That was the best lamb I've ever tasted," he said. "But you know what would have made it even better? Being carried in on the back of a horse."

I couldn't argue with his logic.

17. Shkodër / *Chickens of the Accursed Mountains*

Having bid a fond farewell to Reloland, Irmira , and Tirana, Rich and I headed to the far northern reaches of Albania, to a city dating back to the Bronze Age and perched in the foothills of the Accursed Mountains. With a pedigree like that, you'd think the city would be dramatic, or at least a little picturesque, but you would be wrong. My first impression of Shkodër was that it was one of the most relentlessly unremarkable towns ever built. I stepped out of the bus in the central Sheshi Demokracia (Democracy Square) into a landscape of uninspired hotels, blandly modern apartment buildings, and shabby little shops, garages, and cafés. Possibly an OK place to live, but (I thought then) who would want to visit there?

However, as I collected my bag from underneath the bus and dragged it to the curb, I began noticing some rather unusual folks passing by.

While people in the modern uniform of jeans, t-shirts, and sneakers were visible everywhere, sprinkled in among them were some who appeared to have ridden in on horseback from the remoter villages of the Accursed Mountains. I saw several robust matriarchs in traditional outfits dating back centuries (the outfits, that is, not the matriarchs): spotless white cotton blouses and skirts layered over loose white trousers and topped with striped aprons. White caps sat atop shoulder-length hair so stiff and black I wondered if they touched it up with shoe polish or soot. Men in ancient waistcoats and cloth caps drove horse carts piled with coarsely woven sacks filled with grain or charcoal.

I began to realize that Shkodër was the borderland between modern Albania and the land of the ancestors. Yes, there were high-rises, cell phones, and many other trappings of twenty-first century life, but just a few miles away people were still going out to the barn to kill something for dinner and cooking it in a stove fueled with wood hewn from the forest outside their door.

"I've heard," Rich said, "that you can arrange for farm stays around here. We should look into that."

"Absolutely." But right then all I could think about was a recombobulation coffee and a taxi to our lodgings.

The Hotel Tradita turned out to be a marvelously atmospheric Ottoman-style inn built around a sprawling courtyard. Tables were set beneath old olive trees, waiters in striped sashes served traditional fare cooked over open fires, and musicians played folk songs late into the evening. This was a mixed blessing, as our no-frills room overlooked the courtyard, but I found I quite liked drifting off to sleep hearing ancient melodies mingled with low-voiced talk and laughter. Nothing seemed to have changed much since Ottoman times; I was told that parts of the hotel dated back to 1694.

"I'll tell you what part dates back to 1694," grumbled Rich the next morning. "It's these pillows. What are they stuffed with?"

"Slabs of old tractor tires, maybe? Whatever it is, I think it's permanently imprinted on my neck."

I scrounged up some elderly but more pliable throw pillows from a bench in the corridor and tucked them into our pillowcases. This was a decided improvement, although no doubt the hotel maids puzzled over this curious American eccentricity. Every morning they replaced the throw pillows with "real" ones, and every night I switched them back.

The courtyard restaurant was popular with travelers, and I soon learned that nearly every foreigner in Shkodër was passing through en route to the Accursed Mountains, specifically to a tiny village called Theth. The more I learned about it, the more determined I was not to go there.

According to local legend, Theth was founded in the seventeenth century by Ded Nika, who was seeking a safe place to practice his Catholic faith. The village grew to a few hundred families and maintained its isolation and traditional lifestyle until quite recently. And then, incredibly — and I know you'll be as shocked by this as I am — the younger generation decided they didn't want to get up at five in the morning to milk the goats. They wanted to move to a city, get tattoos, drink cocktails, have wild sexual adventures with inappropriate strangers, and do everything else they saw in the movies. The town's modest population began dwindling at an alarming rate. What to do? Why not start marketing the town to tourists?

Perhaps the biggest draw (besides the name Accursed Mountains, of course) is the monumental difficulty of getting to Theth. You can't drive there at all in winter, and in summer there's a legendary twenty-five-kilometer stretch of rough, unpaved road requiring an all-terrain vehicle and an exceedingly strong stomach. One intrepid-looking, twenty-something British couple told me all about it, shuddering as they recalled the endless, wild lurching over narrow passes above sheer, instantly fatal drops.

"After a while," one of them told me, "we just put our heads together, closed our eyes, and held on to one another until it was over."

Travelers who survived the ordeal earned all sorts of street cred and bragging rights. Or at least, they used to.

The glory and glamour dimmed as the crowds grew. #Theth began trending on social media. Hoards descended on the village. Now even with half the homes converted to B&Bs, visitors were advised to book well in advance to secure lodgings and a seat on one of the muscular vehicles plying the rough road to Albania's hottest rural destination. A visitors' center was under construction, and no doubt villagers were already standing by selling maps to the trailheads for that genuine, unspoiled Accursed Mountain hiking experience.

I'm never keen on following the crowd, so every time someone asked brightly, "You're going to Theth, of course?" I shook my head thankfully and ignored their quizzical looks when I explained that I was finding plenty to interest me right there in Shkodër.

Early on, I arranged to interview the young chef who cooked at the Florian Shkodra Guest House. Emanuela was one of the new breed of Albanian farm women; she had a career of her own cooking meals for an institution in town, then returned home every evening to prepare dinner for her family and whatever visitors were currently in residence at the guesthouse run by her brother, Florian.

During our initial exchange of emails, Florian told me his was the first guesthouse ever to open in Albania, and that his family had lived in the home since the late 1940s, growing nearly everything they ate on their modest plot of land just a few miles outside the city. Florian was the family entrepreneur, running the guesthouse, organizing guided tours, renting out cars and bikes, and arranging cooking demonstrations like the one I was about to see.

Florian sent a car and driver to fetch us, and in no time the drab high rises of downtown Shkodër were disappearing in the rear view mirror; for a city of 135,000, it was remarkably compact. Now I was surrounded by green fields where farmers were tilling the old-fashioned way, by horse or hand-held hoe. In the uncultivated patches I saw lush meadows dotted with grazing cows and sheep. The deep silence was broken only by the hum of insects, the occasional barking of a distant dog, and the rumble of the car's motor.

The driver — who spoke not a word of English — pulled up in front of a big, gray metal gate flanked by walls on which someone had carefully spray painted "GUEST HOUSE" in large red and white letters. Rich and I climbed out and stepped through the gate.

I found myself on a flat stone path shaded by grapevines and lined with flowers. To my left stood neat rows of vegetables, and on my right was a small vineyard where Florian's father, Zeff, clad only in a pair of denim shorts and plastic shower shoes, was busy digging in the dirt at the base of the vines. He nodded politely as I passed but didn't pause in his labors. I later learned that he'd spent twenty years building concrete defense bunkers for the mad dictator Hoxha — somewhere around 200 of them, Zeff calculated. Now he was retired and tended the family's vegetables, herbs, and grapes.

The cook, Emanuela, was a young, dark-haired woman who greeted me pleasantly in excellent English, led me to a table in the garden shaded by overhead vines, and got right back to work. She was tremendously energetic and efficient, never pausing in her labors, always rushing on to the next task. Rich, who loves gardening, was delighted to pass the time puttering around looking at the plants and occasionally chatting with Florian, who strolled about barefoot, smoking cigarettes and taking his ease.

Ema, as the family called her, began by grating zucchini for fritters, tossing the scraps into the pen where the chickens made a mad dash for them, clucking excitedly. Setting the grated zucchini aside, she prepared dough for *burek*, the Balkans' beloved pie. Her version involved making fourteen tiny balls of dough and rolling each one out to a circle that was paper thin and precisely the size of her pan. Seven layers of dough went on the bottom, then came the filling of nettles and onion, then another seven layers on top. Ema ran inside the house to put the *burek* in the oven, then returned to the table to make the fritters by adding egg, onion, fresh milk, salt, pepper, garlic, and flour to the grated zucchini.

Then the action moved from the garden table to the outdoor kitchen, which consisted of a pair of burners sitting on a table under a wooden overhang. The timing was perfect, as the light, intermittent drizzle was now gathering strength and becoming serious rain.

Ema's mother rounded up the chickens, chasing them to a sheltered little corral behind the outdoor kitchen, where they'd be protected from the downpour and out from underfoot. A few stragglers, too hysterical to follow their companions to safety, tore off in the opposite direction and ran around clucking madly. Eventually Ema's mother shooed into the main pen, where they stood in the downpour glaring at everyone, living embodiments of the phrase, "mad as a wet hen."

In the outdoor kitchen, Ema already had vegetables simmering on one burner and oil coming to a boil on the other. Now she quickly dropped globs of the fritter dough into the oil, where it bubbled, hissed, and turned golden brown. Meanwhile, she took the vegetables off the stove and began spooning them into bell peppers. This done, she dashed back inside the tiny indoor kitchen, removed the *burek* from the oven and slid in the stuffed peppers. While they baked, she assembled a zucchini cake for dessert.

She never measured anything except by eye and hand, and although she wore no watch and never seemed to glance at a clock, timer, or phone, she always knew precisely the right moment to remove something from the oven or a burner. It was a remarkable performance, and as everyone was gathering at the table, I asked Ema if she did this every night, after working her eight-hour shift in the downtown kitchen.

"Yes, of course." She then confided that she was saving up to marry her boyfriend and move to Switzerland. And who could blame her? As charming as it was to cook in the garden with the scent of freshly turned earth and the soft clucking of the hens, I thought it would get very old, very quickly if you had to do it every day.

I pictured Ema in a sleek Swiss high-rise apartment, sitting in one of those yellow Ikea armchairs with her feet up on a footstool, eating take-out and drinking beer. Or a martini. Would she, I wondered, get a tattoo or two? I thanked her for sharing her recipes and wished her well in her next life.

Back in Shkodër once more, Rich and I found plenty to keep ourselves entertained. We explored mosques, churches, quirky shops, plazas, and the market where live fish waited in buckets of water to be sold for someone's dinner. In the Marubi Photography Museum, the work of several generations of a family of photographers made it clear that the city and its people hadn't changed all that much since 1856.

People-watching was a constant delight in Shkodër, and I loved the mix of rugged country folk and street-smart urbanites. At a café-bar near the hotel, I often saw one heavyset character sprawling at an outdoor corner table nursing a late-morning beer. I could never decide whether this was a feminine-looking man, a masculine-looking woman, or that peculiarly Albanian non-gender individual known as a "sworn virgin."

The concept of a sworn virgin dates back to the bad old days, when women were defined as chattel and couldn't sign contracts, vote, wear a watch, smoke, or do much of anything else without a man's permission. (Don't get me started on how I feel about this.) Traditional *Kanun* law was strict but provided a single loophole for a woman wishing to change her status.

Under special circumstances — for instance, if she needed to run the family business after her father or husband died — a woman could officially become a sworn virgin. This was a legally binding contract with society in which she agreed to adopt the dress, demeanor, and legal rights of a man and to remain celibate for the rest of her life. For some, this was a last resort driven by dire necessity, while others viewed it as the freedom to be their authentic selves in public.

Today, there are few sworn virgins around because — to give the mad old dictator his due — Hoxha overturned *Kanun* law, educated women, and brought them into the work force, where they held positions of considerable power, including important government posts. Females didn't have to give up sex, cut their hair, or dress in trousers to be taken seriously in the workplace anymore. But there were still a few sworn virgins around, people who found the lifestyle more comfortable than the gender role they were assigned at birth. If the person at that café-bar had made such a choice, more power to her. Or rather, him. According to historian Marina Warner, the sworn virgin's "true sex will never again, on pain of death, be alluded to either in her presence or out of it."

I could certainly see the practical advantage of gaining autonomy after a lifetime of being subjugated by male relatives. As if any more proof of this were needed, there's a strange and gruesome legend associated with Shkodër's ancient stronghold, Rozafa Castle. Perched on a promontory above the city, the castle offers spectacular views of the vast Lake Shkodër and the rugged grandeur of the Accursed Mountains. Some say there's been a castle on the spot for 4,000 years, but the oldest remaining walls date back "only" to the fourth century. If the original walls would talk, here's the story they'd tell.

According to legend, three brothers were in charge of the castle's construction, and while they worked industriously every day, every night the foundations would collapse again. Eventually an old man came by, watched them for a while, then told them he knew how to solve the problem. The brothers naturally pressed him for details.

"Are you all married?" he asked.

They replied that yes, they all were.

"If you really want to finish the castle," the old man said, "you must swear never to tell your wives what I am going to tell you now. The wife who brings you your food tomorrow — you must bury her alive in the wall of the castle. Only then will the foundations stay put and last forever."

The three brothers swore on the honor code of *besa* to not say anything about all this to their wives. But the older two ran right home and told their wives everything, instructing them to stay away the next day. So it was the youngest brother's wife, Rozafa, who showed up with the midday meal and was told that she was required to make the ultimate sacrifice for the good of her people.

She allegedly agreed without protest, adding, "I have but one request to make. When you wall me in, leave a hole for my right eye, for my right hand, for my right foot, and for my right breast. I have a small son. When he starts to cry, I will cheer him up with my right eye, I will comfort him with my right hand, I will rock him to sleep in his cradle with my right foot, and I will feed him with my right breast. Let my breast turn to stone and the castle flourish. May my son become a great hero, ruler of the world." And so it came to pass, and they named the castle in her honor.

Really? That's how it went down? I don't know about you, but I have some serious issues with this story.

First, it was the men's fault they couldn't build decent foundations, so why wasn't one of them walled up in the building (preferably the incompetent chief designer)? How did the older brothers and their wives get away with violating the allegedly iron-clad rules of *besa*, while the honorable younger brother lost his good wife? Why did the wife agree to this insane plan? Because really, how would sealing her up inside a wall strengthen the building's structure in any way whatsoever? And for how long are her eye, hand, foot, and breast going to serve the baby after the rest of her is walled up?

Inexplicably, the ancient tale of Rozafa's hideous (and pointless) tragedy became all the rage in nineteenth century literary circles. An epic poem about it caught the attention of Jacob Grimm (of *Grimm's Fairy Tale* fame), who translated it into German and called it "one of the most touching poems of all nations and all times." It was published by Johan Wolfgang Goethe, acclaimed as Germany's greatest and most influential writer, who never really warmed to the tale, calling it "superstitiously barbaric." Ya think?

This story rather put me off Rozafa Castle and I considered giving it a miss. But it's one of the major sights in the city, so in the end I agreed we really ought to pay it a visit.

You'll recall that this was the hottest summer in European history, and like sensible travelers, Rich and I made a huge effort to get out the door early, when it was marginally cooler. But despite our best intentions, it must have been nearly noon by the time we finally got across town to the base of the hill on which the castle stood.

I remember stumbling up the steep, rocky trail to the castle and arriving, breathless, at the first courtyard. I staggered to the parapet, intending to look out at the stunning view, but found my vision beginning to blur and darken. "I have to …" I muttered. "I'd better…" Seconds later I was sitting on a fragment of fourth-century wall with my head between my knees.

And it was in this moment that it truly hit me that I was aging. All my life I've been remarkably heat-tolerant and able to soldier on no matter what climb or climate presented itself: the Himalayas, the Amazon jungle, volcanos, pyramids, Seville in August. But now I simply, physically couldn't take another step. The spirit might be willing, but my body was saying, "Sit down, you idiot. Drink some water. Catch your breath. Then go find some shade." And above all, *"Don't do this again."*

It was a pivot point in my travel life. I vowed to make an effort to show a little common sense from now on. (In this I was only partially successful, as you'll see later.)

"This view is totally — hey, are you OK? What's wrong?" said

Rich.

"I'm having an epiphany." I drank more water and filled him in.

"We should go," he said.

"Yes, we should," I agreed.

I was sorry that I wouldn't get to see the stunning view from every angle of the battlements, but there was no shade anywhere, and I needed to be sensible. Besides, leaving now would let me avoid the museum, which I had been dreading. It housed a life-sized modern sculpture showing poor Rozafa half-buried in the castle wall, with her various body parts sticking out. It sounded hideous on so many levels; I was relieved not to have that image seared into my brain forever.

I rested a few more minutes, took one last glug of water, and hoisted myself to my feet. As we began the long downhill walk, I noted five powerful all-terrain vehicles, heavily splashed with mud, parked near the entrance. No doubt they'd just arrived carrying a load of white-faced tourists fresh from the bone-jarring, death-defying roads of the Accursed Mountains. At least the travelers been spared the long, hot uphill climb to the castle on top of that ordeal.

Around the next bend in the trail, we came upon an accordion player, a man of about my own age who gave me a merry grin and struck up a lively tune. Without an instant's hesitation, Rich raised his arms and began to dance. It was a marvelous moment, and all three of us were laughing as Rich came panting to a standstill, hand over his heart. Just then I noticed three young Albanian men walking past, staring at us disapprovingly. I could almost hear them thinking, "I am never going to be that old or that uncool." Which just made me laugh even harder. Oh yes, you will, boys. Trust me.

Later that day, as I lay on the sofa drinking glass after glass of cool water, Rich brought up the idea of the farm stay again. "I've read about one place where the traditional food is said to be exceptional. It's a couple of hours away in a chestnut forest."

At least there would be shade, I thought. "Do we need a four-wheel-drive vehicle to get there?" I asked suspiciously.

"Nope, just a taxi."

"I'm in!"

"And I thought we'd go luggage-free. I mean, it's just one night. What do we need besides a toothbrush?"

What indeed? Rich sat down at his laptop to fire off an email. The timing was perfect; he arranged to go in a couple of days, on what would be our next-to-last night in Albania. It seemed a good way to wrap up this portion of the trip.

As the confirmations flew back and forth, Rich passed me his laptop, and I added a note to our hosts explaining about the Mediterranean Comfort Food Tour, my desire to see traditional dishes being prepared, and the fact that Rich and I had light appetites. We'd be delighted to sample everything but hoped they wouldn't be disappointed or offended if we couldn't finish everything they set in front of us. They seemed agreeable on all points.

The car service next door to the hotel was happy to take us to the farm in time for lunch and collect us after breakfast the following day. The burly driver didn't speak any English, but he seemed a jovial fellow and was clearly a competent and cautious driver. Where were they keeping all the drunk and disorderly motorists I'd read about in the guidebook? What little traffic I saw seemed pretty tame. Don't think I wasn't grateful.

After an hour or so on major roads, we entered the foothills of the Accursed Mountains, and the driver turned off beside a large prison. I was relieved that the journey didn't end there but continued on through green fields, up thickly wooded slopes with ever taller trees, past tiny farms, and into the great chestnut forest of Pylli I Gështenjave, for which we had Alexander the Great to thank.

As his nickname suggests, Alexander was a chronic overachiever. While running around shifting the balance of world power, he happened to be in the Turkish city of Sardis and came across the sweet, nutritious "Sardian nut." The trees were fast growing, hardy, and capable of providing carb-laden food at altitudes too high to grow wheat. He began planting the seeds across Europe on his various campaigns. From then on, countless mountain villages stepped back from the brink of starvation because of "Zeus's acorns" — or, as later Europeans would call them, chestnuts. Nice work, Alex!

The driver brought the car to a neat a stop in front of a modest white house where two women stood on the shaded porch. Our hostess, Zina, was a bright-eyed, dark-haired woman of about fifty. Her daughter-in-law, Diana, who would serve as translator, stood with a baby on one hip wearing the glazed look of new mothers everywhere. The driver got out and exchanged a few words with the women; as usual in Albania, *besa* required that guests be officially handed over to the care of the next person responsible for them.

"Would you like coffee?" Diana asked.

When I said yes, Zina made a gesture inviting us to sit at an outdoor table set beneath a wooden roof. She disappeared into the house and returned moments later with a tray bearing tiny cups of espresso and — apparently this was so automatic that it didn't need to be discussed — small glasses of *raki,* homemade fruit brandy. She set out coffee and *raki* for us and for our driver, who sat down with pleasure to refresh himself after the long journey.

I took a cautions sip of the *raki*, which had a throat searing flavor and an alcohol content somewhere to the north of zowie. When I recovered my powers of speech, I said to Diana, "This is wonderful." She nodded.

As I would soon learn, she was a woman of few words. In an effort to keep the conversation going I added, "I can never tell when to drink *raki*. Some people say before a meal to prepare the stomach. Others say after to improve digestion. Last night someone suggested it with our meal. I've also heard it's always drunk with coffee." I realized I was babbling and closed my mouth.

"I have *raki* every morning with my coffee," said Diana. "It helps me start my day."

"Where do you work?" I asked, hoping it didn't involve driving or operating heavy machinery.

"I teach English in a school."

I wondered if any of my old schoolteachers ever did the same. It would explain a lot. Especially about some of the nuns.

The farmhouse was spacious and impeccably clean, every window offering views of mountains, cornfields, and the vast chestnut forest. Our bedroom held old-fashioned wooden furniture including a wardrobe big enough to contain all of Narnia. It was wasted on us, of course, as we were traveling without luggage, but I appreciated the thought.

The online description had mentioned a private bathroom, but as I'd learned the hard way, "private" doesn't always mean attached to your room for your exclusive use. It can also signify "not open to the general public but everyone here may use it." In this case, the bathroom was down the hall, but as Rich and I were the only guests, and the only people sleeping on our floor, it hardly mattered.

After settling in, which obviously didn't take long without any luggage, Rich and I decided to go for a short walk while Zina finished preparations for lunch.

"Would you like to see the chestnut forest?" Diana asked. I nodded.

Her father-in-law, Mirash, beckoned. We followed him into the woods, where he pointed to the path and then to a red and white arrow crudely painted on a fencepost. I took this to be a signpost leading us … somewhere. Mirash turned back toward the farm house, and Rich and I set off in the direction of the arrow, heading deeper into the canopy of huge chestnut trees.

Diana had told me that each family in the community was assigned a section of trees from which they could harvest the chestnuts as a cash crop. This enabled them to buy a few luxuries such as salt and sugar; everything else was raised on their own handful of acres. My mind boggled at the thought. Farm to fork sounds wonderful when you're at the fork end of the process, but here was the labor-intensive farm end, with its countless hours of drudgery and no guarantees that some storm or blight won't ruin you overnight. I was profoundly grateful that this was not my destiny.

Splashes of red and white paint on various rocks and tree trunks guided the way through the forest and out to the narrow road, where I had a fine time photographing ancient barns, rough wooden gates, and chickens hunting up their lunch. Returning to the house, I saw ours had been laid out on the garden table. It was a splendid meal, with platters of roast chicken, tomato and cucumber salad, sauteed mushrooms, spinach-stuffed *burek*, cheeses, breads, and yet more.

Zina and Diana fussed around, pouring fruit juice, accepting compliments with modesty and grace, adjusting the position of the plates until perfection was achieved. Then they retired to the house, leaving us alone — unless you count the eight or ten chickens wandering about underfoot. I felt a little guilty to think I was eating one of their mates, who I must say was delicious.

After a long siesta and another short stroll along the winding lanes, it was time for the main event: making dinner. Zina welcomed us into her kitchen, and it was soon clear she was justifiably proud of her ability to create a feast from simple ingredients — milk from Lara their cow, vegetables from their garden, meat from their pigs. I was pleased to see Mirash pitch in, cheerfully helping with the cooking and minding Diana's baby.

Over the next few hours, Zina ruled the kitchen, chopping, stirring, frying, directing the work of the others. She frequently fed the woodburning stove, a rather terrifying process in which she shoved each piece of firewood deep into the blazing inferno, seemingly impervious to the heat engulfing her hand and wrist. She was one tough cookie.

Cheese was the star of the show. Zina whipped up a batch of *maze e zier*, which translates as "boiled cheese," even though it's made in a frying pan. The ingredients are super simple: cheese, flour, and water. The technique, however, involved a complicated series of flips to keep the edges moving toward the center so it cooks to precisely the right viscous consistency. When she was satisfied, Zina poured it into bowls and drizzled it with honey. This is traditionally served to greet guests, and I can tell you it certainly made me feel welcome.

Another of the main dishes was *kaçimak*, a sort of cornbread with extremely stiff dough; Mirash was recruited for the long, arduous beating process. When she judged the desired consistency had been achieved, Zina dropped clumps of the dough into a pan, close-packed like biscuits; they would merge into a bumpy round loaf while baking. She prepared two batches, one with butter-cheese topping, the other topped with bits of pork from the smokehouse.

Dinner was served in the garden, and once again Rich and I were left to eat in solitary splendor, with only the chickens and some hopeful cats for company. We gorged ourselves to bursting and still felt horribly guilty that we weren't able to consume more than a small fraction of what was on the table.

"At least they'll have plenty of leftovers," I said, surveying the remains. "This has to be a week's worth of food for the family."

By now the sunset had reached its colorful zenith over the chestnut forest, turning the sky a breathtaking mix of purple, orange, and gold; against this flaming backdrop, the trees turned a deep emerald. The little wooden feed shed at the clearing's edge was visible only as a crooked silhouette, like something from an old woodcut in a book of fairy tales. I jumped up to take a photo and Rich wandered after me. We gazed in awe at the beauty for a moment and then I turned around.

"Aughhhh!" I shouted. "Oh my God, the cats!"

In the short time my back was turned, the cats had seemingly multiplied from three to a dozen — or was it a hundred? — and were swarming all over the table, gulping down the leftovers. I grabbed my napkin and began flapping it at them, shouting, until they jumped down and disappeared into the darkness. I felt I'd been horribly lax to allow food to be stolen by the animals. No doubt Zina and her family were inside, watching the whole episode, rolling their eyes and thinking, "City slickers. Americans. What can you expect?"

The next morning the cats were nowhere to be seen. Rich and I ambled around making friends with the family's other animals. I spent some time thanking Lara the cow for her contributions to last night's feast; she ignored me and kept on grazing in her little field. I greeted two engaging young pigs with lively eyes and tried not to calculate how long it would take for them to plump enough to qualify for the smokehouse.

By the time we returned from the walk, Zina had prepared an enormous breakfast of pancakes with homemade fruit compote and honey, fried eggs, slabs of smoky cheese, and large glasses of hot, fresh milk with little pools of butterfat floating on the surface.

As soon as we were alone, I said to Rich, "It's like drinking it directly from Lara's udder. I really can't."

To my astonishment and admiration, Rich manfully downed his glass. "My parents gave me warm milk as a kid," he explained with an

213

offhand shrug. "I'm not crazy about it, but I can drink the stuff."

And that's the beauty of travel. You learn things about each other that somehow never came up, even in more than three decades of conversation.

Rich may credit his upbringing, but I know the real reason he was able to belly up to that milk so cheerfully: before breakfast, he'd already downed a glass of *raki* along with his early morning coffee.

"I can never figure out when to drink what," he said. "But I know why I'm drinking it: because it's there."

And I suppose that's as good a policy as any.

BOSNIA & HERZEGOVINA

18. Trebinje & Mostar / *Ćevapi (Never Call It Sausage)*

Having enjoyed Albania far more than I'd dared to hope, I was having a difficult time working up much enthusiasm for the next item on the itinerary, a brief stopover in Podgorica, the capital of Montenegro.

I'd visited the city in 2013 and found it heartbreaking. The incredible natural beauty of the landscape, with a winding river at its heart and dramatic hills in the distance, was crushed beneath the weight of giant blocks of brutish Soviet architecture marching across the plane, with the occasional low, grim bunker for visual relief. It looked like the set of a cheesy, low-budget dystopian movie. How could anyone, at any time in history, actually choose to create human dwellings and workplaces that were so thoroughly soul-blighting? I understood the Soviets were making a point about workers being insignificant cogs in the great machinery of the State, but still.

On that first visit, Rich and I had arrived by a late train and taken a taxi directly to a pleasant if unremarkable hotel in a non-descript part of town. The next morning, after an early breakfast at the hotel, we took a walk, strolling past a handful of small shops, a few cafés, and a broad, empty plaza with a modest fountain. At that point, having exhausted the delights of the neighborhood, I suggested going back to the hotel for a map that would show us how to get downtown, where they must be keeping the exciting stuff. (This was in the dark days before everyone had GPS on their phones.)

"Map?" said the desk clerk. "There is no map."

I'd never been in a capital city that didn't have some kind of a map. How were visitors supposed to find their way around? How was I going to pass the four hours until my train left? I asked if she could direct me to the center of the city.

"This *is* the center of the city."

I reeled for a moment, gobsmacked by this news, then soldiered on. "Can you suggest some things to see or do? Museums? Monuments? Historical buildings?"

She looked at me blankly. "You could go to a café and have a coffee," was the best she could come up with.

But that was years ago. Would time have done anything to improve the Montenegrin capital? Would I find it much different now?

Encouragingly, there were several new, gleaming, high-rise hotels, and Rich had booked us into one. I arrived to find it clean, modern, and decorated with the conventional elegance favored by corporate owners everywhere on the planet.

As the dinner hour was fast approaching, I suggested staying in and grabbing a bite in the hotel's main restaurant. This was on an upper floor offering sweeping views of the brutalist architecture, which didn't look any less ominous than it had in 2013. Too bad Edi Rama wasn't around to paint everything in persimmon and rainbows. The distant hills shimmered softly in the twilight.

The menu was as determinedly international as the decor, but I was pleased to see one traditional dish, Montenegro's favorite comfort food, *Njeguški pršut* (smoked ham). Living in Seville had given me plenty of opportunities to enjoy Spanish *jamón,* and I was curious to try the

Montenegrin version, which was produced in the southern village of Njeguški and modeled on Italian *prosciutto* — hence the name.

I placed my order, and after a suitable interval for the hand-carving ritual in the kitchen, the waiter returned bearing a plate on which lay beautifully arranged slivers of rich red ham. Although not as tender as Spanish *jamón*, *Njeguški pršut* had a robust flavor, with a pleasantly salty tang and just enough fattiness to give satisfaction.

The morning bus carried us north across the border into Bosnia and Herzegovina and dropped us off in the small city of Trebinje. Established in medieval times, the city was lucky enough to have escaped the twentieth century's brutalist architectural craze and had preserved its historic buildings, most notably in the eighteenth-century Ottoman center where we'd taken lodgings. Our apartment was small and bland, but its location couldn't have been better.

A few blocks away stood a large park shaded by tall trees, and every morning people gathered there to sell fruit, vegetables, walnuts, honey, and other farm fresh foodstuff. My fondest memories of Trebinje are of waking in the cool morning, throwing on some clothes, buying fluffy white rolls in the nearby bakery, then browsing through the park's market for ripe peaches and little jars of honey. Having gathered our breakfast, Rich and I would then carry it into the big, tree-shaded outdoor café and order coffee. Nobody ever objected to us bringing in food or being eccentric enough to drink coffee with the morning meal.

I loved sitting under the shade of those tall trees, lazily sipping coffee and drizzling honey over the still-warm bread. Often there were honey-drenched walnuts at the bottom of the jar, and fishing them out was a messy but rewarding business. The town planners had thoughtfully placed a spring-fed fountain nearby, so I could rinse my hands clean in cool fresh water afterwards.

Breakfast was the least complicated meal of the day, the only time

I could order without feeling I was walking a cultural tightrope over a minefield. I did my best, and people were kind enough to overlook my occasional faux pas, but I was aware, all the same, that every dish on the menu was served with a side order of social and political implications.

Take *ćevapi*, for instance, about which many online articles had warned, "Don't ever call it sausage!" Just because it was shaped like a sausage, looked, smelled, and tasted like a sausage did NOT mean … you get the idea. Bosnians were touchy on this point because sausage is associated with pork, which is prohibited for Muslims, who comprise fifty percent of Bosnia's population. *Ćevapi*, on the other hand, is a theologically neutral mix of ground lamb and beef with a bit of onion. It's formed in an oblong shape (giving rise to the dreaded sausage comparisons) before being grilled and served on a flatbread called *somun*. "Don't ever call it pita bread!" Why? It's all about cultural identity.

That's life in the Balkans, where even the simplest meal has geopolitical and religious implications. And perhaps this is the right moment to touch on the complexity of identity in the Balkans. This will take a little while; you might want to stop and put the kettle on. Wait, skip all that; it's too exhausting. For now, I'll just give you a few quick highlights.

You've probably been wondering about the double name, Bosnia and Herzegovina. The word Bosnia goes back more than a thousand years and means "running water," a reference to the region's major river. Herzegovina derives from an Ottoman title equal to duke, which eventually became grafted on to the original Bosnia to emphasize who was now running things around here. For short, it's called Bosnia-Herzegovina, BiH, B&H, or simply Bosnia.

To ensure maximum confusion and inefficiency, Bosnia is led by three presidents, officially speaks three languages (Bosnian, Serbian, and Croatian), and is divided into three political entities. Roughly half the land in the nation of B&H belongs to the Federation of Bosnia and

Herzegovina, and nearly all the rest comprises the Republika Srpska, which is subdivided into two regions, one in the north the other in the south, with the Federation in the middle. Those of you with good math skills may have noticed that's just two entities; well done! There's a tiny third entity called the Brčko District, which was created in 2000 out of bits of land from the other two. Brčko officially belongs to both, is governed by neither, and functions under a decentralized system of local government.

Are your eyes glazing over yet? I know mine are. Bosnia is a very, very complicated place, and its 12,000-year history is filled with ancient feuds, religious wars, ethnic divisions, and boundary disputes. The constant, simmering friction occasionally boils over into widespread rage and violence, most recently from 1992 to 1995 in a conflict known simply as the Bosnian War. Since then the country had been at peace, at least in the sense that armies were no longer shooting at each other.

That sweltering July in Trebinje, peace prevailed in an atmosphere of heat-induced somnolence, with life moving at a leisurely pace. I spent a lot of time simply drifting around the city, enjoying the passing scene and taking long siestas through the hot afternoons.

Occasionally I bestirred myself to do more. I knew that Trebinje, being in the Republic of Srpska, was largely populated by Serbian Orthodox Christians, who were famous for their sumptuously decorated churches. One of the most dazzling could be seen at Tvrdoš Monastery, just three miles west of town, so one morning after breakfast, Rich and I hopped in a taxi and went to check it out.

The first thing I learned was that my sleeveless summer shirt offended the norms of modesty prevailing at the monastery. Clearly I wasn't the first, as a monk was standing by to provide me with a thin, royal blue cloak to toss over my shoulders; I felt rather dashing in it. Rich and I strolled about for a while, enjoying the lovely gardens and wondering how many of the legends about the place might actually be true.

Was the fourth century monastery really founded by St. Helena, Queen of Serbia, Empress of the Holy Roman Empire, mother of Constantine the Great? Had Helena discovered the True Cross in Jerusalem and given a fragment of it to Tvrdoš Monastery? Did the monastery contain one of her hands, as a relic? Wasn't she supposed to be buried, intact, somewhere in Rome? Even Google couldn't answer these questions for me.

Sadly, the original fourth century church had disappeared long ago, leaving behind just a few foundation stones and its name. The monks now worshipped in the "new" fifteenth century Church of the Dormition of the Most Holy Theotokos, which meant the Death of Mary, Mother of God.

The church was modest in size, but the paintings on the inside walls were glorious, a riot of Bible scenes showing stiff figures with magnificent, jewel-colored robes and big, glittering halos. There was an astonishing amount of gold leaf, wood carved into fantastic arabesques, and white linens embroidered with flowers and the face of Jesus. Not for the first time, I was struck by how creative and industrious we humans can be when we really put our backs into it.

The whole effect was so exuberant and dizzying that when I'd looked my fill, I stepped outside and sat down on a small bench to catch my breath. I was in a lovely, shaded, deserted little courtyard filled with flowers, and for a while I lost myself in the simple pleasure of absolute stillness.

When Rich emerged, we wandered on, finding a flight of stairs leading down to a cool, dark wine cellar. Standing beside the giant wooden barrels was a sommelier who told me Tvrdoš Monastery had been famous for its wines for 1700 years and asked if I'd like to taste some. In fact, he kept plying me with free samples until it became clear I'd better call a taxi and head back to the apartment for a siesta.

Trebinje was my kind of town: warm in its welcome, cool beneath the trees, brimming with history, and setting an easy, undemanding pace. I would be sorry to see the last of it. But now it was time to head north, out of the Republika Srpska into Federation territory, to the town of Mostar. I wanted to see the most famous bridge ever built and destroyed and rebuilt again.

It all began in 1557 when the Ottoman sultan Suleiman the Magnificent decided to replace the rickety old wooden suspension bridge over the Neretva River with a crowd-pleasing dazzler. The result was the longest hump-backed bridge in the world (at the time), and for centuries, people came to gawk — and stayed to do business. The villages on either side prospered and grew into a flourishing city in which Muslims, Christians, and Jews were all stakeholders.

Fast forward to the 1990s and the Bosnian War. Suddenly everyone became keenly aware that bridge — now known as Stari Most, or Old Bridge — not only connected the two sides of the river but divided the population into enemy camps. On the eastern side you had your Bosnian Muslims, and on the western side were two Christians groups: Orthodox Serbs of Eastern heritage and Catholic Croats who embraced the traditions of Western Europe. The city's thirty Jewish residents wisely stayed out of the fray, but everyone else seemed to be itching for a fight. A year into the war, for various strategic reasons that are now generally viewed as completely boneheaded, six Bosnian Croat generals got together and blew up the bridge.

The world reeled in horror. Mostar's bridge was a symbolic link between east and west, showing the potential for unity in a divided land. Was it a legitimate military target? Or was this a war crime? This being the Balkans, where there are five people you'll have ten opinions.

After the war, UNESCO oversaw the rebuilding of the bridge, and today, the new Old Bridge is the darling of the tourist industry, a guaranteed feel-good moment for all. In 2019 the city of Mostar, home to a population of just over 100,000, welcomed a million visitors. And all those visitors did exactly the same thing: walked through the old historical district taking selfies with the bridge in the background, stepped onto the bridge to take selfies with the historical district in the background, then found a bar where they could slake their thirst and wax eloquent about how the bridge's reconstruction reflected favorably on the resilience of the human spirit and our ability to turn swords into ploughshares.

Arriving in Mostar, seeing the massive crowds, I felt my heart sink. As a travel writer and photographer, I'm always trying to find a unique perspective. Standing in a crowd of a hundred people all jostling to take the exact same shot of an iconic monument, so they can say the exact same thing about it on social media, ranks high on my list of things to avoid. Mostar was clearly going to be a challenge. With some difficulty Rich and I elbowed our way through the throng and went to check in at our hotel.

Stepping through the front door, I found myself in a large, cool, dim lobby that was actually more of a parlor and one of the most overdecorated rooms I've ever seen. Every square foot of space held couches, tables, and armchairs; every piece of furniture — including the piano's keyboard — bore a fussy slipcover.

The manager strode forward — no small feat in the obstacle course of that overcrowded room — and greeted me with gracious condescension. She was a formidable woman with jet-black hair, a booming voice, and no hesitation in expressing her opinions. After a few welcoming remarks, she proclaimed, "You will, of course, wish to dine in a restaurant with a view of the bridge." And proceeded to mention several I'd read about online, the kind of "safe" cookie-cutter tourist restaurants I'd walk a mile out of my way to bypass.

As she led the way to our room, she laid out the house rules. No cooking in the room, despite the fact we had booked a suite with a full kitchen. No guests in the room, which made me wonder why the table offered seating for four and the massive leatherette sectional couch could easily hold eight or ten. No doing laundry in the room, even though there was a washing machine in the bathroom; she'd snapped off the washer's door handle so I wouldn't be tempted to transgress. Her suspicious glare made it pretty clear she viewed us as potential troublemakers and would be keeping a close eye on us at all times.

I found her attitude unnerving, especially after months of warm, make-yourself-at-home-have-a-glass-of-homemade-brandy hospitality I'd encountered all through Greece, North Macedonia, Kosovo, Albania, and Trebinje. Doing my best to radiate innocence, I meekly accepted the laminated card that restated the regulations and added a few more. "Guests," it warned sternly, "are required to report and compensate for any damage caused by their inappropriate behavior."

As soon as she was gone, Rich said, "Whatever you do, don't cross her."

"If I do, I'll make sure she never finds out."

Over the next two days I engaged in all sorts of "inappropriate behavior." I snuck food into the room in my purse and did clandestine laundry in the sink, draping it over the furniture on the balcony to dry. Feeling like a criminal, I smuggled out empty food packages and tossed them into public bins. I hid my laundry, dry or not, in the closet whenever the housekeeping service might come in. I was actually rather proud of covering my tracks so thoroughly.

And then, on the next-to-last day, I finally fell afoul of our hostess.

My friend Honey and her wife Sandy happened to be in Bosnia with their dog Scout, and we'd arranged to rendezvous at our hotel. I was looking forward to seeing all of them, including Scout, a well-traveled, beautifully trained, exceptionally good-natured older service animal, with kind eyes and tail-wagging charm. Everyone falls in love with Scout, who was clearly as dumbfounded as the rest of us when the manager reacted as if she'd found a snarling werewolf with blood-dripping fangs on the hotel's doorstep.

"No, no! Impossible!" she cried out, reeling back a step. "Dogs? In a hotel? No! Impossible! It must be outside! Outside! Get it away from here!"

Rich, Honey, Sandy, Scout, and I took off down the street as fast as our legs would carry us, followed by a few parting shouts from our hostess. I felt like Dennis the Menace, caught in a prank. "Gosh, Mr. Wilson, I didn't mean nothing by it," I muttered as I flew through the cobblestone streets of Mostar.

As soon as we were out of sight of the hotel, we stopped and collapsed with laugher. Scout sat down in a patch of shade and grinned at us.

When we'd recovered sufficiently to continue, Rich led the way to a little restaurant we'd discovered the day before on the other side of the river. It didn't have a vista of the Old Bridge, wasn't listed in a lot of guidebooks, and certainly wasn't recommended by the hotel manager (obviously a point in its favor). I'd liked the rich scent of the food and the humble yet inviting look of the place. When the proprietor assured me Scout would be most welcome, I'd booked a table.

The restaurant proved every bit as delightful as I'd hoped. The proprietor welcomed us back like old friends. He showed us to a table that overlooked the river and was conveniently close to the large electric fan and tub of water that he used to spread a cooling mist over his guests. As soon as the humans were in their seats and Scout was curled up at our feet, he produced complementary aperitifs. These were soon followed by platters heaped with roast lamb, grilled chicken, crispy fried potatoes, rice, yogurt, and round patties of ground meat that I suspected were some form of *ćevapi* (don't call it hamburger!).

"You do realize," Rich said, helping himself to another slice of lamb, "that on Monday, we'll have been traveling 100 days. That's the longest we've ever been on the road."

"So what have you learned about long-term travel?" Honey asked with interest.

Rich began talking about minimalist packing, how to find comfort food that's as heartwarming as it is tummy satisfying, and staying longer in places to absorb the atmosphere more deeply.

I agreed with everything he said but found it hard to listen closely because I was still a little giddy with the exhilaration of our headlong rush away from the hotel. It reminded me of times in my childhood when I'd experienced the thrill of sneaking around and escaping wrathful adults. To me, road wisdom starts with ignoring bad advice, breaking ridiculous rules, and enjoying getting away with it.

I reached down and petted Scout, who gave a tiny wag of his tail and drifted back to sleep.

19. Sarajevo / *The Secret of Okra*

On the bus from Mostar to Sarajevo, I wondered if I'd find Bosnia's capital as bullet-riddled as it had been during my first visit in 2005. Of course, that was just nine years after the war, when the landscape was battle-scarred and the surviving citizens were literally shell-shocked. And even then Sarajevo had contrived to be charming. Like the Mostar bridge, the city was designed by the Ottomans to dazzle and delight, and it still did. As for the people I met, everyone treated me with courtesy and kindness. I'd considered myself lucky to be there.

The reason for that visit was a volunteer project providing business consulting to a microenterprise funded by an international charity. From time to time the charity felt one of their projects might need a bit of assistance and sent us in to investigate and advise. This particular charity also sent us to Kenya, Mexico, and El Salvador; we'd spent six months in the Republic of Georgia for another organization. In Bosnia we would be working with a knitting collective in Tuzla, an industrial city in the northeastern part of the country. The projects were always loads of fun and I couldn't wait to get going.

To get there required flying into Sarajevo, and Rich and I arrived one evening just before dusk. As our taxi threaded its way through the darkening city, the sporadic light of streetlamps revealed bullet holes scattered across just about every building — except for those that had been reduced to rubble, of course.

THE GREAT MEDITERRANEAN COMFORT FOOD TOUR

The cab driver didn't speak much English but managed to ask where we were from. "Ah, America," he said. "George Bush, bang bang. Bill Clinton, kiss kiss."

After this pungent political analysis, he fell silent until it was time to deposit us on the doorstep of the Holiday Inn.

This blockish yellow high-rise hotel was once a symbol of optimism, built in the heady run-up to the 1984 Winter Olympics in Sarajevo. Bosnia's communist dictator, Josip Broz Tito, had died a few years earlier, and by the time the games began, Yugoslavia and the Soviet Union were crumbling. Bosnians were daring to dream of independence and a larger presence on the international stage. Which they achieved, just not in the way they'd hoped.

Seven years after the Winter Olympics, Yugoslavia split apart and Bosnia promptly declared its independence. The Bosnian Serbs were furious; despite being in the minority, they'd hoped somehow to turn all of Bosnia into a Serbian state. Refusing to let go of the dream, the Bosnian Serbs decided to round up an army and lay siege to the capital — because that's always a good way to win hearts and minds.

Nestled a shallow, bowl-shaped valley, Sarajevo offered the perfect fish-in-a-barrel target. The Bosnian Serbs posted 13,000 soldiers in the surrounding hills and sent shells and bullets raining down on the populace. The city's water was cut off. Roads were blockaded. No food, medicine, or other supplies could be brought in. No one was allowed out. And that was how the Bosnian War started.

"It was literally unthinkable," the head of the knitting collective told me when I got to Tuzla. "We were modern Europe. We'd just had the Winter Olympics there." The city was cut off from the outside world for nearly four years — a total of 1,425 days, the longest siege of a capital city in the history of modern warfare. On a typical day three hundred shells fell on the city; on the worst, three thousand. And then there were the snipers.

During the war, the Holiday Inn's once-prestigious address on Zmaja od Bosne (Dragon of Bosnia Street) placed it squarely on "Sniper Alley," one of the most dangerous roads in the city. And its yellow color made it an inviting target. But nowhere in the city was safe, so the international press continued to live and work in the hotel.

"Many times it was shot by artillery fire, mortars were fired that landed on or near it, windows were broken regularly," CNN's Christiane Amanpour recalled afterwards. Despite the risks, and often the lack of hot water or electricity, she said, "We considered the Holiday Inn our recreation, our home. It was where we woke up, where we went to sleep, where we visited each other, sometimes in each others' rooms. It was where love affairs blossomed, it was where we worked, it was where we escaped death. It was really everything to many of us."

My experience of the Holiday Inn was considerably less exciting. Nine years after the war, I found it reassuringly free of damage and functioning much like any other international chain hotel. Rich and I passed a quiet night there, and in the morning a driver came and took us to Tuzla for our meeting with the head of the knitting collective.

"At the start of the siege I happened to be away, visiting relatives here in Tuzla," she told me. "It was nearly four years before I could go home. I knew I needed to do something with my time, and I heard about a Swedish project helping war widows. Most of the women knew how to knit and crochet, and I thought it would be good therapy for them. There were charities that would donate yarn. Some of the women were really, really good. After a while I decided to see if we could sell the things they made. Nobody had any money; any income would be a huge benefit." By the time I got there, the collective was so successful their products were being sold in the upscale Sundance catalog started by Robert Redford.

This was a rare success story in Tuzla, a city distinguished by a remarkable history of misfortune. The Ottomans built the town in 1510 over a vast, unstable salt mine, and ever since then, whole buildings had been sinking abruptly into the earth or collapsing in ruins. Nowadays, the salt was used to manufacture soap, and the factory run-off flowed into the river that wound through town. The first time I crossed one of the wooden bridges spanning the river, the eye-watering stench stopped me in my tracks. I peered over the railing, certain I'd see a large, dead animal floating in the water. I was reassured it was "just" chemicals from the soap factory.

Oh good, was that all? I vowed to breathe as little as possible while I was in town.

"We have a joke here," said one of the knitting collective administrators. "A guy from Tuzla goes away for a wedding. He finds himself so lightheaded from the air quality that he has to put his mouth on the tailpipe of a car and breathe deeply to feel like himself again."

But the thing that really tore the heart out of the city was the massacre of the kids. It happened about six months before the end of the Bosnian War, on a day when the city's youngsters had gathered to celebrate a traditional youth day. Why anyone thought this was a good idea in a war zone remains a mystery; obviously I couldn't ask. Were they relying on their attackers' sentimentality and good sportsmanship? Really?

No doubt the Bosnian Serbs could hardly believe their luck as they saw hundreds gathering in Kapija Square. They fired a high-explosive fragmentation shell into their midst, killing seventy one people, mostly students and a few teachers, wounding two hundred and forty more.

I was shown the very spot where the shell landed and the hillside cemetery's long rows of graves bearing the school photos of the dead; seeing the smiling young faces was heart-rending. Their funerals were held at four in the morning to avoid further shelling. Nearly ten years later, sorrow still hung over the city like a fog.

During the days I kept busy with the work project, but in the evenings there was little to do. The movie theater had closed down two years earlier, after the last of the UN peacekeepers pulled out, and by the time we finished dinner, the streets were deserted. In our tiny hotel room, Rich and I played cards and watched Bosnian TV, making up our own translations for the incomprehensible dialogue on screen.

One public service announcement needed no translation. It began with a man walking in the forest. Then the camera angle shifted to ground level, as the man's foot come down and … Boom! Landmine! At the end of the war there were still millions of mines buried in the countryside, and although efforts were being made to remove them, it was slow, expensive, dangerous work. Every year a few unlucky Bosnians were killed while walking in the woods.

The charity's chief administrator had warned me about the land mines and advised me not to go wandering about in the forest. No fear of that! I made sure to stay on well-trodden concrete paths at all times. Even in downtown Tuzla, where I knew every inch of land had long since been searched and cleared, I held my breath whenever I saw a child run across an empty lot or patch of lawn. Nothing happened, of course, but it was nerve-wracking every single time.

All things considered, when the project was over, I was only too happy to return to Sarajevo. The head of the knitting collective drove us there herself and took us to lunch at a charming traditional restaurant in the Ottoman quarter. When she heard we planned to return to the Holiday Inn, she instantly overruled the idea. "You must stay at a Bosnian hotel. I will take you to the best in the city."

This turned out to be a gracious and hospitable hotel, with spacious rooms, massive dark wood furniture, and the most hideously uncomfortable bed of my long and varied experience. Clearly efforts at reconstruction and modernization had not yet reached inside this establishment. The pre-pre-war mattress was rutted like a bad road; the metal springs inside it had long since broken free of their moorings and now thrust their jagged tips upward, directly into my kidneys and other tender parts of my anatomy. I'm pretty sure I still have internal scarring.

I considered sleeping on the floor until I took a closer look at the carpeting with its rich patina of substances I didn't care to think about. After briefly eyeing the ancient bathtub, I sighed, lay down again on the bed, and waited for the 5:30 am taxi to the airport.

Not surprisingly, returning to Sarajevo many years later, I found vast improvements. The rubble and bombed-out ruins had been cleared away, and the lovely old Ottoman section, which I remembered as subdued and deserted, was now thronged and vibrant.

There were still bullet holes in lots of buildings, including the one in which we were staying, a mid-century apartment block not far from the old Ottoman district. Inside, the apartment proved to be bright and comfortable, with tall windows offering a dramatic view of the hills where snipers had been stationed. I could only assume the curtains had been kept firmly shut for every minute of those 1,425 days of siege. I asked our hostess if leaving the bullet holes on the outside of buildings was a deliberate act to keep alive memories of the war.

She laughed. "No, not at all. It's because there are endless arguments between landlords and tenants over who is responsible for paying for the repairs. It's just economics."

Apparently plenty of those disputes had been resolved, as many buildings, especially in the bustling downtown, now presented a smooth facade to the world. But others still bore the scars of war, as did the city's sidewalks, on which bloomed the famous "Sarajevo roses" — shell craters filled in with red resin as a memorial to those killed there. Calling them roses made them sound almost romantic, but in fact they looked like blood spatters at a crime scene.

Feeling the need to strike a more visually cheerful note, city officials were currently installing a new mosaic on the pavement of the main pedestrian street, Ferhadija. Workers were laying stones showing a compass and the words, "Sarajevo Meeting of Cultures." On one side of the street stood centuries-old Ottoman coffee houses, on the other smart European-style shops and wine bars. The mosaic was nearly finished by the time I left Sarajevo; since then, it's become one of the city's iconic landmarks.

For old times' sake, Rich and I stopped by to see another Sarajevo icon, the hotel we'd known as the Holiday Inn. It had already started its slow decline when we'd stayed there in 2005, and later it hit the economic skids and lost the Holiday Inn franchise. Eventually it was shut down by Bosnia's State Investigation and Protection Agency for reasons I probably don't want to know about.

Optimistic new management had now reopened it under the name Hotel Holiday, allowing them to capitalize on its fame without technically violating any statutes pertaining to the terminated franchise agreement. Nice tap dancing around the law, guys!

The moment I stepped through the doors, I saw the Hotel Holiday was in fine fettle, the lobby gleaming with fresh paint, polished brass, and glossy guests. I always evaluate hotels on the state of the ladies' room, and I wasn't surprised to find the lobby contained one of the city's best efforts. A stand-alone structure inside the vast open space, it was constructed of solid wood planks and required passing through a series of three substantial doors to reach the immaculate interior.

"That ladies' room is a fortress," I told Rich. "If the shelling ever starts again, I'm heading directly in there. It could be the most impregnable spot in the entire city."

Much of our time was spent exploring the old Ottoman district, where ancient wooden buildings housed shops, restaurants, a school, a library, a mosque, and much more, all fully restored and humming with activity. I noticed that a number of buildings, including the spectacular sixteenth-century mosque, bore signs crediting someone called Bey for their construction. As soon as I got the chance, I asked a Sarajevo woman who this Bey was.

"Ah, that would be Gazi Hüsrev Bey," Dalida said, smiling the way you do when someone mentions your favorite uncle. "Bey was his title; it means governor. Gazi Hüsrev Bey was the great benefactor of Sarajevo."

Memories are long in the Balkans, and the fact that the Bey had been dead for 500 years did nothing to lessen the affection and respect the town felt for him. I soon learned that Hüsrev came from money and power; he was grandson to one sultan, and after a string of successes on the battlefield, chosen by another — our old friend Suleiman the Magnificent — to govern Bosnia for the Ottoman Empire. As *Game of Thrones* fans know only too well, aristocratic grandsons and popular war heroes don't always make the best rulers. But Gazi Hüsrev Bey rose to the occasion, undertaking a string of public works that caused Sarajevo to become known as "a flower among cities."

The scope of the Bey's projects was astonishing. He not only built the splendid mosque for his Ottoman constituents but helped finance the Old Orthodox Church and a Franciscan monastery as well. He started a school (originally for boys, although later open to girls, too) with plenty of scholarships and an emphasis on "the rational and traditional sciences." The library housed important manuscripts, many from Hüsrev's personal collection. He built public bath houses, a drinking fountain that was still in regular use (Rich and I drank from it), gracious parks, and a caravansary where visitors to the city could stay several days for free. Sadly this last was now defunct, which is why I was in the rental.

I was staggered to discover that the public toilet Hüsrev had had installed in 1530 was still in operation. Clearly I owed it to my readers to pop in, have a look around, and report on its condition. You'll be glad to know that the plumbing had been upgraded since the Bey's day. I found individual stalls, clean ceramic squat toilets, modern sinks, and an optional donation tin. What more could you ask for?

Obviously the Bey had a keen grasp of the essentials, because in addition to all that, he fed his people. "He opened a soup kitchen, a free place to eat," Dalida told me. "It was meant for the poor, but the food was so good everyone went. They say even Gazi Hüsrev Bey himself ate there."

What did he eat there? We can't be sure, but it could easily have been the dish Dalida called "the ultimate comfort food of the Balkans: *begova čorba*." She explained, "It means Bey's soup. We eat it in every season, at the holidays, for special occasions — all the time really."

Dalida was an expert on local cuisine and put her skills to work at Balkantina, a small company running food tours, cooking classes, and a gourmet shop. When I dropped by the shop to ask about cooking classes, her friend and employer, Uliana, offered to host a dinner in her home so I could learn how Dalida prepares traditional Bosnian fare. Rich and I were delighted with the plan and arranged to go over the following evening.

"We always begin with a *meze* plate," Uliana explained, leading the way to a sitting area with a sweeping view of the city and the surrounding hills. A low wooden table held a platter of cheese, tomatoes, paper-thin ham, olive oil, and honey. "And of course, *rakija*." The traditional tiny servings of high-octane, homemade fruit brandy were poured, and everyone raised their glasses to toast the occasion.

After I'd nibbled the honey-dipped cheese, sipped some *rakija*, and been introduced to Max, Uliana's enormous Maine coon cat, Dalida got down to business. As she told me about Bey's soup, she was carefully assembling her ingredients, starting with a long string of dried okra.

Now, I don't know how you feel about okra, but I confess I don't always love it. In some dishes it's scrumptious, but there are times that okra, as one of my fellow journalists so delicately expressed it, "has the consistency of snot." I need not have worried; it turned out that when okra was dried it lost its sliminess, leaving a delicious vegetable bursting with vitamins and antioxidants.

Dalida slid the okra off the string and put it to soak in water, then chopped onions, carrots, and potatoes. She sautéed the onion until it was translucent then dropped in chicken thighs. "Ideally," she told me, "this would be a domestic chicken from your own backyard." She added the okra (technically a fruit) and the vegetables along with garlic, lemon, and bay leaves for flavor, and left the pot simmering.

Next she made a batch of *dolmas* (grape leaves and small yellow peppers stuffed with ground beef and rice). Then she tossed together a salad of tomatoes, cucumbers, and sour cream. By this time the soup had simmered sufficiently, so she removed the skin and bones, then thickened the broth with a roux made from flour and water. Dinner was ready.

The results were marvelous, a full-bodied, delicious chicken soup bristling with nutrition, and a robust way to nourish even the weariest traveler or to welcome a stranger to your home. Did Gazi Hüsrev Bey ever actually eat this soup? Who knows? But like the city of Sarajevo itself, the soup has become a permanent testament to his generosity. I think he would have enjoyed knowing that.

A year into his reign, Hüsrev set up a *vakuf* (endowment) to make sure the city had the policies and funds it would need to keep his legacy going. "Good deeds cause evil to flee," said the official *vakuf* paperwork. "and the loftiest of all good deeds is charity. The loftiest of all charities is the one that lasts forever... The efficacy of the *vakuf* will persist for as long as this world exists, and its work will continue until Judgment Day."

I don't know what to expect on Judgement Day, but it's pretty clear to me that if anything can survive until the End Times, it's the pleasure of sitting down to hearty bowl of chicken soup. It has certainly comforted the people of Sarajevo through good times and bad.

And let's face it, Sarajevo has had its share of bad times. One day

I went and stood on the spot where the heir to the Austro-Hungarian Empire was shot, sparking World War I. I was surprised to learn this epic event was the result of a series of mind-boggling screwups and numbskull decisions. A little common sense anywhere along the line could have avoided the whole disaster. If only.

For a start, the Hapsburg royals, Ferdinand and Sophia, should never have gone to Sarajevo. People were still furious over the way the Austro-Hungarian Empire had "annexed" Bosnia six years earlier, when the Ottoman Empire started collapsing in earnest. This drove the next-door nation of Serbia ballistic, as they'd planned to grab Bosnia for themselves. Bosnian Serbs poured over the border into Serbia demanding that something be done. Serbian agitators poured over the border into Bosnia, itching for action. Things got pretty lively for a while.

Then, in the summer of 1914, Ferdinand announced he and his wife would visit Sarajevo to raise morale — a sort of victory lap to celebrate successfully bringing Bosnia into the Hapsburg family fold. The royals would ride slowly through the city in an open car to give all his loyal subjects an opportunity to pay their respects. Sure, Ferdinand knew he wasn't universally popular. A few days before the event he remarked, "I wouldn't be surprised if there were a few Serbian bullets waiting for me." Even so he loftily refused to change his plans.

The local military commander (I always picture him sweating profusely in what must have been a very difficult interview) begged Ferdinand to let him line the route with troops. But the archduke overruled the idea, insisting such measures would offend the loyal citizenry.

As the motorcade set off, six would-be assassins were waiting at key points along the route. These were not steely eyed professionals but disaffected youths, some mere teenagers. Three of them were dying of tuberculosis. All were filled with the kind of jittery insecurities, dark thoughts, and heroic fantasies that nowadays send American youths into schools with assault rifles. Members of the sinister Black Hand and other

Serbian nationalist groups had been only too happy to give them weapons, pep talks, suicide pills, and some basic but (as you will see) not very effective training.

The archduke's convoy passed directly in front of the first two would-be killers, who froze and did nothing. A few blocks later Nedeljko Čabrinović managed to act, tossing a hand grenade at the motorcade. But his aim was off, so the grenade struck the back of the archduke's car, bounced off, rolled under the car behind it, and exploded, injuring twenty people. Čabrinović then swallowed his suicide pill and jumped into the river. However, the pill only made him sick (oops!), and the river was just four inches deep at that point (oops, again!), so the police hauled him out and threw him in jail.

I know, right? I couldn't make this stuff up.

Meanwhile, responding to the hand grenade, the archduke's driver slammed his foot down on the accelerator, racing past the other would-be assassins, including Gavrilo Princip, who was standing on Franz Josef Street. Incredibly, the motorcade continued to the town hall where the archduke carried on with his planned speech, reading from a paper retrieved from the damaged car and covered in the blood of his assistant. When it comes to maintaining a stiff upper lip, the British have nothing on the Hapsburgs.

After the speech, Ferdinand decided to visit the members of his entourage injured by the bomb. But nobody mentioned this to the driver, who continued along the original route, which meant turning onto Franz Josef Street, where Princip was still hanging about, cursing his luck at not being able to kill anybody so far today.

One of the officials in the archduke's car shouted to the driver he shouldn't have turned. So the driver stopped the car and was trying to put it into reverse when the engine stalled and the gears locked.

The car was directly in front of Princip. This was his moment. He knew he had to act. The street was so crowded he didn't think he could take out his bomb and hurl it with any accuracy. So he pulled a gun from his pocket, stepped forward, and fired two shots at point blank range.

"Where I aimed I do not know," he later testified. "I even turned my head as I shot."

If so, the gods of war took a hand in the day's proceedings, because both shots were fatal, one catching Sophia in the stomach, the other severing Ferdinand's jugular vein. Both royals were dead in minutes.

Bosnia erupted in anti-Serb riots and the Austro-Hungarian Empire declared war on Serbia. In the days that followed, the vast network of alliances that defined Europe conspired to entangle more than thirty countries in the conflict. Twenty million people would perish before the war ran its course.

Standing on Franz Josef Street, I tried to imagine a world in which Princip's trembling hands had fired just slightly more wildly, missing his targets. Today he would be a mere dusty little footnote of history, if that. Would those twenty million people have lived? Or were tensions so great that there was no avoiding World War I? Was the Bosnian War of 1992 equally inevitable?

Walking past bullet holes and stepping over those "roses" on the sidewalks, I kept trying to picture what life had been like for the Sarajevo people during the long siege, cut off from the outside world. I'd read that after the initial shock, one of their first moves was to start digging a tunnel out of the city. The best place to do it was clear: right under the airport, which two months after the start of the war came under UN control and was less likely to be attacked.

For the next four months, soldiers and citizens worked around the clock using nothing but picks, shovels, and wheelbarrows. Planning was hurried, engineering was sometimes sketchy, and heartbreaking setbacks occurred. But eventually the diggers created a passage 875 yards long, 3.3

feet wide and 5 feet high, and the Tunnel of Hope was open for business.

"Everything came through the tunnel — food, electricity, military matériel, fuel, medicines and wounded," said Edis Kolar, whose family home served as the tunnel's entrance. "Sarajevo would not have survived without it."

After the war, the Kolar family turned their home into a museum, and here the bullet holes were certainly left intact for effect. There was nothing slick or professional about the exhibits, but the harrowing tale they told was all the stronger for that. Photos and homemade videos showed the stories nobody wanted to talk about. I remember sitting in a little dark room watching shells blasting the city, hitting the beautiful city hall, Vijećnica street, and shops and restaurants I recognized. I saw women and children dodging behind cars for cover, and men carrying the wounded into makeshift clinics.

They let you walk through a section of the tunnel, which even for someone of my modest height was too short to pass through upright. It was hard to believe this cramped underground passageway had been the city's single lifeline to the outside world for nearly four years.

Another major priority of the besieged capital was organizing the city's water supply. Fortunately Sarajevska Pivara, the local beer brewery, was built over an abundant underground spring, and water was made available to all. A few water trucks served the city, but most people had to come and collect it themselves, risking their lives with every step. In one neighborhood, a deep trench was dug and cars were upended along the sides to serve as a shield, protecting people on their water runs. Often the task was entrusted to fleet-footed older children.

One searing July day, Rich and I made the long hike from our apartment to Sarajevska Pivara in hopes of seeing their famous spring. Even without having to worry about shells or snipers, I found the trek arduous, and by the time I finished the last uphill stretch, I was red-faced and short of breath. Disappointingly, the brewery wasn't interested in allowing visitors to see the spring and their tiny museum pretty much ignored the war.

In fact, nobody I met wanted to talk about the siege. And who could blame them? Those were dark times for Bosnia. One hundred thousand dead, more than two million displaced, tens of thousands of women raped. Reconciliation would take generations, if it came at all. The fact that the former enemies could somehow manage to live side by side again was a miracle.

Luckily there was one thing that united the community, something everybody could get behind, transcending all ethnic, religious, socioeconomic, and political divisions. I am talking about, of course, Sarajevo's hottest new tourist attraction, the Bosnian Pyramids.

On my first morning in Sarajevo, I happened to walk past a lurid poster promoting this newly discovered aspect of the nation's ancient heritage. Catching a glimpse of it out of the corner of my eye, I did a doubletake. Growing up in California, I was steeped in the culture of goofy roadside attractions involving ghosts, aliens, Bigfoot, and ancient, unfathomable mysteries recently invented by hucksters who'd like to sell you a ticket and a t-shirt. I could hardly wait to check out this one.

"They're supposedly much bigger and way older than Egypt's pyramids," I reported to Rich after skimming the text on the website. "Apparently they are energy amplifiers that can heal your body, your chakras, and your aura."

"I would expect nothing less," he said.

The now-famous Bosnian Pyramids were "discovered" (naysayers claim invented) in 2005 by Sam Osmanagich, a Bosnian entrepreneur who told the world that those two pointy hills a half-hour's drive from Sarajevo were actually "the greatest pyramidal complex ever built on the face of the earth." His announcement (made wearing an Indian Jones-style hat, because why be subtle?) caused a sensation, providing a huge boost to national pride — and tourism — in the aftermath of the war.

Supporting Osmanagich's claims became a litmus test of patriotism in many circles. One Sarajevo man told me the pyramids were a national treasure and the first thing I should visit in the region. He said he took his little daughter there every year for a general aura cleansing. Dalida told me with pride that her husband worked there as a tour guide.

The scientific community vigorously protested that Osmanagich was perpetrating "a cruel hoax on an unsuspecting public." Boston University archaeologist Curtis Runnels said, "All of the 'finds' being made by Osmanagich are either natural features like rocks, or the result of long occupation in these valleys by people since the Greco-Roman period. As for the supernatural powers he claims for these 'pyramids,' one only has to note that Mr. Osmanagich published a book claiming the Maya came from the Pleiades constellation."

Yet people happily continued to flock to the site, and Osmanagich happily continued to collect their entrance fees, sell them t-shirts, and assure them their auras have never looked better.

"We should go to the pyramids," I said to Rich. "Maybe we'll be the first to see Bigfoot there."

But before organizing an expedition to the pyramids, I thought it would be fun to find out if Sarajevo boasted any other roadside attractions. And it turned out the town had some doozies.

The first I visited was the ICAR Canned Beef Monument, which stood as a shabby, ironic tribute to the horrendous food sent over as so-called humanitarian aid during the siege. Yes, the UN meant well. But they delivered rations left over from the Vietnam conflict that were 20 years past their expiration date. They shipped in tins of pork, which couldn't be eaten by the Muslim half of the population. But the very worst atrocity was a canned product called ICAR beef, reportedly so foul even starving dogs wouldn't touch it. One blogger wrote that his grandfather told him, "If there is another siege, I would rather die than eat ICAR."

I pictured the sweating transport team, backs bent, laboring to haul food packages through the 875 yards of the Tunnel of Hope, only to find more rank, foul-smelling, indigestible ICAR beef inside. As novelist Margaret Atwood put it, "Stupidity is the same as evil if you judge by the results."

After the war, a meter-high replica of the ICAR beef can was set on a pedestal with the snarky inscription, "Monument to the International Community by the grateful citizens of Sarajevo." Perhaps appropriately, by the time I saw it the ICAR beef can was in a dreadful state of disrepair, paint peeling in so many places I could scarcely make out the words on the label. Since then, it's been fully cleaned and restored and is now standing sarcastically on its plinth behind the Historical Museum of Bosnia and Herzegovina.

For another blast from the past, Rich and I stopped for coffee at the Caffe Tito, a tongue-in-cheek tribute to the former Yugoslavian dictator. The man was surprisingly popular. His strongarm tactics kept squabbling factions in line and forged them into a socialist state with a powerful market economy. Many Yugoslavians considered themselves lucky to have him running things.

During a free walking tour, our guide, Adis, explained it this way. "Yes, Tito was a dictator. And yes, he imprisoned people and had his political enemies killed. But sometimes that's necessary to keep a country together."

"Now that Tito's gone, I hear there's a lot of corruption," someone said.

Adis grinned. "You call it corruption, we call it a free market."

Caffe Tito was situated in a park with a playground, where I spent a few heartwarming moments watching little children climb around on old tanks and artillery weapons thoughtfully provided in lieu of a jungle gym. Inside, the walls displayed a wealth of memorabilia honoring the man and his era, starting with WWII when Tito was the leader of the Yugoslav Partisans, generally viewed as the most effective resistance movement in German-occupied Europe. Cult-like portraits of Tito and vintage weaponry rubbed shoulders with dial telephones, mid-century radios, and vinyl record albums, including a few I'd owned myself.

Rich and I sat down beneath a 1946 LIFE magazine cover naming Tito Man of the Year. While we waited for our coffees, I held a glass of cold water to my forehead. It was ninety degrees, with humidity somewhere around sixty percent. I was wishing I had the nerve to dump the water over my head right there at the table. Maybe I could slip outside and do it behind one of the armored tanks.

"Do you remember what I said back in Skopje, and again in Shkodër, about the wisdom of not climbing to high castles in hot weather?" I asked Rich. "I'm thinking that might apply to pyramids, too."

After some discussion, we agreed to ditch the Bosnian Pyramid expedition in hopes of avoiding outright heatstroke on my part. Obviously it was a shame I wouldn't get my aura cleansed. I felt sure it needed a good brisk scrubbing after all the grubby bus rides and sweaty weather. And now I would never be able to motivate myself to finish the excruciatingly dull video "Bosnian Pyramid SHOCK: Ancient Civilization Received Knowledge from SPACE." I'd just have to resign myself to never knowing how aliens figured into the story.

"I hate to miss a major roadside attraction," I said to Rich. "But it seems the stars are just not in alignment on this one."

Oh, weren't they?

Call it fate, call it destiny, call it one more Sarajevan who had drunk the Kool-Aid. Half an hour after leaving Sarajevo, the bus driver rolled to a stop opposite two pointy green hills that seemed vaguely familiar. Where had I seen them before? Somehow I kept picturing them surrounded by cheesy lettering.

"Hey, look," said Rich. "Aren't those the Bosnian Pyramids?"

Yep. There they stood in all their alleged glory. The bus idled there for a several minutes, letting all the passengers gaze in wonder at the marvel. Did my aura feel just a little cleaner? Were my chakras easing into better alignment? Was I picking up subliminal messages from ancient extraterrestrials? I certainly didn't notice anything like that with my conscious mind. But then, what did I know about paranormal pyramid effects?

Eventually the driver shifted into gear and headed north on the open highway. And then it was time for me to turn my thoughts to the next destination: Zagreb, capital of Croatia.

CROATIA

20. Zagreb, Croatia / *Mlinci, Strukli, Deer Goulash*

The Croatians like to say, "*Bez muke nema nauke*," that is, "Without suffering there is no wisdom." And if there is a perfect embodiment of the value of hard-won lessons, and the keen Croatian sense of humor, it's Zagreb's whacky Museum of Broken Relationships.

This collection of unusual artifacts was inspired by the epic break-up of Zagreb artists Olinka Vištica and Dražen Grubišić. As they picked their way through the wreckage of their romance, the ex-couple started wondering what people are supposed to do with love tokens from failed relationships, the kind of mementos that are too significant to throw away and too painful too keep around. Eventually they had an idea: Why not put these objects on display, along with their stories?

Friends began adding to the collection, and in no time Olinka and Dražen had developed a traveling exhibition. When word got out about the project, they were inundated with contributions from all over the world and soon established a permanent museum in Zagreb; later a sister museum opened in Los Angeles. Today Zagreb's Museum of Broken Relationship houses a quirky collection of unworn wedding dresses, smashed furniture, and other mementos of romantic disasters, each with its painfully funny backstory.

One of my favorite exhibits displayed a small plastic statue with this text: "A holy water bottle shaped as the Virgin Mary. 1988, 2 months,

Amsterdam, the Netherlands. In the summer of 1988 I met my transient love in Amsterdam. He had a stopover during his travels. He was from Peru and discovering Europe by train. We met at the Buddha Disco. Not long after we bumped into each other on the street, and he went home with me and stayed for about two months. Suddenly he was gone. I found a goodbye note and this little statue, which he had specifically brought from Peru in the hope of meeting a new love. What he didn't know was that I had once opened his bag, and found a whole plastic bag full of these bottles. I never saw him again."

Like the exhibitions, the museum's gift shop reminds us that breaking up may be hard to do, but it can also be funny as hell. Sea salt is sold in trendy bottles labeled, "Salt. Rub it into the wound." Chocolate bar wrappers say, "I hope your ass gets bigger," and "Forget love, I'd rather fall in chocolate." A shower gel called "Pain Down the Drain" explains it's there for you "when you need a little extra help getting rid of your ex's smell and having a fresh start."

The exhibition is constantly changing, occasionally touring, and, yes, still accepting contributions. Do you have a side-splitting splitting-up story? A poignant artifact that deserves a wider audience? You'll find the contributor's guidelines on the museum website.

Rich and I first visited Zagreb and the Museum of Broken Relationships three years before the Mediterranean Comfort Food Tour, and I considered it one of the highlights of the city. But by far the most fun we'd had on that trip was dinner in the home of Lidija, a local dentist.

Lidija had just qualified as EatWith's first Zagreb host, and Rich and I had the honor of being her inaugural guests. Joining us at table were her daughter Doris and long-time friend Mladen, who immediately produced a test tube of orange *rakija* (brandy) and passed it around. From there, the evening flowed forward, the conversation rolling around the table as easily as if we had known each other for years.

Dinner was served on Lidija's balcony to take advantage of that September's unseasonably warm weather, known there, Mladen told me, as *kraj ljeta*, or "old woman summer." The meal began with *viška pogača*, bread topped with olive oil, onions, and anchovies. "The recipe comes from the island of Vis, in southern Croatia," Lidija told me. "Traditionally it is made with a second crust on top, but that is too much bread, I think."

A summer salad of tomato, cheese, and olives followed, and then Lidija brought out the main course, fresh *skuša riba* (mackerel), a dense yet flaky fish cooked to perfection and surrounded with glistening roasted potatoes. The side dish was a vegetable Rich and I couldn't identify and nobody else knew how to translate.

"It's like kale, but it's not," was the best Doris could come up with.

One of the things I loved about that dinner was nobody reached for a phone to look it up; we were having way too much fun to bother with such technical details. Later, a reader saw the photo on my blog and identified the mystery ingredient as *blitva*, the same spinach-like vegetable that we'd gone with Mladen to buy at the Old Bazaar in Bitola, North Macedonia, so Victoria could bake into her *zelnik*.

Sitting on Lidija's balcony in the gathering dusk, we finished off the meal with *rožata*, a cross between flan and *crème brûlée*, topped with sour cherries soaked in *rakija*, accompanied by small, sweet purple grapes grown in her garden.

The evening was so much fun we all got together again a few days later and then kept in touch. Three years later, when I wrote to tell Lidija that Rich and I were coming to her town on our Mediterranean Comfort Food Tour, she instantly replied that she'd take the week off from work and introduce me to the tastiest classic fare in Zagreb. I was astonished and delighted by her generosity. As soon as we met up, Lidija began offering suggestions about which of Croatia's favorite comfort foods I should sample first.

"*Strukli*, of course," she said. "And *mlinci*. Have you tried deer goulash? No? The best place to find such dishes is Zagorje." This was a rural area north of the city, and to get there LIdija, Rich, and I set forth one morning by car, leaving the city behind to roll along country roads that wound through forested hills and sleepy valleys dotted with small family farms.

"This was the center of the Peasant Revolution of 1573. It all started right here," Lidija told me. "The nobility demanded that each family contribute food to them. People were living on the edge of hunger, but the lord had an army, and they had to pay. Like today we are forced to pay taxes. So the peasants staged a revolt. It lasted only twelve days. And they took the leader of the rebellion, Matija Gubec, and said to him, 'You wanted to be king. Here is your crown.' And they put upon his head an iron crown that was heated red-hot in the fire. And then they tore him into four pieces." Ouch!

Gubec became a folk hero, inspiring various political movements, the first Croatian rock opera, and the career aspirations of young Josip Broz, who was born in a humble Zagorje farmhouse, adopted Tito as his *nom de guerre*, and went on to become Yugoslavia's President for Life.

As you can imagine, Zagorje's cuisine was designed to fortify hard-working agricultural families attempting to subsist on what was left after the powerful had taken the lion's share of everything produced on the land. It was robust, made from fresh, inexpensive local ingredients, and bristling with the fats and carbs you'd need for long hours of physical labor. "Not thinning," as my grandmother used to say of such dishes, but a glorious indulgence I knew I'd never regret.

"Here we will eat *štrukli*," said Lidija, pulling up at a 1938 country inn called Villa Zelenjak Ventek. When the staff learned this was to be my first taste of this classic dish, a young, English-speaking manager named

Dora stepped forward to describe how *štrukli* is prepared. She explained that you make a basic dough, roll it so thin that it completely covers the tabletop, stuff it with a mix of cottage cheese, eggs, sour cream, and salt, and bake it. When it arrived at our table, hot from the oven, I discovered *štrukli* was the savory Balkan cousin of cheese strudel; every bite of the flaky pastry and creamy filling simply melted in my mouth.

After lunch, Rich, Lidija, and I worked off a few calories strolling around Kumrovec, a charming village of restored nineteenth-century homes that included Tito's birthplace and a museum honoring his legacy. The atmosphere was dripping with "Yugonostalgia," fond memories of simpler times when everyone had a job, a place to live, and enough to eat.

"Were you better off then?" I asked Lidija.

"In many ways, yes," she said, with a philosophical shrug. "Things are much harder for us now."

Our final stop of the day was Gresna Gorica, a rustic restaurant nestled in vineyards below the fairytale towers of Veliki Tabor castle. Like so many ancient citadels, the castle had a long history with some gruesome chapters.

In the fourteenth century, it was home to the powerful Hermann II, Count of Celje, whose son Fridrik fell in love with Veronika, a minor noblewoman of slender means. The two young people eloped, and when he found out, Count Hermann threw his son in prison then accused Veronika of witchcraft and had her drowned. Her body was walled up in the castle, where locals claim they still occasionally hear her weeping. Fridrik was then released from prison, welcomed back into the family, married off to a more suitable noblewoman, and restored to his proper place as his father's successor. It really was a man's world in those dark old days.

Such horrors were the furthest thing from my mind as I sat peacefully on Gresna Gorica's vine-covered terrace eating lard laced with bacon. (Did I mention traditional Croatian cuisine is not exactly health food?) This appetizer was followed by one delectable dish after another: cottage cheese topped with *crème fraiche*, *gulaš* (deer goulash, seasoned with paprika and simmered for hours), beans drizzled with pumpkin seed oil, and duck served over something called *mlinci*. I may have been a bit muddled by the staggering heat, my exhaustion from all the sightseeing, and the stupor brought on by overeating, but I simply couldn't seem to grasp Lidija's explanation. *Mlinci* is not pasta, it is a kind of bread and you boil it? Really?

"Come to my house day after tomorrow and I will make it for you," Lidija said. "Then you will see how it works."

After that, the conversation meandered around and eventually alighted on one of Rich's pet interests: experimental micronations. A few years earlier he'd become fascinated by the discovery that the world contains a remarkable number tiny, self-declared nation-states born out of some offbeat philosophy and a maverick attitude. Some have quasi-legal standing, others are mere figments of the founder's imagination, but all have something quirky to contribute to the definition of "nation."

One of the most famous is the Republic of Užupis, a small, bohemian district tucked inside a loop of the river winding through the Lithuanian capital, Vilnius. Rich and I had visited it some years earlier and were charmed by its whimsical yet idealistic attitude. Dedicated to creativity and freedom, Užupis had its own flag, currency, constitution, president, anthem, and someone authorized to stamp our passports. The Republic of Užupis wasn't recognized by any official government, and no one (including, I suspect, the ringleaders) was quite sure where on the spectrum of serious to tongue-in-cheek the whole enterprise fell.

I kept Užupis' constitution posted in my office for years. Some of my favorite articles read: "Everyone has the right to make mistakes … A dog has a right to be a dog. A cat is not obliged to love its owner but must help in time of need … No one has the right to make another person guilty." Recently a new phrase was added: "Any artificial intelligence has the right to believe in the good will of humanity." Drafted with the help of Roboy, a Swiss robot, this phrase makes it the world's first constitution to mention artificial intelligence. Translated into twenty-five languages and etched into big metal sheets, the constitution hangs on a wall in Užupis; Pope Francis gave it his blessing when he visited in 2018.

You won't be astonished to learn that when it comes to oddball micronations, America has more than its share. One of the most colorful is the Republic of Molossai, which claims territory in Nevada, California, the Pacific Ocean, and a 49,881-acre strip of land on the planet Venus. Instead of the gold standard, Molossai pegs its currency to Pillsbury cookie dough and is currently in a state of war with East Germany, which of course, ceased to exist in 1990. As you can see, being tethered to mainstream reality is not a requirement for any micronation.

Over the deer goulash, Rich told Lidija he'd heard there was a micronation right there in Zagreb and asked if she knew anything about it.

"Of course, the Republike Peščenice," she said with a grin. "Everyone knows it."

Twenty years earlier, Zagreb's irreverent comedian Željko Malnar had created this mini-nation as a long-running gag on his late night "anti-TV" talk show. His political parodies regularly lampooned government inaction. During a Slovenian-Croatian border dispute, for instance, he claimed Republike Peščenice's military was taking over the area in question and restoring it to Croatia's control, "because our friendly neighbor Croatia doesn't have balls to do it herself." He was a cross between Stephen Colbert and Howard Stern, and I was sorry to learn he was no longer among the living.

Luckily some of Republike Peščenice's "senior government officials" were still alive and at large, and Lidija managed to track down one called Hamdija. He agreed to a meet us in the micronation's capital —

a carwash in an obscure Zagreb suburb. To put it in Croatian slang, the location was *bogu iza nogu*, a delightful expression signifying in the middle of nowhere but literally translated as "behind God's legs."

Lidija managed to find the carwash, and we settled down with cups of coffee in the tiny café attached to the it. We were the only ones there until a back door opened and a tall, balding man with a mustache came in trailed by a couple of friends. Hamdija, delighted to have a new audience for the old schtick, settled in to a nearby booth and entertained us with descriptions of pranks and jokes they'd devised to keep the nation on its toes.

Political lambasting is a popular sport everywhere, and Croatia offered Malnar plenty of scope. A member of the European Union and NATO, Croatia sits at the crossroads between Central and Southeast Europe and, according to many, marks the place where Eastern Europe ends and Western Europe begins. It shares borders with Hungary, Serbia, Bosnia and Herzegovina, Montenegro, and Slovenia, and has unresolved border issues with nearly all of them. As you can imagine, Malnar and his merry pranksters didn't lack for material or pull any punches.

Hamdija produced a copy of a book Malnar wrote about the Republike Peščenice and flipped to photos of stunts they'd pulled, including fake interviews with members dressed up as world leaders. He lingered with delight over photos of the red-letter day they received a visit from basketball's bad boy and Malnar's kindred spirit, Dennis Rodman. When Rich asked if he could buy a copy of the book, Hamdija said they were now very rare and cost $300. Then he roared with laughter and gave Rich two free copies. I was still chuckling as Lidija drove us back downtown and dropped us at our rental apartment.

By now the dog days of August had set in, and the somewhat cooler evenings enticed everyone outside. To keep the populace entertained after dark, city leaders had invented something they called the Zagreb Time Machine. Sadly, it wasn't an actual time machine but a program of dance parties, street theater, and other public entertainments designed to "bring the romantic spirit of past times to life."

One evening, Rich and I wandered over to the bandstand in Zrinjevac Park to check out the action. Settling in a chair at one of the tiny wooden tables, I gazed around. On a nearby lawn, kids were chasing each other through the twilight. Jugglers practiced their moves under the trees. Women sat in small clusters on park benches, languidly cooling their faces with paper fans. A few couples slow-danced as a band played golden oldies, mostly sentimental American hits such as the Drifters' "Under the Boardwalk" and Louis Armstrong's "What a Wonderful World." Lights were strung in the branches overhead, casting a warm glow on the couples dancing dreamily in each other's arms. Pretty soon Rich and I got up to join them.

"It feels like Hometown, USA," I said. "It's like the best part of every summer I can remember."

On another evening, as Rich and I were strolling toward the park to see if a band was playing yet, I heard the unmistakable strains of "The Chicken Dance" wafting our way. It was too infectious to resist, and before I could say "Dignity? What dignity?" Rich and I were flapping our wings and shaking our tail feathers right there on the sidewalk. In my defense, we weren't the only ones; several Croatians were right there with us, dancing and grinning their heads off. We all got plenty of amused glances from passing drivers and fellow pedestrians; it seemed we were part of the public entertainment that evening.

And then it was time to go to Lidija's to be initiated in the mysteries of how to make *mlinci*, the not-pasta, bread-like substance you cook by boiling.

On this occasion she was serving it with chicken. "You want a nice chicken from the village. This one was marinated overnight in onion, garlic, and herbs, and will roast in the oven while we make *mlinci*."

Lidija mixed white flour, eggs, oil, water, and salt with an electric beater then kneaded the dough by hand until it reached just the right consistency. She put it in a covered bowl to rise, and turned her attention to the chicken. Removing the marinade, she drizzled the bird with olive oil and wine, covered it, and put it into the oven to bake for an hour.

Glasses of wine were distributed to help sustain us during this interval, while the chicken baked and the dough rose.

As the kitchen filled with the delicious scent of herbs and roasting chicken, Lidija took the *mlinci* dough out of the bowl and reached for a rolling pin. And that's when I realized we really had crossed over from Eastern to Western Europe, because it wasn't the long, skinny, dowel-like rolling pin I'd been seeing for months, but a fatter version much like the one in my own kitchen. She rolled out the dough until it was so thin I could see through it, and then she cut it up into irregular rectangles roughly eight to ten inches long.

By now the chicken was done and cooling on the counter. Lidija took out the oven rack and placed a sheet of parchment paper on the very bottom of the oven. Here she distributed the rectangles of dough, in batch after batch, to bubble, brown, and crisp. The end result was a sort of flatbread, much like Turkish *lavash* or *chapati* from India. It was then broken into pieces, boiled, soaked in chicken drippings, and topped with pieces of chicken. Our *mlinci* dinner was ready.

How good was it? Rich started doing the chicken dance right there at the dinner table. Luckily our friends Lidija and Mladen were no strangers to this kind of silliness, and if they thought Rich had lost his mind, they were too tactful to say so. We all stuffed ourselves and then sat for a very long time, blissfully picking over the remains.

"One thing is clear," I said to Rich as we strolled back to our apartment in the warm night. "If we're going to keep eating like this, we're going to have to do the chicken dance a lot more often to get enough exercise."

Rich just made happy clucking sounds and kept on walking.

To me that evening was, as the Croatians like to say, *tko to može platit* — priceless.

ITALY

21. Parma, Modena & Bologna / *The King of Cheeses*

Crossing the border from Croatia into Italy, I looked forward to being on more familiar culinary turf and enjoying some of the most satisfying comfort food on the planet. I certainly never expected to be plunged into a flashback, reliving the hideous Cheese Knife Debacle from my past.

Excuse me for a moment while I pause to shudder at the memory. OK, I'm back with you now.

Hosting dinner parties in a foreign country inevitably involves pitfalls, pratfalls, and faux pas, and I've certainly made my share of them. This one took place shortly after Rich and I had moved to Seville, when I'd invited some Spanish friends over for drinks and tapas. I walked into the living room carrying a cheese platter and started to pass it around, only to have all my guests throw back their heads and roar with laughter.

I stared at the simple wooden cutting board, the neat wedges of Manchego and cheddar, the graceful little fan of commonplace crackers, and one of the three cheese knives that had come with the cutting board I'd purchased the day before.

The farmer next to me was among the first to recover his equanimity. As he sat wiping his eyes with a cocktail napkin, I asked what the fuss was all about.

"This," he said, holding up my new cheese knife, "is what we use for castrating the pigs." And then he was convulsed with laughter again.

Aghast, I instantly offered to fetch another knife, but my guests wouldn't hear of it, chortling softly and exchanging amused glances every time they passed the platter. Needless to say, that knife was retired, never to be seen again. Until I arrived in Parma, Italy, where its twin showed up in the hand of my hostess at an EatWith dinner party.

When I'd recovered from my shock at seeing that knife, I asked my hostess about its unusual blade. Stefania explained the *tagliagrana's* teardrop shape was perfectly designed to break hard cheeses into shards, making it ideal for serving the region's most famous product, Parmigiano-Reggiano cheese. Having grown up shaking pre-grated parmesan out of a green carboard tube, I had never seen anyone use a *tagliagrana* to slice chunks off a block of cheese. (Or to castrate a pig, for that matter.)

As an adult, I've had plenty of genuine Parmigiano-Reggiano cheese *in* stuff and *on* stuff, but until then I'd never thought of it as a stand-alone food. Stefania expertly wielded her *tagliagrana* to hack off bite-sized wedges as she explained aging gave Parmigiano-Reggiano its characteristic flavor — sharp, savory, complex, fruity yet nutty — and its traditional faintly gritty texture. She drizzled the pieces of Parmigiano-Reggiano cheese with her homemade balsamic vinegar, which was thick, tangy, and nearly sweet as molasses. The combination was sensational.

I was beginning to understand why Parma had been a culinary mecca for centuries. Rich and I hadn't found it easy to tear ourselves away from Zagreb, but we still had a few countries on our to-visit list, and the summer was quickly slipping away. I'd had my eye on Parma from the start, curious to know why people everywhere went into such raptures over Parmigiano-Reggiano, the "king of cheeses."

European laws protected the name and strictly defined the region — mainly Parma, and the neighboring city of Reggio Emilia — where it could legitimately be produced. Other parts of the world (yes, USA, I'm thinking of you) aren't bound by these laws, and they can — and do — call just about anything "parmesan." Production and quality vary considerably, and cheap cheddar, Swiss, or mozzarella are often added for bulk. A scandal erupted a few years ago when US authorities finally noticed that major producers had been diluting their so-called parmesan by adding hefty amounts of powdered wood pulp; the label referred to it as cellulose, to give the illusion it was appropriate for human consumption. That's no way to add fiber to our diet, people!

I knew I didn't have to fear Stefania would ever serve me wood pulp; she was a true believer in the joy of eating real food. While I was nibbling on the vinegar-drizzled Parmigiano-Reggiano, Stefania's husband wandered through the kitchen and was put to work slicing Prosciutto di Parma. This cured ham is slightly sweeter and less salty than prosciutto from other regions and is served in the traditional paper-thin, nearly translucent slivers. Naturally, I mentally compared it to Spanish *jamón Iberico,* which to me tastes a bit more robust and has a richer texture, although I admit I am far from an objective observer. However I could — and did — say, with all honesty, that Prosciutto di Parma was delicious.

Dinner included local tomatoes, eggplant, and the squat, sweet *borettana* onions that have been grown in the nearby town of Boretto since the fifteenth century. There was creamy veal scallopini in lemon sauce. But the star was succulent *coniglio alla cacciatora* (hunter-style rabbit).

Rabbit isn't a popular menu item in most parts of the USA — probably due to our early childhood exposure to Walt Disney's Thumper and the Beatrix Potter stories — but it's an enduring staple of the Mediterranean diet. When I first moved to Seville, I was appalled to see the furry bodies of lifeless bunnies hanging by their paws in the local butcher shops. I asked a friend why they didn't prepare them for sale in the modern fashion, skinned and trimmed so you could think of them as meat instead of Flopsy, Mopsy, Cotton-tail, and Peter. She explained the custom dated back to the Hunger, the lean years after the Spanish Civil War when nobody had enough to eat.

"They leave the fur on so you know it's not cat," she told me. "In those days, you wanted to be sure it wasn't the neighbor's pet. Or your own." Whoa! Enough said.

Stefania reassured me that for those who are squeamish about bunny-based dishes, the *coniglio alla cacciatora* recipe worked just as well with chicken. She then showed me the rabbit, thankfully already skinned and cut up — taking some of the "me" out of "meat," as animal rights people like to say — and now marinating in white wine.

She put chopped celery, onions, carrots, and garlic into a pan with olive oil, and as they began to cook, she lightly coated the rabbit pieces with flour and placed them on top of the vegetables. After adding tomato sauce, tomato paste, water, and seasoning, she let it all simmer for an hour. Toward the end, she tossed in sprigs of rosemary from her garden.

When I asked Stefania how she'd learned to cook, she said, "When I was seven years old, my parents gave me the Easy Bake Oven, and it was the best gift I ever received. So I started to cook, to bake." She grinned. "To sell cakes to my brothers." Her love of cooking for fun and profit led her to offer EatWith dinners and food tours.

"Parma is the cradle of Parmigiano-Reggiano, the cheese that was born in this area some eight centuries ago," she said with pride. "The process has not changed." There are only three ingredients: milk, salt, and rennet (a natural bovine enzyme that helps curds form). The resulting cheese is soaked in a salt bath then stacked in aging rooms for years.

"But you and Rich should see this for yourselves," Stefania said. As it happened she was taking house guests to a local cheese producer the very next morning, and it didn't take much persuasion to get us to join in.

Somehow I had expected an old-school operation, housed in an ancient barn and run by a portly fellow with kind eyes and a big grey mustache. Possibly I was imagining Disney's Geppetto, although wasn't he a shoemaker? No matter, I was utterly mistaken in any case. When I arrived the next morning, I found a starkly modern, super-efficient facility run by men with advanced degrees and a no-nonsense attitude. One of them handed out plastic hats, jackets, and booties for us to wear, and only when properly attired in protective gear were we admitted to the sacred precincts — a large white room in which stood enormous steel vats lined with copper.

Stefania kept up a running commentary. It all started with the milk, she explained, which had to be from local cows eating nothing but local fodder. Within hours of extraction it would be poured into the copper-lined vats and mixed with rennet, which helped it achieve the desired dense texture.

I didn't actually know what rennet was, so I looked it up later, and I have to say, I rather wish I hadn't. Rennet is a complex set of enzymes found in calf stomachs — specifically the inner mucous membrane of the fourth stomach chamber of young, nursing calves. Yes, regrettably, this requires butchering baby bovines to extract it. Nowadays, most manufacturers have abandoned this approach in favor of more modern methods. They employ genetic engineering to extract rennet-producing genes from calves' stomachs and then use those genes to grow rennet in bacteria, fungi, and yeast. Either way, the gross factor is considerable. Try not to think of it next time you're sitting down to a plate of veal parmesan.

OK, back to the production process. The milk and rennet were heated in the vats until curds formed and clumped together to form giant, soft, white blobs. In the time-honored manner, a couple of brawny workers then slipped a length of muslin under each massive blob, tied the corners of the muslin to a wooden pole, and gently lifted it out. The watery milk left behind, known as whey, was later fed to pigs destined to become Prosciutto di Parma.

Each blob, which had now attained the status of young cheese, was placed inside a form that would imprint its outer edge with the Parmigiano-Reggiano name, the producer's name, and the date. The forms were set in a preservative salt bath where they'd float gently for three weeks. After that, the wheels of cheese — each precisely thirty-seven kilos, or just over eighty-one pounds — would be taken out of their forms and placed on wooden shelves to age. Once a week, each wheel was carefully wiped down and turned; this facility, which had hundreds of rows of shelves, now assigned that task to machines instead of humans. In one year or three, the cheese wheels would be deemed ready for sale and make their way to the world's markets.

It seemed incredibly labor-intensive, but who was I to argue with eight hundred years of tradition? After the tour, as we were pulling off our protective gear, Stefania said, "My country home is close to here. Would you like to see it?" Of course, there was only one answer to that invitation!

The house, nestled in a small village in the Lesignano de' Bagni area, proved to be an old, rambling, gray stone building thickly festooned with vines and surrounded with flowering shrubs. I picked my way across a stone-paved courtyard, up the few steps to the terrace, and into the house. The rabbit warren of rooms was filled with lovely old wooden tables and chairs, the kind of comfortable country furniture that always makes me want to sit down, kick off my shoes, and open a book, preferably with a cup of coffee at my elbow.

I followed Stefania, climbing ever higher up flights of stairs until she announced, "And here is the attic," in a tone of voice that let me know this was the main event. It was a simple, airy, whitewashed room filled with barrels, but for the first few moments I only had eyes for the view. The single arched window, framed by rough stone and even rougher plaster, revealed cultivated fields glowing in the sunlight, stands of old trees, the occasional red tile roof, and distant, blue-shadowed hills.

When I could tear my gaze away, I realized Stafania was

explaining about the barrels. "This is the *acetaia*, the place where the grape must — that is, the newly crushed grapes — will be aged in barrels for many, many years to become balsamic vinegar. Each set of barrels," she waved to rows of barrels in ever decreasing sizes, "is called a battery. You see the opening at the top, covered with a linen cloth. That allows evaporation."

She explained fermentation took place during the summer heat, while each winter the older, more condensed vinegar was transferred to the next smaller barrel. In accordance with local tradition, she'd set up a battery for each of her two daughters at birth, so vinegar and child would grow to maturity together.

"I will let you taste the difference," she said. "Here is nine-year-old vinegar." She handed around spoons and filled each one from a small bottle. I trickled the dark liquid into my mouth and felt an explosion of brash flavor. "And this is the vinegar that has aged for twenty-one years." It was thick, dark, and tangy-sweet, lingering delectably on the tongue. "You can see why people here serve it drizzled over ice cream."

The net effect? Stefania had just ruined American balsamic vinegar for me; I'd never again be satisfied with the cheap knock-offs I was used to. Italian law protects the most famous labels such as *Aceto Balsamico Tradizionale di Modena* (Traditional Balsamic Vinegar of Modena), enforcing such restrictions as age (at least twelve years) and additives (none). You probably won't be surprised to learn that America has no such constraints. Bottles labeled "balsamic vinegar," even those specifying "barrel aged in Modena, Italy," often contain juvenile liquids laced with corn syrup, guar gum, or worse.

Parma had plenty to offer besides great food, and Rich and I spent days exploring the older neighborhoods. Like most great cities it was built on the banks of a river; five thousand years ago, Bronze Age people were living on the site in a *terramare*, a village of wooden houses on stilts surrounded by substantial mud walls and a moat. Nobody knows why they wanted stilts, as the land wasn't subject to flooding. Fashion? Superstition? A way to provide comfortable, shady accommodations for the pigs?

The Bronze Age settlers chose an excellent location, with a good water supply and plenty of fertile land, so naturally it was invaded by every army passing through the region. Yet somehow, despite the occasional burning, sacking, and pillaging, the city continued to prosper.

During Medieval times, war was just one of the exciting tools in the arsenal of international power brokers, and in 1061 Parma became embroiled in another — Vatican politics — when its bishop became the antipope. At the time, the Roman Catholic Church was the most powerful organization in Western civilization, but in recent centuries the Holy Roman Empire — claiming to embody the best of Roman achievement and Christian virtue backed by serious military muscle — was giving it serious competition. When old Pope Nicholas II went to his reward, the Holy Roman Empire wanted to be involved in (meaning: be in control of) choosing his successor.

The Church pointed out they'd done just fine electing their own popes for a thousand years and saw no reason to change. The dowager empress Agnes, ruling the Holy Roman Empire on behalf of her minor son, forcefully pointed out the many ways they were wrong about that. The Church, after politely suggesting the Empress mind her own beeswax, promptly gathered the cardinals, held an election, and announced they had a new pope, Alexander II.

Irate, the dowager empress called a meeting of her most loyal German and Lombard bishops, and they selected Pietro Cadalo, Bishop of Parma, for the job.

At the time Cadalo was just sinking his teeth into the massive project of building Parma's cathedral. That alone would ensure his place in history, but it didn't hold a candle to the title he was now being offered:

Bishop of Rome, Vicar of Jesus Christ, Successor of the Prince of the Apostles, Supreme Pontiff of the Universal Church, Primate of Italy, Archbishop and Metropolitan of the Roman Province, Sovereign of the State of Vatican City, Servant of the Servants of God. (You'll notice the word "pope" doesn't appear in this official list of titles; it's actually a nickname meaning "papa.")

Flattered beyond his wildest dreams, Cadalo naturally accepted the position. Agnes and her supporters assembled an army, placed their antipope at its head, and sent the whole lot of them marching south to take the Vatican by force.

They got further than you might expect, winning a skirmish with Roman soldiers and briefly taking over the Basilica of St. Peter within the Vatican itself. But no one in Rome had any doubt who wielded the real power, and an army assembled quickly, defeated the imperial force, and send Cadalo back to Parma.

Key powerbrokers on both sides met in the Council of Mantua, and no doubt there was a free and frank exchange of ideas across the table for some considerable time. When the shouting stopped, the dust settled, and the bloodstains were all mopped up, concessions had been agreed upon — among them, that the Church still held the absolute right to elect its own popes. Representatives of the Empire were forced to accept the decision with as much grace as they could muster.

Cadalo refused to acknowledge the demotion, and to his dying day insisted, to anyone who would listen, that he was the real pope, and they had better call him "Your Holiness" while kissing his ring. When the cathedral he'd built was destroyed by an earthquake in 1117, there were those who felt God, as was so often the case, had had the last word.

I was seeing Parma in far less exciting times. It was late August, and just about everybody in the city was away on vacation. Those who remained moved through the long, hot days at a slow pace. Rich and I drifted through the ancient monuments and sunny cafés, absorbing the peace and tranquility that is always particularly precious in a town that has known so much strife.

One morning I summoned a little extra energy and proposed a visit to nearby Modena, hometown of Luciano Pavarotti, such flashy sports cars as Ferrari, Lamborghini, and Maserati, and of course, the iconic balsamic vinegar that bears the city's name.

It was a Sunday in August, so naturally most of the town was closed down, shutters drawn tight against the hot sun. But a few restaurants and shops were open, as were major monuments and at least one well-known balsamic vinegar tasting room. But first I wanted to get a quick look at the cathedral, home of the object that kicked off the War of the Bucket in 1325.

As they had in antipope Cadalo's day, tensions were running high between the Holy Roman Empire (which Modena backed), and the Roman Catholic Church (to which Bologna had pledged its loyalty). For months there had been scuffles and skirmishes between the two city-states; a few outposts were torched, the occasional unlucky soldier got ambushed, and plenty of bravado and braggadocio was voiced on all sides.

Then, according to local legend, a few pranksters from Modena's army had the bright idea of sneaking into downtown Bologna and stealing the oak bucket from the main well. They slipped back out the gate and, having made sure they were beyond arrow range, brandished their trophy, voiced considerable ridicule and derision, then rode home.

Bologna hotly demanded the return of their property.

Modena merely laughed.

Bologna officials delivered sternly worded warnings to return the bucket — *or else.*

Modena laughed even harder and outdid themselves making

snarky remarks.

Goaded beyond endurance, the Bolognese declared war on Modena.

Bologna assembled 30,000 foot soldiers and 2000 mounted cavaliers and marched to the advantageous high ground near what's now the town of Zappalino. Modena gathered just 5000 men at arms and 2000 horsemen on the plane below. But these were battle-hardened veterans who knew a thing or two about tactics. And by now, they were pretty fed up with the Bolognese attitude. It was just a bucket, for heaven's sake! Where was their sense of humor? Time to get this over with.

The battle ended just hours after it had begun, with 2000 dead on the field and the surviving Bolognese fleeing in disarray back to their city. Whooping and hollering, Modena's soldiers nipped at their heels the whole way back to the main gate. Then, rather than lay siege to the city, as would have been customary, they spent the rest of the afternoon taunting their enemies by holding a mock *palio* (a local form of horse race) outside Bologna's walls and tossing the occasional jeers over the battlements at their vanquished foe.

After wallowing long and hard in their victory, the Modena army packed up to head homeward. Some versions of the tale claim that at this point they stole another bucket from an outlying well and waved it at the walls of Bologna in a mocking manner. I wouldn't put it past them.

The original bucket is said to reside in a secure location somewhere in Modena's cathedral, while a replica remains on display in the belltower. For centuries, the good citizens of Modena have regarded the whole affair as a terrific joke, and the Bolognese have tried to live down their mortification.

After Parma's exuberantly overdecorated cathedral, Modena's struck me as beautifully understated, a serene and graceful work of geometric stone with sculptures by an artist named Wiligelmo, who evidently had a puckish sense of humor. At the base of several pillars he'd carved little men sitting on what appear to be stacks of books, hunched forward, carrying all of the pillar's weight on their bent backs. It would be hard to devise a more hideously uncomfortable way to spend the centuries, and I can only assume Wiligelmo was paying off old scores by carving the faces of his enemies into these grumpy-looking pillar bearers.

The rest of the time in Medina passed pleasantly enough. At a shop offering samples of the town's famous vinegar, the *commessa* (saleswoman) seemed overjoyed to have someone drop by to alleviate the tedium. We explained we were not there to buy, but she brushed that aside and offered sample after sample of her best. The first few were on a par with Stefania's, but I have to admit the last was mind-blowing — as it should be, at $160 for a bottle containing less than three and a half ounces of vinegar.

Another morning I suggested hopping the train from Parma to nearby Bologna. The trip turned out to be a lot more exciting than I expected.. But as Rich always says, "Any one you can walk away from..."

The drama began en route from the railway station to the city center. Most Europeans place their train stations downtown for convenience, but Bologna — perhaps feeling its citizens needed to work off their consumption of the sausage for which the town is known — put theirs about a mile and a half away. On a morning that was already growing uncomfortably hot, I found the walk into town a tedious slog along streets that were largely deserted and lined with nondescript buildings. I know they can't all have been beige, but that's how they are in my memory of that morning.

I stepped off a curb, noticed a car speeding in our direction, and casually laid a hand on Rich's arm. About to step past me, Rich checked his stride for a split second — and the car shot by, the fender missing him by less than six inches. The driver slowed slightly, gave a little apologetic wave out the window, and disappeared down the street.

It took a lot longer for my heart rate to decelerate.

"Is it true that when you save someone's life, it means you are responsible for them forever?" I asked, when I got my breath back.

"It means I'm going to be more careful in this town."

Ten minutes later we reached the center of town and I discovered where everybody was. The crowds of vacationing Italians and visiting foreigners that had been so noticeably absent in Parma and Modena were thronging the streets of Bologna. It was a physically charming city, full of attractive shops and cafés, but I couldn't enjoy it properly surrounded by heaving masses of people.

Eventually Rich and I fetched up in front of the cathedral of Saint Peter and stumbled through its ancient doors into the cool, dim, peace of the lofty nave. I sat down gratefully on an old wooden pew, caught my breath, and looked around.

The décor was pure, overwrought Baroque, a statement about the kingdom, the power, and the glory on the grandest possible scale. Much of it was beautiful, but occasionally an artist overreached himself. For instance, the sixteenth century sculpture *Compianto su Cristo Morto* (Lament Over the Death of Christ) was executed with such theatricality that each of the eight characters seemed to be vying for our attention like ham actors trying to upstage each other at an audition. But hey, it was that kind of era, and when it comes to holy art, I always prefer over-exuberance to dullness and sanctimonious piety.

When lunchtime rolled around, I was more than ready to get out of the city center in hopes of finding a more tranquil atmosphere. Earlier, during the walk from the railway station, Rich had glimpsed a side street with a shady arcade and clusters of café tables. Somehow he found his way back there, and I was overjoyed to find several small eateries serving lunch. We chose the unpretentious Trattoria Tony where a few Italians, neighborhood folks by the look of them, were already seated before large plates of pasta.

Tony welcomed us with enthusiasm and free slices of *mortadella*, the grandfather of bologna sausage — which we kids called baloney when it was our school lunchboxes. To follow, I ordered cold white wine and the city's iconic pasta. Luckily I didn't embarrass myself by using its international name, *spaghetti bolognese*; tipped off by some knowledgeable food bloggers, I asked for *tagliatelle al ragù* and got the classic dish of broad, flat noodles with a slow-cooked meat sauce flavored with tomato. *Deliziosa!*

We left Tony's in a haze of post-prandial bonhomie that made me think that maybe I could start warming to Bologna. This rosy viewpoint lasted right up until Rich was assaulted.

The guy came angling toward us as we were crossing a large, open, deserted plaza. He was a small, scruffy fellow who kept darting sideways glances at us. When he drew near, he demanded something — I'm guessing money. Rich shook his head and kept walking. And then the guy grabbed Rich's arm.

Rich pulled away, trying to dislodge his grip, but the fellow was stronger than he looked and clung like a demon trying to drag a soul into hell.

As they tussled, I threw back my head and shouted at the top of my lungs. "Let him go! Back off! Get out of here! Stop," I roared. And yes, there might possibly have been some stronger language in there as well. For once, I didn't care about getting the wording right; it was all about shock value.

Rich's attacker recoiled as if I'd flung boiling holy water in his face and took off at a dead run.

"You notice he paid no attention to me," Rich remarked. "But it was pretty clear you scared the hell out of him."

"Happy to be of service," I said. I've found shouting to be remarkably effective on the rare occasions I needed to respond to anything like a physical threat. It was rather exhilarating, to be honest. "You know, I'm beginning to think this town has it in for you. Let's get out of here before anybody else decides to mount an attack."

On the train back to Parma, we began discussing our next destination, the small (but mighty) city of Asti in the Piedmont area of northwestern Italy. Among its most well-known and beloved cultural contributions were Asti spumante, Martini & Rossi, and white truffles. But the city was also famed for the wild, no-holds-barred horserace that's been an annual tradition since the thirteenth century. And this year, as luck would have it, Rich and I would be there just in time to catch it.

22. Asti / *What Wine Goes with Horse?*

Long ago, in an era that took enemy-taunting to the level of an Olympic sport, Asti was a hot contender. As we have seen, Modena really distinguished itself in the jeering department during the War of the Bucket. Sculptor Wiligelmo mocked his enemies for all eternity by carving them into hideously uncomfortable poses at the base of cathedral pillars. Of course, when it came to the magnificent medieval put-down, the Bard of Avon is the grand master.

Who but Shakespeare could have written, "Thou leathern-jerkin, crystal-button, knot-pated, agatering, puke-stocking, caddis-garter, smooth-tongue, Spanish pouch!" or the pithy, "Would thou wert clean enough to spit upon," or the somewhat mystifying "Scurvy knave! I am none of his flirt-gills. I am none of his skains-mates." Even without knowing that a flirt-gill is a loose woman and a skains-mate is a cut-throat companion, when someone flings such mockery in your direction, it's clear you've had what the British call a proper bollocking.

Sometimes actions sneer better than words. For reasons that have been lost in the dim mists of time, on one particular day back in the thirteenth century, Asti wanted to taunt their long-time rival, the city-state of Alba. As Modena had done after winning the War of the Bucket, Asti held a *palio,* a freewheeling, bareback horse race, just outside their enemy's walls, trampling the city's vineyards in the process. You can imagine how that went down with the wine-loving citizens of Alba.

The *palio* was so much fun Asti decided to re-enact it every September, only they would hold it in their own downtown and skip the vineyard trampling. For centuries the race was a breakneck dash through city streets, and you can imagine the pandemonium of thundering hooves, shrieking residents, falling masonry, and the hysterical barking of every dog for miles around. Today it's held in the enormous, triangular Piazza Vittorio Alfieri surrounded by temporary bleachers holding cheering thousands. Twenty-one teams, based in and around the city, take part, and competition is fierce.

Arriving in Asti the day before the race, I felt the buzz of excitement everywhere; voices were raised, steps were buoyant, colorful parish banners fluttered overhead. Checking into the Lis Hotel, a small family-run place just a short walk from the Piazza Vittorio Alfieri, I asked my hostess, Caterina, about buying tickets to the race. Would there be any difficult getting seats now, at the last minute?

She reassured me seats were still available and gave me directions to the nearby ticket office. I asked her about *palio* traditions besides the race itself and learned there would be parades of residents dressed in medieval costumes and displays of synchronized banner-waving and banner-tossing by local youths. Each of the competing parish would be holding a pre-race banquet that evening as part of the festivities.

"I have a friend," said Caterina, "who is helping to organize one of the banquets. If you would like to attend, I can inquire if it is possible."

Naturally I leapt at the chance, and by the time Rich and I got back with our tickets for the race, Caterina and her friend had organized everything.

"The parish is Cattedrale," Caterina said, handing me a slip of paper with the banquet's address. "It means cathedral. They have not won in 42 years, but this time, they are hopeful." Great; nothing I like more than rooting for an underdog. It's more thrilling if they win and easier to shrug off if they lose. Rich and I showered, dug out some passably clean clothes from the depths of our suitcases, and went to the feast.

Long tables had been set out in the courtyard of an enormous old building lined with porticos and hung with Cattedrale's colors, sky blue and white with a black eagle. As I paid the modest fee for dinner, I saw people of all ages, dressed in everything from jeans to suits, chatting in small clusters as they drifted toward the tables. I picked a spot more or less at random and sat down a few seats away from a group of eight or ten middle-aged men and women. They shot covert looks in our direction and held a low-voiced discussion. Eventually a woman detached herself from the group and came over to sit next to me. She introduced herself, in passable English, as Judy; clearly she'd been elected to help the two clueless Americans navigate the evening. I was deeply grateful.

Wine was being passed up and down the table — always a good start, in my view — and soon servers appeared with the first course. We each received a disposable plastic plate holding a salad, a wedge of cheese, and a blob of what I took to be steak tartare until Judy explained that it was horse. Raw horse. Probably *pesto di cavallo*, raw horsemeat marinated in lemon juice with fresh garlic and chopped parsley, although Judy didn't go into this much detail. However it was prepared, my dinner included — and I cannot underscore this enough — *raw horse*.

Just then, Judy turned away to greet a friend, and Rich leaned over and whispered, "You realize we don't have a choice. We have to eat it."

"I know. The demands of hospitality … And I'd hate to screw up our team's karma." Judy turned back to us, and I smiled and picked up my fork. Too bad this wasn't a genuine medieval banquet, with hungry dogs under the table just waiting to wolf down any stray scraps.

I suppose I shouldn't have been so surprised. All through Northern Italy I'd seen specialty butcher shops selling nothing but horsemeat. In that part of the world, it was valued as lean, wholesome protein, high in iron and nutrients, and particularly beneficial to youngsters and invalids. Equine consumption was not some new fad. The oldest known human artwork, the 31,000-year-old Chauvet-Pont-d'Arc cave painting in France, shows our Cro-Magnon ancestors hunting horses for meat. For the next 25,000 years or so, everybody considered them fair game.

And then, as is so often the case, religion got into the act. Jewish dietary laws, which took written form about 3000 years ago, prohibited eating horses; they don't have split hooves or chew their cud, so they're non-kosher. Better minds than mine have wrestled with the question of exactly why that's the case; I'm staying out of the debate. Then in the early seventh century, the Quran also took horsemeat off the table due to religious scruples.

The Christians, however, kept on cheerfully chowing down on horse without a thought about how it might affect their immortal souls. And then suddenly, in 732, Pope Gregory III declared that eating equines was a mortal sin.

Why? Because the pontiff was making a major effort to convert some Germanic tribes who consumed horse in their ancient rituals. He figured if he made horse-eating taboo, it would serve as a handy litmus test for judging true conversions — much as eating ham would later be used by the Spanish Inquisition to gauge the sincerity of converts from the Muslim and Jewish communities. Horsemeat, which had graced many a clergyman's Sunday dinner table for centuries, was suddenly prohibited throughout Christendom. Pope Gregory's proclamation echoed down the centuries, causing people all over the world to view eating horsemeat as not only immoral but nearly as abhorrent as cannibalism.

On top of all that, Americans, and especially my relatives, tend to view horses as companion animals — not just pets, but members of the family, if not outright soul mates. As children, my mother and her sister, Beverly, lived in the country, riding horses daily, and they put us kids in a saddle as soon as we could sit upright. Whenever old, obscure family photos were passed around, my mother and aunt could instantly identify every one of the horses and dogs but were often vague about the humans. I knew, as I started to raise the first bite of *pesto di cavallo* to my lips, that if it turned out there actually were ghosts, I was in for a quite a scolding from Mom and Aunt Bev.

Of course, it was quite possible I'd already eaten horse without even knowing it. In 2013 there was an enormous scandal when European officials discovered horsemeat was being passed off as beef by major food suppliers. Such giants as Burger King, Tesco, and Ikea found themselves scrambling to pull potentially tainted products off the shelves. I did eat meatballs at an Ikea in Spain during that time, and I'll go to my grave unsure about what was in them.

Outraged consumers complained about the violation of religious principles, the horror of being tricked into eating these noble animal companions, and legitimate medical concerns over the possible presence of veterinary drugs unfit for human consumption. When traces of pork were also discovered in this so-called beef, the uproar rose into the stratosphere, especially in the Jewish and Muslim communities. As heads rolled up and down the food chain, everyone scrambled to distance themselves. One West Yorkshire pub put a sign outside saying, "Neigh horse in our burgers."

But unwittingly eating meatballs or hamburger with a pinch of pony is a far cry from sitting down to a plate of horse tartare. I can now report from personal experience that it is much like beef tartare but slightly sweeter and more tender. If I could just stop picturing the amiable face of our old Shetland pony, I could almost like it. I told Judy it was delicious; she beamed.

"Look," she said suddenly, " the man who will ride tomorrow." A slender figure was making his way to the head table amidst cheers and shouts of encouragement. He turned and addressed a few brief remarks to the crowd, eliciting hearty applause, then sat down among the dignitaries.

I soldiered on, eating my *pesto di cavallo,* washing it down with copious amounts of white wine. Later I learned that horse is traditionally paired with red wine, but at that point I was beyond caring. I kept wondering what they'd serve for the next course. Pasta with puppy sauce? Kitten stew? Fortunately it turned out to be a conventional cheese ravioli, so I could enjoy it ,with a clear conscience and stop looking over my shoulder for the angry shades of my ancestors.

Aside from horse, I loved the cuisine of Asti. The next morning I discovered our hotel had a truly lavish breakfast buffet, and while I was browsing happily among the rich cakes and fluffy pastries, my hostess, Caterina, materialized at my side.

"Try the, *torta de nocciole,*" she suggested, indicating something that looked like a flourless chocolate cake. "A specialty of the region. The name means hazelnut cake, because they are traditional, but I make it with walnuts and chocolate, so it is even richer. I will send you my recipe." Who could resist? "It's normally served as a dessert," she confided. My kind of breakfast.

Rich and I spent the morning wandering about, enjoying the festive atmosphere. Medieval costumes were much in evidence, with civic leaders dressed as nobles and rich merchants dressed as rich merchants. Women sported elaborate headdresses and long satin skirts that trailed behind them over dusty cobblestones; I was glad I didn't have the job of cleaning those gowns afterwards. Men in gorgeous cloaks and velvet hats rode by on well-mannered, prancing horses. Youths in doublets and hose waved large flags, tossing them in the air and catching them again with practiced ease and satisfied grins. Everyone seemed to be having grand time.

I peered into the cathedral where mass was being celebrated and saw that every pew was full. No doubt some very intense praying was going on, especially by my team, easily identifiable by their satin scarves of sky blue and white emblazoned with the black eagle and the word

"Cattedrale." I've read that when the town of Siena holds its *palios*, they bring the horses right into the church for a special blessing, and horse droppings on the floor are considered a sign of good luck. If Asti has the same traditions, I saw no evidence of it.

At last it was time for the main event. Rich and I climbed up to our nosebleed seats and settled down to enjoy the fun. As it turned out, Asti's *palio* was the most disorganized mess I'd ever seen on a racetrack. I loved every minute of it.

At the beginning of each race, the jockeys, helmeted and riding bareback, guided their mounts toward the thick rope that marked the starting line. Before they were all in place, one horse ambled off, a second had a skittish moment, and a third began eyeing the crowd, sidestepping and shaking his mane in a flirtatious manner. As these animals were encouraged back to the rope, two more backed out of line. A large bay took a few practice spins in place, displacing his neighbors. Then another horse flitted away with a flourish of his tail. As if that were a signal, the whole lot of them began milling about, shaking their heads and stomping their feet importantly. After a small eternity of this, there was a single golden moment when a fair majority of them were nudged into ragged alignment at the starting rope. It dropped and the race was on.

The horses thundered around the track, slewing wide on the tight turns of the triangle's corners, the jockeys bent low, whipping them forward. A rider fell off, the first of many who would hit the dirt that day; at least one or two tumbled off during each heat. Most of the fallen managed to scramble to their feet and stagger to the relative safety of the railing. A few had to be carried off, and astonishingly only one had to be hauled away in an ambulance. The riderless horses continued hurtling around the racecourse; they seemed to know the rules allowed them to win even without a jockey on board, and they kept up the frantic pace right to the finish line.

Winners of earlier heats competed in the final race, and I was delighted to see the sky blue and white colors at the lineup; Cattedrale had made the cut. The atmosphere was electric. Plenty of glory was at stake, to say nothing of the massive amounts of money changing hands in wagers. The official prizes for the winning jockeys were symbolic rather than monetary. First prize: a large, colorful cloth banner, suitable for flaunting. Second prize: spurs. Third prize: a modest pouch of coins. Last place: an anchovy, the sign of mockery and dishonor.

Before the final race could began, the horses had to spend even more time prancing and pirouetting about. Eventually, the competitors arrived at a haphazard semi-alignment. The rope fell, and they were off as if shot out of cannons.

They passed by me in a blur of color, thundering around the track again and again, hooves flying, jockeys flattened along the animals' outstretched necks. Everyone in the stands was on their feet and shouting, including me. And when they shot across the finish line, who should be first but the jockey wearing sky blue and white.

"Cattedrale!" announced the loudspeaker.

"Oh my God, we won!" I shouted, jumping up and down, hugging Rich and laughing. "We won!"

It was a heady afternoon indeed.

Rich and I celebrated that evening with a horse-free dinner at the elegant Campanaro Restaurant. I ordered a lovely zucchini frittata, roast chicken with carrots, and the region's popular dessert, *pesche ripieno all' Amaretto* (peaches stuffed with Amaretto cookies and chocolate). To accompany the dessert, I ordered one of the sparkling wines for which Asti is so famous, going with the waiter's suggestion of the 2013 Paolo Berutti Moscato d'Asti, which was a rich, slightly fruity delight.

All in all, Asti had been tremendous fun. The next morning, as Rich and I were walking to the railway station with our suitcases to catch a train for Turin, I heard a shout and saw someone waving at me from across the street. It was Judy, my friend from the banquet.

She ran over and flung her arms around me, shouting, "We won! We won!"

And that was the perfect ending to my time in Asti.

23. Turin / *Santa Polenta*

In Turin, I found a simple, sure-fire way to break the ice with people you don't know well: commit a social faux pas. As if the efficacy of this approach hadn't been amply demonstrated by my Cheese Knife Debacle, I proved it all over again the night I met Carlotta and Paolo.

Shortly after arriving in Turin (or Torino, as it's properly known), I was, as usual, flipping through the EatWith site and found Carlotta's menu. "This one sounds fabulous. Salami and cheese with truffle honey … risotto with sausage … that weird dish we liked the other day, veal with tuna sauce … and for dessert? Hazelnut cake with a sauce I can't pronounce."

"You had me at risotto," he said. "Sign us up."

I sent Carlotta a note explaining about the Mediterranean Comfort Food Tour and asking if I could come early and watch her cooking. She kindly agreed, and even though I knew wine was included in the meal, I thought I'd bring along a bottle as an extra courtesy to express my gratitude. Days earlier I'd chilled a couple of bottles of crisp, pleasant white in our rental apartment's refrigerator, and on the way out to dinner I grabbed one and threw it in a carrier bag. I now pulled the bottle out of the bag and presented it to Carlotta and her partner Paolo with a little flourish.

And then I did a double take.

"Oh, my God," I exclaimed in horror. "I brought the wrong wine."

In my haste, I'd grabbed the bottle we'd opened two nights earlier. I was beyond mortified. An unopened bottle of wine says, "Thanks for your hospitality." I'm not quite sure what a partially drunk bottle says. "We're barbarians who don't know the first thing about social niceties" perhaps?

Fortunately, Carlotta and Paolo were kindhearted, easygoing hosts with a lively sense of humor. As I fell all over myself apologizing, they just kept laughing and reassuring me it was fine.

To move us all past the moment, Carlotta produced a bottle of Rocca dei Forti, a delicious, dry, sparkling white wine. "Would you like to try it with a little vermouth?" she asked. The Torinese are proud of having invented vermouth back in the eighteenth century and will slip it into a drink at the drop of a hat. In a spirit of journalistic inquiry, I felt I should accept her offer. The tiny dash of vermouth gave the wine a pleasing depth and zing — much as it does to the gin of a martini.

The combination of Carlotta's drinks and our little icebreaker soon had us all talking and chuckling like old friends. Note to self: Perhaps make a point of doing something idiotic at the start of every social occasion? Additional note to self: No need to make an effort, this is likely to happen all on its own.

Black and green olives accompanied our wine-and-vermouth aperitif, along with some of the slender breadsticks known as *grissini* wrapped in *prosciutto di Parma*. Carlotta then produced a platter with local salamis and cheeses, slivers of golden pear, and two sauces — grape compote and honey with truffles — which combined divinely with the cheese.

While nibbling and sipping, I learned that Paolo was an architect, and that Carlotta had a small tour guide business called Torino Discovery which, in addition to traditional sightseeing, offered market tours, vermouth tastings, and expeditions to sample the city's famous chocolates. (I noticed Rich's eyes lighting up over this last and knew I'd be learning a lot more about Torino's chocolate confections in the near future.)

Carlotta asked where in the city we'd eaten so far, and I mentioned we had our eye on a bistro called Santa Polenta. Carlotta and Paolo fell about laughing.

"What?" I asked, hoping this wasn't local slang for pig castrating. Or worse.

"Here in Turin, that's an expression you use when you want to swear, but need to make it a mild swear," explained Carlotta. How delightful! I collect minced oaths of this kind, such as gadzooks, Jiminy Cricket, zounds, tarnation, and a childhood favorite from Snagglepuss, heavens to Murgatroyd. Lovely to add another to the repertoire.

The conversation rolled on, mostly revolving around food, and Carlotta confided that she'd had a passion for cooking since she was a young girl. Which made it especially challenging when she had learned she'd have to give up gluten altogether.

"At first," she told me, "when I was diagnosed with celiac disease, I thought it was the end. Not only of my good eating, but also of my cooking. But actually, I would say it was a blessing in disguise. Because it helped me to look at things in a different way. And to adjust recipes, even traditional recipes, and to do more research about the science that is behind baking especially, and about cooking in general. All in all it was something that made me progress in my cooking, in my passion, and in my knowledge."

Her skill and passion became abundantly evident as I watched her prepare the centerpiece of the meal: risotto with sausage. After browning onion in a large pot with a sprig of rosemary, she added ground sausage and when that had browned, she cleared a spot in the bottom of the pan and tossed in handfuls of carnaroli rice (arborio's slenderer cousin). When the rice had seared, she mixed it with the sausage, then added broth and red wine, simmered the mixture until the rice was al dente, stirred in some butter and cheese and served it.

Of all the wonderful recipes I was given on this trip, Carlotta's risotto with sausage turned out to be the one I would make most often when I got home. I use the easier-to-get arborio rice, white wine instead of red as I usually have it on hand, and vary the sausage depending on who is at the table. For carnivore friends I use a robust pork sausage as Carlotta did. For vegans I go with plant-based pseudo-sausage and replace the butter and cheese with extra olive oil. No matter what I do with it, this dish is always a huge hit.

Along with the wonderful risotto, we ate *vitel tonnè* (veal with tuna), a star of the Torino summer menu. Slices of braised veal are served cold topped with a marvelously creamy, slightly salty sauce. To make it, you simmer fresh or canned tuna in white wine, vinegar, onion, and garlic, then purée the mix with olive oil and egg yolk to form a sort of thick mayonnaise, which is then enlivened with anchovies, capers, and lemon. It's prepared a day or two in advance so the flavors have a chance to really come together.

And then, just when I was sure I couldn't consume another mouthful, it was time for dessert. "My hazelnut cake is of course flourless," Carlotta said. "And really quite simple. It has just three ingredients: hazelnuts, eggs, and sugar. On top I put *Moscato zabaione*. Would you like to watch me make this sauce?"

Leaving Paolo and Rich chatting at the table, Carlotta and I went into the kitchen, where she proceeded to put egg yolks and sugar in one of those fancy food processors that's also a cooker, an Italian brand much like a Thermomix. "I use one egg yolk and one tablespoon of sugar per person," she said, "And for every egg yolk I add one eggshell of Moscato." And with that she picked up a half eggshell and used it to measure sweet Moscato d'Asti dessert wine into the mix. "I make sure the machine heats it enough to destroy any bacteria but not cook the egg." In minutes the thick, sweet, creamy sauce was ready to serve.

Rich and his sweet tooth were in their glory. "This is incredible," he said, finishing his own piece and eyeing the remains of mine. I had slowed to a halt, having reached my consumption capacity halfway through the *vitel tonnè*. I passed my plate to him and he tucked in with a happy sigh. "You see?" Carlotta grinned. "You can eat a full Italian meal that is just as good as a gluten-y meal."

Santa Polenta, was that ever the gospel truth!

"Food is part of our social life," Carlotta told me thoughtfully. "So sitting down at a table and having good food, comforting food, and eating it slowly with your friends and your loved ones while you have a conversation about your life, about the important things, silly things, is part of the everyday life." Sitting with her, Paolo, and Rich, I was stuck again by the Mediterranean genius for making every meal feel like a manifesto for Life as It Is Meant to Be Lived. We talked about everything and nothing, and rose from the table deeply satisfied.

I got to thinking about how the mix of social connection and mouthwatering goodness has made Italian cuisine a favorite just about everywhere on the planet — proof that, as the Weird Italy blog put it, "in a culinary sense at least, the Romans managed to take over the world." And their reach is still expanding. A few years ago, Italian astronaut Luca Parmitano persuaded the International Space Station to provide the crew with a dinner that reminded him of home: lasagna, risotto, parmigiana, and tiramisu, all re-engineered for space travel.

Parmitano may have found the meal comforting, but I have to confess I consider the idea of reconstituted freeze-dried tiramisu outright horrifying. To me, Italian cuisine is all about fresh, local ingredients, recipes passed down for generations, and hands-on preparation in a kitchen that smells of roasting garlic, fresh basil, and olive oil. Somehow I doubt the International Space Station managed to include any of that. But I give Parmitano full marks for trying.

Torino's cafés and restaurants were only too happy to provide the kind of classic Italian comfort food I love, and during our days there, Rich and I did our best to visit as many as possible, roaming far and wide from our smart Airbnb apartment in the central Piazza Castello. This was a far cry from the way we'd seen Torino on our visit three years earlier, when I was there to write about the city's dive bars.

The American term "dive bar" refers to a well-worn, unpretentious local place that can be anything from a comfy, no-frills neighborhood pub to the kind of squalid gin joint that requires going home and washing (or burning) your clothes, and possibly calling the clinic to update your shots. Those of my friends and relatives who gravitate toward the finer things in life are bewildered by my affection for dark and dingy taverns with peanut shells on the floor, pool players with full body tattoos, and juke boxes belting out country western hits from 1987.

I frequently have to explain that yes, of course I enjoy decent food and up-market drinks as much as the next person. So why am I drawn to dive bars? Because everyone is welcome there. You don't have to wear fancy clothes, hold down a trendy job, or be able to pay $20 for a glass of wine without blinking. Nobody cares about your weight, your hair, or what, if anything, you're driving. In a world where differences so often define and divide us, it's great to know that some neighborhoods still offer places where your own unique voice and quirky character will always be a welcome addition to the mix, no questions asked. It's extremely refreshing.

For our dive bar research trip, Rich booked slightly dodgy lodgings near Torino's railway station. The 1970s furniture was dotted with cigarette burns, the bedside table was almost entirely occupied by an elaborate pushbutton console of unknown purpose and defunct status, and the air conditioning system had been turned off for the year despite daytime temperatures hovering near ninety. On the plus side, the neighborhood was full of downscale bars with neon signs, cheap beer, and colorful characters. The floors were sticky, the bar stools held together with duct tape, and the bartenders friendly enough to drink right along with the customers.

This time around, the Mediterranean Comfort Food Tour took me to an entirely different side of the city, the one devoted to savoring the kind of pleasures reserved for people of wealth and power. In short, I was there to catch a glimpse of the Torino that served for centuries as home and headquarters to the mighty House of Savoy.

The Savoy family had a pretty good run for a thousand years, parlaying control of a key Alpine transit route to dominion over nearly all of the Italian peninsula — right up until Mussolini's fascists marched into power. The Savoys expanded their power by a mix of military might, shrewd business sense, and political cunning that included a gift for making a splashy statement when it counted. As they did by introducing chocolate to everyone in Tornio.

As you likely know, the Spanish discovered cacao in Mesoamerica and brought it home, hoping to keep it secret and to themselves. But the Savoys naturally got word of the exciting discovery and set about accumulating their own supply. When the Duke of Savoy relocated his headquarters to Torino in 1560, the public celebrations included treating everyone in the city to a cup of chocolate. As you can imagine, it was love at first sip.

Just over a century later, Duchess Consort Marie Jeanne Baptiste made chocolate history by graciously granting Torino's candy makers a special license to produce chocolate in solid form, ushering in the era of morsels and bars. And the rest is gluttony. Sorry, I meant history.

Today the city's signature treat is a hazelnut chocolate called *gianduiotto*, which comes in a small, foil-wrapped bar shaped like an ingot. The first coffee I ordered in Torino came with one tucked on the side, and it was easy to see why everyone adored them. For dark chocolate lovers, Torino offers *baci di Cherasco* (Cherasco kisses), crunchy, irregular blobs of total scrumptiousness. Another local favorite, which I confess I never got around to trying, was the liqueur-filled *Alpino*, named for their resemblance to Italy's old-style military hats. So many chocolates, so little time.

I knew I couldn't get around to them all, but I felt compelled, for my readers' and my husband's sake, to sample the city's most famous chocolate beverage, *bicerin*. This divine mix of hot chocolate, espresso, and cream debuted in 1763 at Café al Bicerin across the street from the aptly named Santa Consolata, (Holy Consolation) church. Technically a drink, not food, *bicerin* could be enjoyed even during Lenten fasting, and as you can imagine, everyone stopped by for one after mass. I found the Café al Bicerin a temple of paneled wood and marble tabletops, and the *bicerin* itself just as heavenly as you might imagine.

There are countless ways the Savoys left their mark on Torino, but perhaps the most remarkable was bringing to the city one of the most famous — and controversial — religious artifacts in Christendom. I can still remember the nuns at school telling us the story. I am talking about, of course, the Shroud of Turin.

The Shroud is a fourteen-foot strip of linen that was placed around the body of Jesus Christ when he was taken down from the cross and buried. It bears the imprint of his entire body, front and back, and the detail is marvelous, although terribly faded now. It has been venerated by the faithful for 600 years.

Naysayers, however, cite a few pesky little inconsistencies. For a start, not long after the strip of linen first turned up in fourteenth century France, it was denounced as a fake by the Bishop of Troyes because he'd found the artist who confessed to fabricating the shroud. It's easy to believe it's art; the image seems a bit too perfect, from the serene expression down to the details of the eyelashes.

With Vatican permission, samples of the cloth were tested in 1988 at the University of Oxford, the University of Arizona, and the Swiss Federal Institute of Technology. All three concluded the linen dated to between 1260 and 1390, which is around the time the Shroud first appeared in Church history and at least 1227 years after the burial in question.

What about forensic evidence, you ask? The positions of the wounds conform to the conventions of church art rather than actual crucifixions of the era. Bloodstain pattern analysis revealed that the flow of blood on the back of the left hand and along the left arm occur at two different angles. Sections bearing the most body weight should be the most pronounced, but in fact the buttocks are barely indicated, as if to preserve the figure's modesty.

Naturally, the faithful refuse to listen to this devil's brew of gobbledygook. It's a miracle. Get over it.

In vain do historians point out that faking sacred objects was a huge business in medieval times. Most were said to have been brought back from the Holy Land by a Crusader, who snatched them from some heathen temple in the tradition that later gave us Indiana Jones. Naturally you can't expect proof of authenticity under those circumstances.

The church's official position is that it has no position. Not long after the Shroud surfaced, French officials entrusted it to the Count del La Roche for safekeeping, with documents calling it an icon, meaning a work of art; there was no reference to it being a sacred relic. But as soon as the Count was laid in his grave, his widow publicly announced the Shroud was the real deal and discreetly let it be known that she was willing to part with it for the right price.

Naturally word soon reached the ears of Duke Louis I of Savoy, who bought it from the countess, giving her two castles as payment. It's to be hoped she spent the rest of her days enjoying her newfound wealth, as the outraged Pope excommunicated her, consigning her to a considerably less comfortable afterlife.

Duke Louis appeared delighted with his acquisition, carrying the folded Shroud along on his travels in a silver case — a larger and more powerful version of the protective St. Christopher statues people stuck on their car's dashboard when I was a kid. Eventually the Duke decided — wrongly, as it turned out — that it would be safer in the chapel of the Savoy's main palace, which at that time was in Chambéry, France.

One day a fire broke out in the palace chapel, and the silver reliquary in which the Shroud was housed began to melt. A single drop of molten silver fell on the folded linen, tearing through every layer. All of Christendom was horrified. The Duke was furious. The Poor Claire nuns volunteered to repair the damage but bungled the attempt with amateurish patches. Eventually the Savoys pulled the shroud out of Chambéry and carried it with them to Turin where it remains today.

In 1983 the Savoy family donated the Shroud to the Catholic Church. Still refusing to speak out on its authenticity, church officials left it in Turin, where it is stored in a climate-controlled case inside the cathedral. No one is allowed to see it except on very special occasions, and incredibly, my visit was not one of them. I had to content myself with a visit to the Museum of the Shroud, which displays a replica said to be quite accurate, which meant it was so faded it was hard to make out anything but the burn holes, water stains, and patches.

No matter. As you have probably deduced, I am a bit dubious about the credibility of the Shroud and wouldn't dream of asking it for a miracle. As for Rich, he felt he'd truly touched glory when he went around Torino taste-testing *gianduiotto, baci di Cherasco,* and *bicerin.* His philosophical view aligns with this popular quote, attributed (probably falsely) to St. Teresa of Avila: "God and chocolate is better than just God." Amen to that.

FRANCE

24. Chambéry / *Blanquette de Lotte*

The small, charming French city of Chambéry, former stronghold of the Savoys, was only 130 miles from Torino, and both were similarly situated in the foothills of the Alps with bracing air, stunning mountain views, and good railway service. But from the moment I stepped off the train, I began to discover Chambéry had distinctly different attitudes about food and culture. It was so much more ... how can I put this? ... French.

Growing up on American McCuisine, and being educated by a Paris-based order of nuns, I was taught to have a deep reverence for classic French cooking. And I'm not alone. In 2010 *cuisine française* was officially designated part of the "intangible cultural heritage of humanity" by UNESCO, which praised the convivial social atmosphere, the fresh, local ingredients, and the diverse culinary contributions of various regions. But like everyone else, they glossed over the fact that much of what we consider contemporary French gastronomy owes much of its original substance and style to the Italians.

Until the sixteenth century, the French (along with most other Europeans) were happily dining in what's sometimes called *service en confusion*, with platters laid out helter-skelter on a table and everyone grabbing food and eating with their fingers. If you were ever seated at an unsupervised kids' table at Thanksgiving, you'll have a general idea of the kind of feeding frenzy that prevailed.

Then in 1533 the fourteen-year-old Florentine princess Catherine de' Medici married Henry duc d'Orleans, the future King Henry II of France. At first, Catherine was largely ignored by everyone who mattered because her husband was so besotted with his mistress, Diane de Poitiers, that he pushed his teenage queen into the background. Catherine was probably too busy trying to survive and, if possible, get pregnant with a royal heir to worry overmuch about what was happening in her kitchen.

The Italians in Catherine's entourage, however, took tremendous interest in matters of the table, and they were delighted to discover a surprising number of kindred spirits at the French court. In those days, the French were often in Italy engaging in minor warfare with various city-states. In between all the fighting, laying siege, pillaging, looting, and occasionally running for their lives, the French took time out to sample the local fare. They liked what they found and brought back fresh ideas, such as serving meals in courses, baking with butter — once ignored as "poor people's fat" — and eating mushrooms. The Italians at the French court encouraged these and other innovations, including the hotly debated introduction of the queen's forks.

Catherine's dowery included several dozen dinner forks crafted by the great Italian silversmith Benvenuto Cellini, and these gradually appeared on the dinner table. The French courtiers teased each other mercilessly over the amount of food they spilled trying to wield these strange new utensils but eventually everyone got the hang of it. Soon fashionable guests were showing up at dinner parties carrying a custom-made box, much like those of dueling pistols, containing their personal fork and spoon.

Although traditionalists held out for years against the unmanly, ungodly, and unnatural practice of finicky forks, over time French dining became transformed from a practical necessity to an art form.

I was lucky enough to experience an elegant gourmet French dinner at the home of a woman named Martine, who lived just outside of Chambéry in the town of Barby. In her family, she told me, cooking was both an art and a necessity. Her grandmother had nine children and fifty grandchildren; with so many relatives around, everyone was expected to pitch in and help. Because her mother had an outside job, Martine was instructed in the culinary arts by her many aunts, and she found she quite liked spending time in the kitchen. Later she took a cooking course at a well-known restaurant and eventually she and her partner Patrick signed up with the private dining group EatWith.

"You are our first EatWith guests," she told me. I assumed that was because she'd joined only recently, but she explained she'd been listed on the website for two years.

I was astonished; wonderful hosts, great food, breathtaking setting overlooking the foothills of the Alps ... what more could people possibly be looking for?

Martine explained that most visitors zipped through Chambéry en route to the ski slopes. In fact, she and Patrick raised their eyebrows when Rich mentioned we'd booked a five-day stay. Their voices murmured something polite, but their faces exclaimed, "Good Lord, what do you DO all day here?" In fact, Chambéry was my kind of town: peaceful, picturesque, and plentifully supplied with congenial outdoor cafés.

When I said so, Patrick grinned. "That's all new in the last year. The buildings are old, of course, but the town decided to expand things that would attract tourists. So now we have outdoor cafés all around the center." I was gobsmacked; I'd assumed the town had always enjoyed a vibrant street life, at least in the warmer months, and that all the winsome restaurants were as long-established as they looked. And maybe they were, but their outdoor seating was sparkling new.

I ate well everywhere in Chambéry, but Martine's dinner was

unquestionably the culinary highlight of my time there. On that warm, mid-September evening we began outside on the terrace, admiring the view of Mont Granier and the Belledonnes. The first course was as much Italian as French: we sipped a delicate rosé and nibbled on ham with melon and thin slivers of baguette with olive tapenade and a cheese-and-anchovy spread.

Martine explained that living in the high mountains, cooking was all about hearty fare that would sustain you and yours through severe weather. The common comfort foods were designed to stick to your ribs: cheese *fondu*, *diot* (sausages), and *crozets* (a small, flat, square-shaped pasta). Given the weather, she was preparing lighter fare: *blanquette de lotte*, anglerfish with mussels and vegetables.

This may have been light by Chambéry standards, but it was the heartiest fish I'd ever eaten, thick slabs of luscious anglerfish and succulent mussels from the nearby Lac de Bourget, topped with a creamy sauce of broth, egg yolks, and crème fraiche. It was served with boiled potatoes and whole carrots roasted with shallots.

The conversation ranged over everything from travel to families to the art of table setting. Naturally we touched upon the region's role as the original power base of the House of Savoy, which was headquartered there from 1295 to 1563. By now I'd learned that Martine came from one of the area's old aristocratic families, and as far as I could tell, she seemed perfectly content to be living a modern life in her smart contemporary apartment.

"This is amazing," I said, busily spooning up the last of my dessert of baked apple stuffed with crème fraiche and topped with vanilla ice cream. "I can't stop!"

Martine grinned. "I never meet American people who don't like to eat," she said. "You are very curious and you all like to eat."

And when you think about it, that may be America's finest gift to world cuisine. Our culinary traditions are all over the place. We have to maintain constant vigilance to keep pernicious corporations from sneaking harmful substances into our diets. Most of us don't know a sous vide precision cooker from a masticating juicer. But we are enthusiastic omnivores who aren't afraid to try new dishes. Our willingness to experiment also gives us the courage to get out there and connect with people around the world, knowing that with luck, we'll discover something to love in the classic dishes that have been cherished and handed down for centuries.

My five days in Chambéry passed pleasantly. I wrote a post for my blog, ate outside in several of the new cafés, cooked in the apartment, and spent hours every day strolling around the old center of town and up into the hills.

On one downtown walk, I wandered into a small plaza and was stopped in my tracks by the sight of a particularly goofy fountain. The centerpiece was an enormous column topped with a male figure posing nobly in old-fashioned clothing. But I doubted whether anyone ever looked at him; I know I didn't because my eyes were riveted on the base, a group of four life-size elephants — well, the front halves of four elephants anyway, each facing outward and spewing water from its trunk.

This fountain had inspired jeers of derision from the local populace when it was foisted upon them in 1838, and frankly, I could see their point.

The man standing atop the monstrosity was popular enough: Count Benoît de Boigne, Chambéry's greatest non-Savoy benefactor. Born plain Benoît Leborgne in 1751, he was one of seven children of a struggling Chambéry fur merchant. He later wrote that his father's shop sign, which showed such exotic animals as tigers, panthers, and elephants, fired his boyish imagination and inspired an insatiable, lifelong wanderlust.

In the eighteenth century, penniless young men thirsting for travel and adventure usually joined their region's army division. But seventeen-year-old Leborgne had just wounded an officer of the local regiment in a duel, generating so much ill will he knew he would never be admitted to their ranks. So he enlisted with Louis XV's Irish regiment in Flanders, and then when peace broke out (what are the odds?), he fought for Russia's Prince Orlov against the Ottomans. That campaign ended in disaster, and Leborgne was captured and taken to Constantinople as a slave.

As luck would have it, Leborgne's owner put him to work for a British official who took a liking to the young soldier and negotiated his release. After that, having heard some rajahs were looking for Europeans to help build their armies, Leborgne sailed to India. But a storm at sea washed all his possessions overboard, including the letters of recommendation and introduction necessary to secure work.

In India, he survived by teaching fencing until a well-connected student helped him get a job as a military instructor. Eventually he was hired to teach modern European military methods to the Maratha Empire's army, and he made a huge success of it. After a long and colorful career, he returned to Europe with riches beyond even his wildest fantasies, honors showered on him by kings and emperors, a beautiful Persian wife and two children, a chronic case of dysentery, an opium habit, and a new version of his name — de Boigne — which he felt sounded more aristocratic than Leborgne.

Sadly, his wife hated Europe, so the marriage was dissolved by mutual consent, and she and the kids went home. Leborgne then married a sixteen-your-old penniless French aristocrat; to no one's surprise that marriage was a total disaster, and she, too returned to her family, taking a good chunk of his money with her. Leborgne retired to Chambéry, where he spent his time managing his vast fortune and financing schools, hospitals, and various other public works helping those down on their luck, as he'd been so often in his checkered past.

In gratitude, the town built him a fountain that everyone loathed. The neighbors considered it a tasteless eyesore, calling it *"les quatre sans culs"* (the four without butts), and the nickname stuck. More than a century later, local punsters made much of the similarity between the fountain's nickname and the title of the famous 1959 François Truffaut film *Les Quatre Cents Coups,* literally *The 400 Blows*, a slang term for raising hell.

I imagine Leborgne would have loved that — having "hell raiser" as a final epitaph from his home town. What a fitting tribute to the adventurer who set out, sword in hand, to seek the exotic places and wild animals he'd dreamed about as a little boy. And in a way, isn't that why we all travel — to capture, if only for a moment, the wide-eyed wonder we felt as kids, imagining the world as vast, thrilling mystery awaiting us?

25. Dijon / *Mustard & Gingerbread*

"I like my gingerbread covered with *pâté de foie gras [chopped liver]*, accompanied by a nice white wine," said Philippe, sighing with pleasure.

And I thought, "I will never get this town."

Dijon was the thirty-sixth city I'd visited during the last five months. The Mediterranean Comfort Food Tour had taken me from Spain through Greece, North Macedonia, Kosovo, Albania, Montenegro, Bosnia and Herzegovina, Croatia, Italy, and now France. Since you've gotten this far in the book, I probably don't need to tell you that the trip through all ten countries had been tremendous fun.

Of course, there had been challenges along the way. I'd struggled to read bus schedules in the Cyrillic and Greek alphabets and navigated such hazardous stairs it was a wonder all my limbs were still intact. And while generally the food had ranged from good to fabulous, a few meals were disappointing, and some — that raw horsemeat in Asti, for one — were literally hard to swallow.

None of that had put me off my stride. But in the city of Dijon, I finally met my match.

Everyone I knew had promised me that I would adore Dijon, the capital of Burgundy and the jewel in its gastronomic crown. Envious comments were made about all the *boeuf bourguignon* (Burgundy beef stew) and *escargots de Bourgogne* (Burgundy snails) I'd be eating, washed down with the region's signature burgundy wine. It would — they all assured me rapturously — be a highlight if not the absolute pinnacle of the entire trip.

My experience was a far, far cry from any of that.

The first hurdle was finding anyone who would even serve me a meal. Naturally, having traveled across so many borders and culinary traditions, I had learned to check the ever-changing local meal schedules, and according to my insider source (Google) lunch in Dijon occurred from noon to 1:30. Rich and I arrived by train in mid-morning, and by the time we'd dropped our bags at the rental apartment and headed into the old center, it was nearly half past noon. I figured we'd be right on time.

Despite all the glowing praise, I hadn't actually received any specific recommendations, so Rich and I just wandered around, passing up several blandly modern places and encountering quite a few signs reading *"Fermé pour vacances"* (Closed for vacation). Nearly everyone in Europe took their holidays in August, but for some reason, the good people of Dijon were bucking the trend and heading to the beach now, in September. I should have realized it was a foretaste of how contrarian this town could be.

It must have been nearly 1:15 by the time we found a promising little bistro, dimly lit, cozy, half-filled with contented-looking customers. I asked, with my few words of French and some sign language, if one could acquire lunch here.

You would have thought I'd asked the staff to strip down and perform the Dance of the Seven Veils. Shock, disbelief, affront, headshaking, and rapid shooing motions with the hands sent us scurrying out the door with cries of *"Non, non, impossible!"* raining down upon our heads.

Similar scenes were enacted in three other restaurants, leaving us as bewildered as we were famished. Eventually Rich recalled passing a downtown department store advertising a food market in its basement, so we made our way there, collected some supplies, and returned to our apartment for a hasty meal. This was hardly the fine dining experience I'd expected in the gastronomic heart of Burgundy, but I was determined not to be daunted by such a minor setback. We decided to stay in, rest up, and give it another try in the morning.

Early the next day we set off to explore the city, which is home to a remarkable collection of half-timbered houses, churches with multi-colored tile roofs in the Flanders style, and magnificent palaces built while the Dukes of Burgundy reigned there from 843 until 1477. Approaching the north side of the thirteenth century Gothic Church of Notre-Dame, I spotted a little oblong blob of stone attached to the corner of a buttress.

"Look, there's the famous Owl of Good Luck," I said. "You're supposed to touch it with your left hand and make a wish."

"It's not in very good shape, is it?"

We stared at the blob. Squinting hard, I could just make out wings and something that might have been legs, but the head looked like used chewing gum. I'd read that the origins of the Owl are obscure; nobody knows who added it to the "new" (early sixteenth century) chapel, or why this traditional figure of wisdom suddenly gained magic wish-granting powers.

"I wonder what its success rate is," Rich said musingly.

"Well, apparently not a hundred percent," I said. "In 2001 it was attacked by a vandal with a hammer — I'm guessing a dissatisfied customer. After that the Owl was restored to its former shape, so I guess this is what it looked like before the attack — worn to a nub by centuries of being touched by human hands."

Rich dutifully placed his left hand on the owl and made his wish. I could tell he didn't think much of a good luck charm that couldn't even keep itself safe, and as I followed suit, I had to admit he had a point.

All in all, Notre-Dame's statuary had not had an easy time of it. The original west façade was decorated with fifty-one gargoyles, one of which promptly fell off and killed a man on his wedding day (that would be the man's wedding day, not the gargoyle's, as you have no doubt surmised). That particular gargoyle was fashioned to look like a usurer (money lender), a character often reviled in the Bible, and by a bizarre twist of fate, this was the profession of the unfortunate bridegroom. Obviously this was a Sign. Of what, nobody was entirely sure, but the Devil's name was freely bandied about in connection with the incident. At the insistence of the victim's colleagues, the rest of gargoyles were removed, and they weren't put back up for another 600 years. When they were, I'm guessing they used much, much stronger adhesive.

Inside the church was another remarkable statue, a former Black Madonna. You may have run across one of these ancient, dark-skinned images of the Blessed Virgin; there are hundreds of them in Roman Catholic and Orthodox churches around the world. Naturally speculation runs rife about why they differ from the more customary lighter-skinned version of the mother of Jesus.

Some say they were inspired by the line "I am black, and I am beautiful" from the Bible's Song of Solomon, although most scholars agree these Old Testament words refer to the Queen of Sheba. Others say the artists were matching her skin color to that of the congregation, which makes sense but isn't customary in Church iconography. Some insist the images were blackened by candle smoke. New Agers believe Mary represents the Mother Goddess and this version harks back to an ancient cultural memory of our common African origin. One blogger connects the Black Madonna with an alleged UFO sight in 1345, but so far that one hasn't gained much traction.

Like the Owl of Good Luck and the west façade's gargoyles, Dijon's Black Madonna has had a rough time over the years. This venerable image — one of the oldest in France, dating back possibly to the eleventh century — was originally seated on a throne with Baby Jesus on her lap. Later the throne was removed, and the back of the statue was sawn off and replaced with a wooden plank. During the eighteenth century her hands were stolen, and later, during the French Revolution, somebody absconded with Baby Jesus. Her skin, originally a pale buff color, was painted black in the sixteenth or seventeenth century; nobody knows exactly when or why.

Interestingly, it was around this time that she performed her first major miracle. The Swiss, apparently a more aggressive nation in those days, were laying siege to Dijon. The entire city was panicking. They didn't think their defenses could hold out for long, and once through the gates, the victors were sure to start the traditional looting, raping, and pillaging. On September 11, 1513 (remember that date) the Madonna (who may have been freshly painted black at the time) was carried around the city so everyone could beseech her for help. Two days later, the Swiss unexpectedly packed up and went away.

Fast forward to September of 1944. The Germans were occupying Dijon, and the French army was on its way to retake the city. While this was, of course, welcome news in the long run, everyone knew the battle was likely to get very bloody indeed, with plenty of bystanders killed and property damaged. On September 10, the bishop made a special plea to the Madonna (who was definitely black at the time), and by the morning of September 11 the Germans were gone. A year later, for reasons no one seems able to recall, she was repainted with lighter skin tones.

I know what you're thinking: if only America had this Madonna around on September 11, 2001, how different the world might look today. And if you're like me, you're also thinking it might be wise to paint her black again, just in case that affects her superpowers. In fact, I'd have voted to do it in 2020 to fend off a different kind of catastrophic invasion. Not that I believe these old superstitions, but hey, it couldn't hurt.

The morning's sightseeing and owl-wishing had given me quite an appetite, but finding a place for lunch proved as complicated as it had the day before. Most places that looked interesting were *fermé pour vacances,* and once again Rich and I seemed to be too late to get in on any actual eating.

And then, by some miracle, Rich spotted an all-hours kabob house around the corner from our apartment and in our desperation we gave it a try. Their chicken taco with yogurt sauce was absolutely fabulous and big enough to split; it became our go-to dish during the rest of our stay. I know, it was a bit unorthodox. Who goes to Dijon for Middle Eastern food? At that point, I was past caring.

The next day we did manage to sample some French fare but only by signing up for a food tour. Naturally we asked our knowledgeable guide, Philippe, about eating schedules, and he explained that on weekdays in Dijon *le déjeuner* (lunch) begins at 12:00 noon and lasts to 1:30 pm. Apparently everyone makes absolutely sure to arrive at the table between 11:59 am and 12:01 pm. Who knew the good citizens of Dijon were such rule followers?

I really shouldn't fault them; they were only complying, if perhaps a bit overzealously, with a rather admirable French law — the one that that makes it illegal to eat your lunch at work.

When I first heard of this law, I naturally assumed this was the brainchild of enterprising restaurant lobbyists, but in fact the original motivation was hygiene. Near the end of the nineteenth century it dawned on health officials that cities had grown so large workers could no longer return home at midday, requiring vast numbers of them to eat in factories and workshops, surrounded by phosphorus fumes, lead paint, mercury, arsenic, tuberculosis germs, and worse. Air vents? Running water? Not so's you'd notice. *Zut!* Something had to be done.

In 1894 workplace lunches were banned by law. As you can

imagine there was a tremendous uproar, especially from female workers, who knew just walking down the street to a café they'd be subjected to all sorts of harassment. And then there was the pesky cost issue. Women were paid less than men. (Can you imagine such inequity? Oh, wait, that's right, it's still that way.) Buying lunch every day took an unacceptable bite out of their slender income. Seamstresses organized the first women's strike in France to demand their God-given right to eat in safety, comfort, and economy at their sewing machines.

But the government stood firm, and after a prolonged and spirited exchange of views, in which everyone freely aired their differences and expanded their vocabulary of scathing insults, the citizenry finally settled down and accepted the idea. Now, lunch outside the workplace is enshrined in French culture and for many is the social highlight of the day. Not for me, obviously, but apparently everybody else in France enjoys it.

Our Dijon food tour started hours before lunch with a sampling of the city's iconic mustard, now sold in various flavors such as tarragon, nut, and gingerbread spice. Mustard had been produced in the region since the twelfth century, as a way of using the seeds from mustard plants that were grown beneath grapevines in local vineyards to add nutrients to the soil.

Sadly, Dijon mustard didn't manage to hang on to its "protected designation of origin" status, as did products such as Champagne and Parmigiano-Reggiano cheese. Today anyone can call their yellow spread Dijon mustard, and they do. Even more sadly, no mustard is produced in the city any more. Dijon's most famous brands, Maille and Grey Poupon, are now manufactured elsewhere by Unilever and Kraft Foods using mustard seeds from Canada. Sort of undermines the romance, doesn't it?

The next stop on our food tour was the gingerbread shop. I'd never associated gingerbread with Dijon, or even France, but that just showed how woefully ignorant I was. Popular in tenth century China, gingerbread was allegedly among the rations of Genghis Kahn's horsemen and was later carried to Western Europe by Crusaders returning from the Holy

Land. Obviously the European version was much manlier than the sugary, soft, cake-like gingerbread I was used to eating at the holidays.

For centuries Dijon was renowned for its many gingerbread makers, but now there remained only one, Mulot-Petitjean. Nibbling samples at their shop, I found it rather dry and bland compared to America's. Philippe explained it was often served with condiments, and that's when he told me he like his *pain d'épice* slathered with *pâté de foie gras* and accompanied by white wine.

Gingerbread with chopped liver? Really? Oh well, fine by me, so long as I didn't have to eat it.

At eleven o'clock, Philippe led us to a café, announcing it was time for a traditional mid-morning *aperitif*. Apparently all of Dijon paused at this hour to enjoy an alcoholic version of elevenses, and who was I to stand in the way of tradition? A platter appeared on the table laden with *gougères*, the crispy, soft-centered cheese puffs which have been justifiable popular in the Burgundy region since the eighteenth century. And then I got to sample Dijon's other most renowned contribution to world gastronomy, *kir*.

This delightful cocktail was named after one of the city's heroes, Félix Kir. Ordained as a Catholic priest in 1901, during World War II he became a resistance leader who rescued thousands of prisoners of war. But his contribution didn't stop there.

Among all their other war crimes, the Germans had confiscated Burgundy's entire supply of red wine. As a substitute, Kir mixed white wine and *crème de cassis* (a dark red blackcurrant liqueur), creating a burgundy-colored drink. It was an instant hit, and today the cocktail that bears his name is enshrined in French culture. A grateful populace elected Kir mayor of Dijon in 1945, a post he held until his death in 1963.

Like the combination of gingerbread and chopped liver, the idea of drinking a cocktail at eleven in the morning seemed a bit strange to me, but when in Dijon…

After this refreshing interlude, Philippe led the way to the colorful nineteenth century Les Halles Market. Weaving his way past artistically arranged produce, cheese, and meat, Philippe stopped at a case displaying the most expensive poultry in Europe: the famous blue-legged Bresse chickens. Epicure Anthelme Brillat-Savarin is said to have called it "the queen of poultry and the poultry of kings." Its fans like to point out that the red comb, white body, and blue legs match the colors of the French flag. Its detractors like to point out the cost, which that day was 28€ a kilo or around $50 to $60 for a whole bird.

Unlike Dijon's mustard, Bresse chickens managed to hold onto their "protected designation of origin" status; they can only be raised in the Bresse region on local feed. For four months they are fed small amounts of cereals and dairy products, leaving them hungry enough to forage for insects, which are believed to give the meat that certain *je ne sais quoi*. Then they go to the *épinette*, a cage in a dark fattening shed where they gorge on corn and milk for weeks before being slaughtered. This regimen is said to give them incredibly tender skin and rich flavor.

"Worth twenty-eight euros a kilo?" Rich asked skeptically.

"Yes, they are expensive. But if you eat this, you really taste *chicken*," Philippe said.

I could tell my husband was far from convinced.

The market's central café, La Buvette, was jammed, yet Philippe somehow contrived to find seats and produce platters of Beaufort cheese, salami, ham, bread, pickles, and glasses of delicious Macon chardonnay. This was the last stop on the tour, and as we nibbled and sipped, Philippe told us how lucky we were to be there during European Heritage Days.

"You get free admission to all the museums, palaces, and historic monuments — and also there is a second-hand market." What fun! Rich and I stopped back at the apartment for a brief rest then returned to the city center only discover the second-hand market dismantled and every one of the museums, palaces, and monuments closed and locked for the day.

It seemed we were fated to be perpetually out of sync with the city of Dijon. It no longer made mustard. They ate gingerbread with chopped liver. The Black Madonna was now beige. The poor mutilated Owl of Good Luck couldn't even help itself, let alone us. The dining hours were brutally enforced and we couldn't seem to get on the right side of them. Even the markets, museums, and monuments had taken to shuttering their doors when they knew we were coming.

"I can take a hint," Rich said. "This town is not for us. Let's go buy train tickets out of here."

"Great," I said. "We can stop for dinner at the kebob place on the way."

SPAIN

26. Seville / *Sweet Homecoming*

On the train from Dijon to Paris, I realized with a small shock that although I still had a few weeks of travel ahead of me, the Mediterranean Comfort Food Tour had, as the Spanish would put it, concluded itself.

In Paris Rich and I were meeting up with good friends vacationing in the city, and my days would be far too full to allow time to finagle my way into anyone's kitchen. Besides, as I'd learned in Dijon, the Mediterranean attitude only extended so far north in France. The traditional warm welcome given to strangers was still evident in Chambéry. The city of Dijon, however, seemed utterly indifferent to me, and I suspected I wouldn't be making much of an impression upon Paris, either.

And that was OK. On this journey, I had already done everything I'd set out to do and then some. I had been invited into an amazing number of kitchens, met incredibly generous cooks and their families, and sampled some of the most comforting foods the planet has to offer. I'd collected countless recipes, photos, videos, and new friends. I'd traveled five thousand miles overland. My job was, for the moment, done. I could relax into the pleasant pastime of renewing long-standing friendships in a city I'd visited many times. As author Kristin Hanna put it, "In Paris, with a glass of wine in your hand, you can just be."

After a few congenial days and nights in Paris, Rich and I started homeward. Trains took us smoothly to Nimes, Barcelona, Valencia, and finally — after 161 days on the road — to Seville.

As always, I was a trifle shocked to return after a long absence and find the city and my apartment just as I'd left them. I felt quite different — renewed and inspired, more engaged with the world than ever, excited by all the fresh ideas rattling around in my brain. I knew it was illogical, but I found it hard to believe the physical landscape had not rearranged itself to a similar degree.

I spent a lot of time getting reacquainted with my home. My closet seemed insanely full of clothes — why did I ever think I needed so many? I stood at my bookshelves gazing fondly at the well-worn spines of favorite works in their familiar editions. In the kitchen, every time I thought about needing a utensil or ingredient, it was ready to hand; that was something I'd missed. At the market, I didn't have to struggle with unfamiliar products labeled in strange alphabets; favorite foods leapt from the shelf into my hand, as if saying, "Well, duh, of course you need me."

I soon began slipping into familiar routines, taking walks in favorite parks and neighborhoods, stopping at my regular cafés, and best of all, checking in with friends.

As you can imagine everyone had lots of questions, including the usual "You really are nuts, aren't you?" and "Are you going to stay put for a while?" (The answers were "Yes" and "Yes.") Of course, it soon became clear what they really wanted to know was how much weight had I gained and when I was going to burn my clothes.

After five months of gorging myself on Mediterranean comfort food, the answer was — *drumroll, please* — I didn't gain an ounce. Rich actually lost two pounds. In the spirit of full disclosure, I will admit I can't provide hard numbers for myself, because after a lifetime of tracking each tiny gain and loss, when I moved to Seville I decided to stop weighing myself altogether. My metric was whether I could button my skinniest jeans, and the answer to that was a definite yes.

Why didn't all that good eating add to my avoirdupois? For one thing, I only ate heartily when I was on the trail of local comfort food; in between, I had salads, fish, and other light fare. I did twenty to thirty minutes of yoga most days. But mainly, I walked a lot. According to Rich's calculations, we covered 735 miles on foot — the equivalent of strolling from New York to Nashville or doing the entire Camino de Santiago pilgrimage one and a half times.

How did our shoes hold up over all those miles? Sadly, only one of the two pairs I brought survived the trip.

Somewhere in northern Greece, I started noticing feelings of mild dizziness; by the time I got to Albania, these spells were getting more frequent, annoying, and disquieting. Finally I realized the culprit was my comfy old sneakers. The soles were worn so slick they didn't maintain proper traction, and I was slipping a tiny bit with every step. Apparently this upset the equilibrium of my inner ear just enough to create a recurring sensation of dizziness. No, I didn't have a medical professional's diagnosis to corroborate this. But I can tell you that as soon as I bought a new pair of sneakers the problem cleared up. That was proof enough for me.

My old sneakers weren't the only things I jettisoned along the way. As you may recall, I got rid of the gauze blouse that suddenly looked entirely too translucent to be worn in decent society. And as the record-breaking heat of that summer wore on, I parted with two long-sleeved t-shirts to make room for one sundress and then another.

As a minimalist packer, I followed the rule that buying anything meant removing an item of equal bulk and weight from the suitcase. I never threw clothes away; instead, I left them somewhere they'd be found — usually sitting on top of a fence or dustbin in a low-income neighborhood or hanging on the back of a restroom door in a train station or dive bar. I liked to think these once-beloved possessions are now leading exciting lives with their new humans.

Among the other casualties were my bedroom slippers, which gradually stretched to the point that I was having difficulty keeping them on my feet. Note to self: Comfortably worn footwear might do for shorter trips, but it simply couldn't stand up to the rigors of long-term use. Broken in enough for comfort yet still in its prime would be the criteria next time.

Which brings me to the question of when I was going to burn my trip clothes.

The answer was — never.

In the past, I had "trip clothes" and "regular clothes," but now I was no longer making that distinction. With the exception of my slippers, all the robust garments I had carried home in my suitcase were keepers. They had plenty of useful life left in them, and far from being tired of the sight of them, as many supposed, I found them cheerful reminders of my road trip. They'd served me well and had earned their place in my wardrobe. Unless of course, any of them become embarrassingly translucent, like the blouse I wore to Kosovo; in that case, they were history.

One of the pleasures of returning from a long trip is telling people all about your adventures, but this gets tricky when you're a travel writer. Roughly half my friends had read my weekly blog and believed they knew everything there was to know about the trip. They didn't, of course, but I rarely had time to explain this. For instance, I tried a few times to tell the story about getting a fish bone stuck in my throat, something I'd never written about. But the moment I mentioned the Albanian horse restaurant they'd murmur, "Yes, yes, of course, Ali Kali…" and change the subject.

The other half of my friends never read my blog, hadn't a clue what I'd been up to, and said things like, "You were out of town? Huh, didn't notice. Go anywhere nice?" And it was difficult to know where to start.

The upside of being a travel writer is that I could now proceed to roll out all my best stories in a book, leaving out none of the quirky details, misadventures, jokes, and loony backstories. I would have the enormous luxury of telling everything properly, from start to finish. I could hardly wait to get going.

From the outset, I'd known one of the book's underlying themes would be the feeling of emotional connection that naturally comes with sharing a meal. Didn't we all grow up envying those Mediterranean families we saw in the movies, gathered around a long table in the garden, the air ringing with laughter and glowing with candlelight and love? Surely this was the answer to the isolation and loneliness plaguing modern society. If only it wasn't so totally out of reach for the vast majority of us most of the time.

But companionship wasn't the only reason all those Mediterranean meals were so wonderful. Part of the enjoyment came from everyone's deep and abiding interest in the food itself. They looked at it, sniffed it, poked it with a fork, and talked about it endlessly: the ingredients, the flavor, how it compared with the way their grandmother made it, other occasions when they'd enjoyed it at this restaurant or that.

Obviously I'd expected that attitude from the cooks, but I was astonished to observe the same enthusiasm in everybody else, too. Old men in cafés. Harassed young mothers with babies on their laps. Middle aged business colleagues on a lunch break together. They took plenty of time deliberating over their choices, even in modest little eateries. Everyone read menus as if they were love letters.

And perhaps this is the most important lesson I'd absorbed on this trip: eating well wasn't about being finicky or a purist or a health nut. It was about eating for enjoyment. I might not like the rigid hours they kept in Dijon, but I deeply respected France's decision to get everyone out of their workplace and into a restaurant serving food that required a fork. The secret to Mediterranean-style eating wasn't being

311

more virtuous, it was having more fun.

In my country of origin, we tend to view cooking and eating as an inconvenience, just one more obligation to squeeze into our day when we'd rather be doing something else. Americans now eat twenty percent of all meals in the car, a phenomena that shocks my European friends. When visiting the US, they report having hostesses overrule the idea of a sit-down lunch, saying, "Why waste time eating? I have so much to show you, and this way we can fit in ..." Too polite to demand an explanation for the strange phrase "waste time eating," the Europeans gamely swallow junk food while hurtling down a highway at sixty-five miles an hour in order to stop at the Birdwatchers Hall of Fame or Bigfoot Museum on the way to Sea World.

Living in Seville, I've learned to view eating as the Spanish do — not as squandering time but as making the most of it. And I'd discovered this same attitude throughout all the Mediterranean countries I visited.

This is good news because eating for pleasure is available to all of us. We don't need a candlelit garden with generations of loving family members gathered around, or a meal that's taken six hours to prepare, starting with catching a live goat. All we need to do is pause a moment to appreciate the food sitting on the table in front of us. Once we really notice our food, it's a short step to viewing it as a friend instead of a chore or an enemy. And that is what Mediterranean comfort food is all about.

I was grappling with how to express this as clearly as possible as I plunged into a rough first draft of this book. At meals, Rich patiently listened to me rambling on about the meaning of food in our lives and how that related to snails and honey laundering and eight different ways to spell *burek*.

From time to time I'd pull up the map showing the route and stare at it a while. Viewed as a whole, the Mediterranean Comfort Food Tour was an enormous undertaking, covering 5,234 miles, or even more impressively, 8,423 kilometers. I could never have done enough planning to organize every part of this journey in advance. Having a broad outline in mind at the start, and then making decisions about next moves as I went along, had really worked. I was glad that I'd started in Crete, skipped Sparta, lingered in Albania's capital, and skedaddled out of Dijon in my own time, not at the dictates of a pre-planned schedule.

I was spending most of my time typing at breakneck speed, trying to corral my notes, thoughts, and memories into some kind of coherent form. As usual when I'm knee-deep in writing a book, I mostly ignored the outside world; news and correspondence could wait. When my online inbox got too full, I'd sit down, answer emails from friends and family, and skim through the rest before deleting it. I remember casually glancing at a blog post about the worrying state of the world and coming across word I'd never seen before: coronavirus. The author sounded so alarmed I decided to look it up.

That's when I discovered a million people were on lockdown in China. Wait, what? When had this happened? And how did I not know about it? Was it possible I'd gotten just a tad too wrapped up in the book? I sat staring at the computer screen. A million people on lockdown. Should I be worried?

Of course, you all know the answer to that.

Within weeks I was on lockdown myself, and my lighthearted book about finding comfort food on the road suddenly seemed irrelevant. Worse, it seemed insensitive, even cruel, to write about feasting with congenial companions in exotic settings when nobody could even go out for coffee.

With regret, I set the book manuscript aside to focus on my blog, where I endeavored each week to find something heartening, helpful, and if possible humorous to say to my readers. I kept thinking of a line from David Whyte's poem, *Loaves and Fishes*: "People are hungry and one good word is bread for a thousand."

Being in Spain, which had the strictest lockdown protocols in Europe, I rarely left the apartment, but I never lacked for things to write about. I took pictures of Rich heading out to buy food swathed in scarves — the stores having long since run out of masks — and wearing, as required in Spanish markets at the time, latex gloves, which we were soon patching and re-patching with duct tape.

I posted my favorite memes of people walking odd pets (goldfish were the biggest hit) and videos of Italian mayors roaring threats at scofflaws and chastising those taking out their dogs five times a day. "Where are you going with these incontinent dogs?," shouted one. "You irresponsible idiots!" Another said, in low menacing tones, "I hear some want to host a party. We'll send armed police, and we'll send them with flamethrowers." Lively stuff!

Then there was the time Rich discovered virtual tours of the world's greatest museums, and I learned just how terrible I am at this kind of online navigation. Watching the screen, I had the dizzying sensation of lurching at warp speed past the great masters and slamming up hard against a wall, from which I extricated myself with difficulty, only to stagger off and do it all over again. It was like visiting the Musée d'Orsay roaring drunk. And not in a good way.

And through it all, I cooked.

For the first time in my life, I was planning twenty-one meals at a time. I gave up my usual slap-dash approach to kitchen management and got serious about menus and recipes, making careful lists of ingredients to be purchased during the single weekly shopping. Suddenly everything that would wind up on my table took on tremendous importance. I developed a much greater appreciation for the careful planning and hard work that went into running a traditional home kitchen.

Naturally, I also spent a lot of time on Zoom, talking with others, trying to get a grip on the new reality. "It's easier for you," one young friend commented during a call. "You've been through this sort of thing before."

Afterwards I said to Rich, "We have? I wonder how old she thinks we are. Old enough to have lived through the 1918 pandemic? The Black Death? Asteroids killing off the dinosaurs?"

But I knew what she meant. While I'd missed out on those exciting times, I remembered other shockers — the assassinations of JFK, Bobby Kennedy, and Martin Luther King, Jr., for instance, and the attacks of 9/11. In the weeks after the Twin Towers fell, I heard a radio story in which a young reporter interviewed people in their eighties and nineties, seeking perspective about how to handle the unimaginable from those who'd lived through the Great Depression and World War II.

One woman of very advanced years cut directly to what the young reporter really wanted to know. "Don't worry," she told him kindly. I always picture her patting his knee. "You will get through this just fine."

Now, two decades later, I found myself saying much the same thing to my readers. Overtaken by world events, we were all scrambling to reshape our vision of the future. We were learning, as had countless generations before us, that life is what we salvage from the wreckage of our plans.

Luckily, humans are amazingly adept at surviving catastrophes. "Resilience is our shared genetic and psychological inheritance," said author Elizabeth Gilbert. "We are each and every one of us — no matter how anxious you feel you are, no matter how riddled by fear you feel — every single one of us is the genetic survivor of hundreds of thousands of years of survivors. Each one of us came from a line of people who made the next correct intuitive move, survived incredibly difficult things, and were able to pass their genes on."

That's a reassuringly solid collective heritage to have at our backs.

Around this time, Rich decided to take a course on happiness. He enrolled in a free, eight-week, online program called the Science of Happiness offered by the University of California Berkeley. For the next two months, he talked of little else. When it was over, I did an interview with him so I could summarize the highlights for my readers.

"What was the most unexpected thing about the course?" I began.

"Probably the biggest surprise," he told me, "was that fifty percent of your happiness is inherited, ten percent is your life situation, such as your profession and how comfortable you are economically, and forty percent is what you do with your life and how you view your life."

"How can you inherit happiness? Is it built into your DNA?"

"A surprising amount is physiological," he said. "For instance, the vagus nerve runs from the brain throughout the body. Some are born with more of it. It's the thing that responds physically when you see a beautiful sky that takes your breath away. Another thing is the dopamine stimulator in the brain; the more it's stimulated, the more caring people are. Again, some of us are just born with more of it."

"Obviously there's not much we can do about our DNA," I said. "But what about the forty percent of happiness that is under our control?"

"Being happy takes a lot of work," Rich said.

"But you've told me that you can't go after it directly."

He nodded. "If you're seeking happiness all the time, you are going to fail. Life doesn't work like that. Happiness is really a byproduct. The ancient Greeks called it *eudaimonia*, human flourishing and blessedness, achieved by a life of virtue and ethical wisdom. Contrary to what it says in the Declaration of Independence, you can't pursue happiness; you pursue something else and receive happiness."

"Like what?" I asked. "What can you pursue in life that will lead to flourishing and blessedness?"

"Help others and show gratitude," he replied promptly. "Kindness leads to compassion. Compassion leads to altruism. Compassion makes you want to do something for others; altruism is actually doing it. All that is totally different from empathy, pity, or sympathy, which don't call you to action. 'I feel your pain' isn't action and doesn't lead to happiness."

"How do we start?" I asked.

"It's the little things. Like the time you helped that old lady up the steps of the café in Greece. Or the other day, when we passed those two panhandlers, and one said, 'Spare any chocolate?' And you had some in your purse so you gave it to them."

I had to laugh, remembering the surprise and delight on the guys' faces. They'd been kidding around with the request, and moments later they were each holding a foil-wrapped square of high-end dark chocolate with sea salt caramel — something I know from personal experience will brighten anyone's day. The four of us laughed together a moment and parted on a little buzz of joy.

"OK, I get how helping others makes you happy," I said. "Where does gratitude fit in?"

"Expressing gratitude is underrated; we rarely do it except in eulogies. The course's presenters recommended keeping a gratitude journal, or developing a nightly habit of climbing into bed and thinking of three things you're thankful for from your day. Even in challenging times, you can find small blessings that make you grateful. And those blessings make it possible to remember that every day is sacred."

My happiness quotient improved markedly as the pandemic finally began to ease. People started traveling for pleasure again, and my thoughts kept straying to this book. Finally I opened up the manuscript file and dove in, losing myself once more in the stories of our culinary adventures on the road. I found the work a cheerful antidote to years of fear and gloom. Before I knew it, I was once again showing up for meals laughing over the War of the Bucket and the history of forks.

Recounting the stories behind some of the Mediterranean region's most beloved comfort foods, I was struck by how many of them were born out of hardship: wars, poverty, shortages. Those dishes helped people endure the dark times, celebrate the bright spots, and give everyday comfort to one another. They provided the feeling, as poet Billy Collins put it, that "tonight the lion of contentment has placed a warm heavy paw on my chest."

When we're paying attention, good food reminds us to enjoy all the pleasures, large and small, that might otherwise slip past unremarked in the hurly-burly of daily life. Kurt Vonnegut wrote about learning this from his Uncle Alex. "So when we were drinking lemonade under an apple tree in the summer, say, and talking lazily about this and that, almost buzzing like honeybees, Uncle Alex would suddenly interrupt the agreeable blather to exclaim, *If this isn't nice, I don't know what is.* So I do the same now, and so do my kids and grandkids. And I urge you to please notice when you are happy, and exclaim or murmur or think at some point, *If this isn't nice, I don't know what is.*"

Rich and I say this to one another all the time. In fact, it's become one of our road rituals, like stopping for a recombobulation coffee and taking siestas. These small rituals are vital to our happiness. Why? Scientists and spiritual teachers agree it's because they offer a sense of stability in a topsy-turvy world. They let us know we are exactly where we need to be, doing just what we need to be doing, at precisely that moment. We come away more grounded and confident, able to see things more clearly, from a broader perspective. They help us relax and reconnect with the sense of joy and adventure that caused us to travel in the first place.

So I'm passing this small ritual on to you, in hopes that you'll find yourself saying it, again and again, as you plan your own adventures and sit down to meals that bring you comfort and joy: *If this isn't nice, I don't know what is.*

And with that we come to the very end of the 5,234-mile sojourn that began with a chat over coffee and took me through ten countries and countless glorious meals. Thanks for joining me on the journey.

Karen McCann

Seville, Spain

EnjoyLivingAbroad.com

PS: Oh yes, I've got another trip in the works. Watch my blog for details.

If you enjoyed this book, please leave a review on Amazon.

ABOUT THE AUTHOR

Karen McCann is an American travel writer who has been living in Seville, Spain for the better part of two decades. Her bestsellers include *Dancing in the Fountain: How to Enjoy Living Abroad* about her transition to life in Seville, Spain; *Adventures of a Railway Nomad*, which tells of her three-month train trip through Eastern Europe; and the ever-popular *Pack Light*. She's traveled to more than sixty countries and volunteered assisting microenterprises in Europe, Africa, the Caucasus, and Central America. She now divides her time between California and Spain — when she's not on the road in pursuit of another great story or more comfort food.

For more visit EnjoyLivingAbroad.com.

As thanks for joining me on the journey, I'm happy to send you
A FREE BONUS GIFT: *PACK LIGHT*
my bestselling short Kindle book, fully updated and revised for 2023.

Just send me your email at
enjoylivingabroad@gmail.com
and I'll send you the Kindle edition.
(Sorry, it's not available in hard copy.)

I invite you to check out my

FREE ONLINE MEDITERRANEAN COMFORT
RECIPES COLLECTION

You can find all the recipes — along with photos, videos, and my notes — on my website, and I hope you'll go take a look. It's fun to see the cafés, farms, restaurants, homes, gardens, and urban rooftops where memorable meals were created. You'll meet the cooks and listen to their advice about making *moussaka, risotto*, wild goat, *bourbouristi* (snails), dragon pie, and other unforgettable fare. And you'll have all the recipes — in both metric and US measurements — so you can experiment with making them yourself.

You'll find this free recipe collection on my website:

EnjoyLivingAbroad.com

Bon Appetit, Ju Bëftë Mirë, Καλή Όρεξη, And Buon Appetito!

Made in United States
Cleveland, OH
18 February 2026

33548007R00194